Contents

Texts used

We are indebted to the following people and institutions for permission to reproduce texts. Any omissions brought to our attention will be remedied in future editions.

L'Arche: an *Arche* shoes advert, *Madame Figaro*, 29 March 1988. Reproduced with kind permission of Arche, Madame Figaro and SC&A, Paris.   133

Le Compte Basique: an advert for *Le Compte Basique* of *L'Union de Banques à Paris*, *L'Etudiant*, October 1990. Reproduced with kind permission of *L'Etudiant* and *L'Union de Banques à Paris*, which, since 1998, has discontinued 'Le Compte Basique', designed for the 1980s, updating and restyling it for 16- to 25-year olds as 'Jeunes'.   139

Duras, M. (1960) 'Synopsis', *Hiroshima mon Amour*, Paris: Gallimard, pp. 9–10. ©Editions Gallimard.   39

ESSEC: an advert for the *École Supérieure des Sciences Economiques et Commerciales*, *L'Etudiant: Le Guide des Métiers*, November 1986, p. 167. Reproduced with kind permission of Groupe ESSEC.   6

Furet, F. (1978) *Penser la Révolution Française*, Paris: Gallimard, pp. 35–36. ©Editions Gallimard.   182

Garnier, I. 'La Comédie musicale du Grand Siècle', *Figaro Magazine*, 24 April 1990, pp. 40–41. Reproduced with kind permission of Le Figaro-Magazine.   90

Gaxotte, P. (1970) *La Révolution Française*, Paris: Fayard, pp. 11–13. Reproduced with kind permission of Librairie Artheme Fayard.   169

Le Clézio, J.M. (1982) *La Ronde et Autres Faits Divers*, Paris: Gallimard, pp. 15–16. ©Editions Gallimard.   120

Pagès, F. 'Victoire du tactico-ethnique', *Le Canard Enchaîné*, 15 July 1998, p. 1.   108

Pudlowski, G. 'La Brie, comme autrefois', *Le Point*, 1 October 1994, no. 1150.   79

Contributors

Robert Crawshaw is Senior Lecturer and Head of French Studies at Lancaster University and a former academic adviser to the European Commission. A graduate in French and Italian, he worked in publishing and studied comparative literature and linguistics at the Universities of Paris and Cambridge. He has published in the fields of French theatre, European educational policy, management studies, applied linguistics, stylistics and discourse analysis and is currently director of a UK government project on the development of intercultural awareness.

Benoît Heilbrunn is a graduate of the Ecole des Hautes Etudes Commerciales and a holder of *Diplômes d'Etudes Approfondies* in Marketing, Semiology and Philosophy. Formerly associate professor at the Ecole Supérieure de Commerce de Paris and lecturer at University College Dublin, he is currently *Chargé de Conférences* at the Ecole de Management de Lyon.

David Scott, who holds a personal chair in French (Textual and Visual Studies) at Trinity College Dublin, has written widely on literature, painting, semiotics and textual and visual studies. The organiser of many exhibitions on the visual arts and design, his books include *Pictorialist Poetics* (1988), *Paul Delvaux: surrealising the nude* (1992) and *European Stamp Design: a semiotic approach* (1995). An editor of the journals *World & Image* and *L'Image*, he is president of the International Association of Word & Image Studies.

David Steel is Senior Lecturer in French Studies in the Department of European Languages and Cultures at Lancaster University. After graduating from Magdalen College, Oxford, he taught at the Sorbonne and at the Ecole Normale Supérieure, completing a *Doctorat ès Lettres* from the University of Paris on the work of André Gide. In post, since then, at Lancaster University, he has published widely in the field of Gide studies, on early influences of psychoanalytical theory on French literature and on the relationship between advertising and literature in France, particularly in the context of Dada-Surrealism.

Karin Tusting is a research assistant in the Department of European Languages and Cultures at Lancaster University. Her PhD analyses the role of written text in the construction of identity in a Catholic parish community. Her research interests are in the field of critical discourse analysis, literacy studies and identity. Her publications include contributions to the book *Situated Literacies*, Routledge, 1999.

Preface

This publication is a project rather than a book. It came about as the result of discussions between colleagues from different departments at Lancaster University and then took on an inter-institutional dimension. As we saw it, within the changing environment of European Languages and Cultures in Higher Education in the UK, North America and Australia, there was an increasing need for courses which brought together language, culture, critical theory and the study of textual variety. Traditionally, in French Studies, the relationship between language and aesthetic expression had been taught through literary commentary or *explication de texte*. But the technical analysis of literary language had a diminishing appeal for students and was rooted in a humanistic tradition which was out of line with recent theoretical accounts of the interaction between text and society. There was an opportunity to provide students with the means to appreciate the potential of the written language and to explore the links between the structures of discourse and the interrelationships between social institutions.

There were centres of expertise at Lancaster which provided a strong knowledge base for mounting a course of this kind, but there was a clear difference of interest within the discipline between literary stylistics and poetics on the one hand, and, on the other, a linguistics whose primary object of analysis was the interaction between discourse, social institutions, ideology and power. This difference of focus, which broadly corresponded to that between humanities and social science, was also reflected in the divergence in France between 'stylistique' and various forms of 'analyse du discours' whose approaches were inspired by linguistic theory or social philosophy. As colleagues from a department whose task was as much to teach students language as to draw their attention to the operations of culture and society, it did not seem to us necessary to separate an appreciation of the expressive resources of French from an insight into the mechanisms of social change. Only tradition and the processes of discursive formation had given them the status of independent subdisciplines. We wanted to examine these processes more closely from the perspective of French and, where appropriate, to question their validity.

Our aim was not purely pedagogical. As authors with different temperaments and backgrounds but having common academic ideals, we wanted to understand the issues better ourselves and to explore their characteristics in the form of an essay which was to become Part 1 of this book. We wanted to make an argument for an eclectic approach which would develop students' knowledge of French while making them aware of the way in which texts reflected social structures and the formation of ideologies. However, we also wanted to provide a source of information and guidance for students following the courses for which we were responsible, at final-year undergraduate and postgraduate levels. In our experience, the main difficulties faced by students were methodological: knowing what to look for in texts and how to describe what they saw. It was necessary to describe and illustrate the features of the written language in a way that would demonstrate their potential value as instruments of expression and, at the same time, to offer a framework within which insights could be coherently presented.

The final component of the project was to implement the approach which we were proposing and to apply the thesis we had explored in Part 1. We wanted to test the principle first explored in depth by Michel Foucault in *Les Mots et les Choses* (1966), *L'Archéologie du Savoir* (1969) and *L'Ordre du Discours* (1971), and since developed by a modern school of discourse analysts, that style was not purely a matter of form but an indicator of social attitudes and a barometer of change. We therefore identified a number of topics which we saw as central to the national way of life in France and, in collaboration with colleagues and students, selected texts which were representative of particular genres and illustrated different aspects of stylistic evolution. From the analysis of their construction and the way in which they 'positioned' their implied readerships, it would be possible to make wider inferences about the way in which French society viewed itself and hence about the character of French national identity.

Commentators bring their own values and perceptions to the act of interpretation, and the cogency of their insights is itself subject to critical evaluation according to different criteria: the internal coherence of the analysis, the degree of linguistic awareness brought to the reading of the source texts, the extent to which the values of the commentator are shared by those of the reader, and so on. By offering a number of commentaries submitted by different contributors on a range of topics and representing different styles and techniques, we wanted to leave the issue of interpretation open to debate by the potential readers of the book. It was our hope that the analyses themselves would be the topic of argument and discussion in seminars and would help students to develop their own approaches.

The book is not, therefore, exclusively designed as an undergraduate textbook on French stylistics. The sections are intended to be used variably by different audiences. Undergraduates may only be interested in individual elements of the first chapter and could be directed to particular points rather than being expected to read the chapter as a whole without guidance. The approach of the first chapter is better suited as an introduction for postgraduates who are relatively unfamiliar with techniques of text analysis and who need some knowledge of the background to the discipline.

The structure of the second chapter has emerged as the direct outcome of a final-year undergraduate course in stylistics and discourse analysis. The sequence of the material in the course has been successively modified in order to take account of the need to reconcile coverage of linguistic features with an insight into their social function. The topics and approach in Part 2 can be used as the basis for an undergraduate programme which can be supplemented as required by additional reading according to the level and degree of specialisation of specific groups. The summary framework on pages 60–62 follows the same structure and is designed to be used by students when writing their own commentaries. It is supplemented by a glossary to familiarise learners with the metalanguage which a course of this kind inevitably demands. We hope that in using the book as a source of reference and in critically discussing the examples of commentary which have been provided, students will gain a new awareness of written French and a better understanding of the interaction between language and society.

Robert Crawshaw
Karin Tusting

Lancaster
July 1999

Acknowledgements

It would not have been possible to embark on this project, let alone complete it, without the support of colleagues and friends, particularly in the Department of European Languages and Cultures and the Department of Linguistics and Modern English Language, at Lancaster University. Only the provision of sabbatical leave and the concomitant burden borne by overworked colleagues allowed it to get off the ground, and our thanks and appreciation go to them, together with the hope that our efforts have not let them down. Unbiased feedback is hard to come by within the academic profession and we are grateful to those who took the trouble to read drafts of the text in detail and to give us honest and always constructive comments at various stages. Special thanks are due to Tony Lodge, who saw early outlines of the original proposal and supported its submission to Routledge; to Anne Judge for her advice and for the loan of her own excellent book on the history of French written style; to Andy Stafford and David Whitton for material on the French Revolution and the postwar productions of *Le Malade imaginaire* respectively; to Graham Bartram and Beth Callen for the pertinence of their comments; and particularly to Sally Johnson for her readings of successive drafts, her participation in numerous meetings during the early stages of the project and her assistance with the glossary. We are also grateful to Malcolm Quainton and Norman Fairclough for their time and comments, and for the patience of the commissioning editor, Louisa Semlyen and the Routledge staff. Our thanks, last of all, to several generations of undergraduate and graduate students. As much as anything else, it was their comments and support which made the project worthwhile.

Part 1

Style, rhetoric and critical discourse analysis

Style, discourse and choice

Robert Crawshaw and Karin Tusting

Stylistics and critical discourse analysis: some assumptions

The study of written language has reached a crossroads. For many students and academics, the analysis of aesthetic or literary writing is felt to be irreconcilable with the study of language, which is perceived to be serving functional or social ends. The two approaches have come to have different objectives and methodologies which reflect divergent views on the relationship between the individual and society. The first, more traditional, approach is based on the belief in the individual's capacity for freedom of expression, the ultimate manifestation of linguistic creativity being writing which is primarily aesthetic or artistic. According to this point of view, works of literary fiction are the result of independent choices made by their authors from the rich and infinitely varied resources of the language. The author's 'style' is a direct reflection of that choice and bears the stamp of his or her originality. 'Stylistics' consists in identifying the images and grammatical patterns – 'stylistic features' – which mark the individual's outlook on the world and differentiate his or her language from what can loosely be described as the norm, and also in making explicit the regularities of form – repetitions, parallel sentence structures, and so on – which are contained within the message itself. The study of style as the means of producing a given 'effect' by way of 'devices' which draw on the intrinsic creative potential of the language has traditionally been seen as a specialised discipline within the broader field of literary studies in which linguistic structure is perceived as a reflection of a writer's intention.

The intentionalist approach to style, which reaches back to the classical humanist and Romantic traditions in European thought, has been called into question since the beginning of the twentieth century by approaches which have caused the focus in the analysis of written language to shift from the author to the structure of the text. More recently, this emphasis has been further extended to include the relationship between the text and the social determinants which have led to its production. In the 1960s, the growing influence of linguistic theory on literary criticism gave rise to analytical approaches whose objective was to describe creative language either in terms of its internal formal structure or in relation to a particular theoretical model. Stylistic 'complexity', for example, could be 'measured' in terms of the number and type of grammatical operations required to produce long sentences (Ohmann 1970). Alternatively, the 'deviance' of literary language could be captured 'objectively' by identifying the grammatical rules which had been broken in a piece of poetry and by describing which new rules were needed for the grammar to be able to accommodate the language of the text (Thorne 1970; Leech 1970). In this way, the centre of attention shifted from the intention or personality of the author supported by appropriate biographical and historical evidence towards what was claimed to be a more 'scientific' form of analysis (Jakobson 1960; Levin 1973). Stylistic analysis was also used to show how literary language, in conforming to a particular genre (novel, short story, sonnet, etc.), would set up expectations in the mind of the reader, who would then be surprised by a stylistic feature which would stand out from the background of the work as a foregrounded marker of the writer's style (Riffaterre 1959, 1971). In this way the act of interpretation could be accounted for more fully.

The focus on structure at the expense of author and reader had the further implication that texts were no longer studied as isolated entities. Their internal patterns were not unique but were part of a wider symbolic fabric in which all texts were in some way related to each other like elements in a huge kaleidoscope. The interrelationship between texts ('intertextuality') could be analysed through time ('diachronically') in the sense that all texts could be seen to re-formulate and be derived from ('re-write') previous representations of similar material. Alternatively, the form of texts could be compared and contrasted to that of other texts which had been produced at virtually the same time ('synchronically'). In this way, certain trends could be identified in the way in which reality had been represented at a particular moment in the development of a culture. In either approach, the interest in the style of the author and the individuality of the text were diminished in favour of understanding the myth-creating processes which were at work within society as a whole (Barthes 1957; Kristeva *et al* 1971).

At the same time, the shift in emphasis from the author to the structure of the text led to a redefinition of the notion of 'intention'. Instead of understanding intentionality as being vested in individual choice, approaches to text analysis saw the writer's linguistic decisions as directed by subconscious or socially determined forces. Psychoanalytical criticism explored the unconscious impulses which lay behind the act of literary creation (Lacan 1966). According to post-Marxist analysis, on the other hand, linguistic selection, and the textual frameworks or 'genres' within which it took place, were more or less predetermined by the interrelationship between political and economic influences, the institutions which resulted from them and the forms of discourse which defined the way in which they were represented (Foucault 1969, 1971). Within this ideological framework, the 'person-centred' concept of 'intention' is replaced by the more objective one of 'function', implying that texts and the structures within them are the outcomes not of creative initiative but of identifiable social interactions which can be systematically categorised and organised into hierarchies (Halliday 1978). Placed within a wider social and cultural context, texts are perceived as instruments which reflect the changing patterns of power relations in society (Fairclough 1989, 1992).

The object of study in the analysis of written text has therefore evolved from one of defining individual creativity to one of making explicit the symbolic processes of social interaction and change. At the same time, a different educational objective has emerged. Whereas the traditional goal of text analysis was to develop the literacy and powers of expression of the individual, that of more recent approaches has been to enhance the learner's understanding of social and political processes. A new discourse has developed, accompanied by new publications and new institutional frameworks. Its objective is to describe the dynamic relationship between texts and the sociopolitical forces which can be seen to be at work within them. In its more radical form, this approach, which has become known as 'critical discourse analysis' (Fairclough 1995; Van Dijk 1995), sees itself as engaged in a political process. Its task is not simply to make the literate public aware of how the forces of oppression and exclusion operate through the manipulation of linguistic media but to urge informed readers to counteract their influence through protest and other forms of political action. This approach has become distanced from a stylistics which focused on the relationship between the writer and the text or on the structure of the text to the virtual exclusion of social considerations.

In this book, we address the issue of whether the apparent schism between stylistics and discourse analysis is either valid or necessary. While calling into question the distinction between literary and non-literary language, we raise the issue of whether, for the purposes of a socially aware consideration of written discourse, the virtual exclusion of the writer's creative input corresponds to the reality of the interaction between readers and texts. Instead we argue for an eclectic approach to the analysis of written style, which draws in a discriminating way on the strengths of different traditions and which acknowledges an inclusive interrelationship between writer, text, reader and the wider sociocultural environment. In seeking to validate our approach and to place it in an historical and conceptual context, we propose first to call into question some generally held assumptions on which the distinction between stylistics and critical discourse analysis is based, and second, to review some of the major traditions in the analysis of written text: to illustrate their strengths and limitations and to identify those elements which may inform the interpretation of written text today.

ESSEC

Se préparer aux fonctions de gestion et de direction des entreprises exige la connaissance et la pratique des techniques les plus avancées dans ces domaines. Et aussi une pédagogie qui développe le sens des responsabilités, le souci de la communication, la passion d'entreprendre. La renommée de l'ESSEC se fonde sur ces deux exigences.

L'excellence dans la formation

La passion d'entreprendre

GROUPE ESSEC

École Supérieure des Sciences Économiques et Commerciales, Établissement Supérieur Privé reconnu par l'État
Avenue de la Grande École - B.P. 105 - 95021 CERGY-PONTOISE CEDEX - Tél. : (1) 30.38.38.00

Source: ESSEC: an advert for the *École Supérieure des Sciences Economiques et Commerciales,* *L'Etudiant: Le Guide des Métiers,* November 1986, p. 167. Reproduced with kind permission of Groupe ESSEC.

Assumption 1: 'Literary language is different from non-literary language'

It is generally taken for granted that there is a distinction between 'fictional' and 'non-fictional' text. 'Non-fiction' claims to represent events which have 'actually taken place' and the reader is more or less prepared to accept this claim as true. 'Fictional' text makes no such claim and the reader imposes no obligation on writers of fiction to be 'truthful' in their representation of reality. The notion of 'truth' instead takes on an ethical, psychological, spiritual or philosophical dimension which distinguishes it from 'accuracy'. 'Literature' is not the same as fiction. The 'literary' quality of a text is not directly related to the question of whether or not it claims to represent experience in an 'accurate' way. Letters, historical accounts of lived events – advertisements and news broadcasts – can be described under certain circumstances as having literary qualities despite the fact that they are claiming to represent reality directly. Equally, texts which create fictional worlds and which are accepted as belonging to what society calls 'literature' – Shakespeare's *Henry V*, Voltaire's *Candide*, Goethe's *Egmont*, Hugo's *Ruy Blas*, Tolstoy's *War and Peace*, Orwell's *1984*, Camus' *La Peste*, Pasternak's *Dr Zhivago*, and so on – refer to people, events and places derived directly from reality and seek to impact on the real world. Many narratives, ancient and modern, combine invention with the description of historical events in which the distinction between 'accuracy' and 'truth' is deliberately confused. What is at first perceived as a qualitative difference between 'literature' and 'non-literature' becomes reduced to one based on convention. Rather than promoting a clear-cut distinction between 'fiction' and 'non-fiction', or between texts which are categorised as 'literary' or 'non-literary', it is therefore more appropriate to think of written texts as having different functions, some of which will be emphasised more strongly than others.

According to most standard definitions, 'ESSEC' could not be described as a literary or poetic text. Its primary function is evidently to promote the *Ecole Supérieure des Sciences Economiques et Sociales*, one of the leading French business schools. The layout of the text and its inclusion in the publication *L'Etudiant* which is designed to inform young people about different educational or professional opportunities earmark it as an advertisement. The assumption on the part of the reader is that the text is not fictional. It serves a clearly defined purpose whose potential impact on the real world is direct and more or less unambiguous. Even so, the text is telling a story, however brief. There are no facts and figures beyond the name and address of the school and the reference to the corporate group which represents it. The text is defining the qualities of the institution and its members in figurative and moral terms. It is creating an image, setting up associations. It would be artificially restrictive to claim that, although primarily persuasive and promotional, the text does not have expressive, even poetic features which are present in the interrelationship between the structures, rhythms and sounds of the language and the ideas which are being conveyed.

Apart from the symmetry of the layout which, if you include the logo and print at the foot of the page, stands out like a wineglass or candlestick, the two strong noun phrases which balance each other in the middle of the piece, symmetrically sum up the two main selling points of the school – '*excellence . . . passion*' / teaching . . . entrepreneurship – the one being received by the learner, the other developed and freely given. Drawn further into the verbal space of the two sub-headlines, the reader is struck by the repetition of /l/ . . . /d/ and by the symmetry of the apostrophes. At the same time, the '*la*' of '*la formation*' is balanced by its repetition in '*la passion*'. The effects of rhyme and assonance -*ence* . . . -*endre* / -*tion* . . . -*sion*, bring the arrangement of the two pairs of lines into relief a . . . b / b . . . a – a classically symmetrical figure which enhances the difference in meaning and association between '*dans*' (passive) and '*de*' (active) and, as suggested, between '*formation*' and '*entreprendre*'.

A closer analysis of the smaller print soon reveals how much care has gone into the composition of this little text. The first half of the piece deals with the knowledge required to be an effective senior manager. The role demands two main areas of expertise ('*fonctions*'): financial management ('*gestion*') and executive control ('*direction*'). As complements of the noun '*fonctions*', the two properties concerned are linked by the coordinating conjunction '*et*' and are perfectly matched by the two objects of the verb '*exige*': '*connaissance*' and '*pratique*'. Likewise, each noun complement in turn governs its own ending: '*des entreprises*' and '*des techniques* . . . ', which together complete the balance of the two phrases. The techniques to be developed are '*les plus avancées dans ces domaines*', the plural of the word '*domaines*' and the demonstrative '*ces*' binding the sentence together by referring back to the twin *fonctions* with which it begins. Each feature of the sentence is matched by a parallel feature which sets the other off and gives the whole a sense of completeness.

Despite the full stop, the sentence does not end. Two prerequisites ('*exigences*') are imposed by the objective of wishing to become an appropriately qualified senior executive: the acquisition of knowledge and technical expertise and a satisfactory approach to teaching which will enable the student to develop the necessary personal attributes. These attributes are listed in a group of three, with the emphasis falling naturally on the last: '*La passion d'entreprendre*', which forms the climax of the sentence as a whole. The dual themes are rounded off by the concise closing statement. The reputation of ESSEC is based on the twin foundations which have just been described. Once again the demonstrative '*ces*' is employed, this time strongly reinforced by '*deux*'. The closure acts as an effective link, which points both ways: backwards to the body of the text and forwards to the two headlines that follow.

The structural features of the text are therefore very difficult to ignore once the reader has embarked on the text. The acronym 'ESSEC' is itself bisyllabic, the two syllables being more or less mirror images of each other closed by a sharp /k/ sound. The logo is a capital 'G', which is also an 'e' – a reminder that the school is part of a privately owned group. The sounds /e/,/s/,/an/ and /ion/ as well as the alliterations of /l/, /d/ and /p/, bind the text together, further underlining its coherence and very self-conscious structure. The message as a whole shows classical restraint in its brevity and balance. At the same time, despite the assumption that this is a text which is not intended to be read as 'literature', it has the quality of a poem, albeit not one which breaks any new ground.

Assumption 2: 'Creativity is an attribute of the individual'

To identify style and stylistics solely with texts written by individuals is to misunderstand the conditions under which much writing takes place. The creative element in writing may well not be the consequence of a single person's contribution. Many texts are the product of collective authorship or are heavily influenced by the system of 'patronage', individual or corporate, which has led to their being commissioned (cf. Lefevere 1992; Hutcheon 1988). Film and television producers intervene directly in the books and screenplays which are made available to the public, just as the texts of advertisements and government reports are the outcome of the interplay between individuals and groups. Institutional forces are always at work in the construction of texts and the balance between personal and collective imaginations can often not be identified.

It is impossible to gauge to what extent the ESSEC text is the product of an individual imagination. Certainly, the decision to build the message around the interdependence and complementarity between '*fonction*', '*pédagogie*', '*entreprise*' and '*formation*' and to develop sentences which combine in such a deliberately symmetrical and harmonious way demanded a single-mindedness of vision which bears the hallmark of individual creativity. Yet the extent to which this factor contributes to the overall quality of a text can never be stated absolutely. Any such statement has to be the outcome of the reader's critical judgement applied to the language of the text supported by as much knowledge and information as may be at her or his disposal.

The extent to which written texts are the product of individuals or institutions impinges on the wider philosophical and ideological question of the relationship between individual freedom and deterministic forces – i.e. social and economic agencies which are outside individuals' control. This is another issue which the ESSEC text may illuminate but in practice does not help us to resolve. The 'deterministic' case is expressed in extreme terms by Foucault:

Décrire une formulation en tant qu'énoncé ne consiste pas à analyser les rapports entre l'auteur et ce qu'il a dit . . ., mais à déterminer quelle est la position que peut et doit occuper tout individu pour en être le sujet.

(1969: 126)

If this analysis is taken literally, there were social, political, economic and linguistic forces at work in 1986 which made the creation of a text like 'ESSEC' inevitable. 'ESSEC' was a text which was 'waiting to be written'. It had a 'position' in the symbolic fabric of society which only had to be filled. In writing it, the author or authors of the text were realising a function whose terms and conditions had been determined in advance.

If taken to its logical extreme, the above position, however attractive from an abstract and strictly theoretical point of view, deprives the individual of any symbolic freedom of manoeuvre, a view which denies the right to liberty inherent in language itself. There are many ways to write an advertisement. How could it have been known that the statement as expressed in 'ESSEC' would have followed precisely the form of this text? Its format and language would inevitably have been the outcome of discussions and decisions in which creativity was placed in the service of an institutional cause but could not, for all that, have been absent. The way in which Foucault resolves this paradox is considered in greater detail later. For the time being, it is sufficient to say that in our approach to text analysis the element of choice is never completely excluded, but finds itself rather in a state of tension or balance with the normative demands imposed by the genre of the message concerned and by the social context in which the communication takes place.

Assumption 3: 'You can't educate for literacy and develop critical awareness at the same time'

One of the primary objectives of 'traditional' stylistic commentary was to enhance learners' insight into works of written art so that they could use the same stylistic devices themselves. Stylistic commentary was, and still is, a descriptive art which is part of a training in writing in the same way that to appreciate the techniques behind fine art is to go some way towards becoming an artist oneself. As has already become clear, discourse analysis, particularly when accompanied by a 'critical' agenda, has a different focus. The text is seen as the symbolic expression of an institution or of an individual acting within an institutional framework. The task of the analyst becomes that of identifying and making explicit the manner in which the text reinforces and mediates the position which the institution occupies relative to other institutions within society. These two approaches are generally viewed as mutually exclusive, but in practice there is no reason why they should be. Imitating the style of a text and appreciating its language do not preclude being aware of its social significance. It is not clear why an inclusive approach to style analysis should not achieve both objectives.

Perhaps the most foregrounded stylistic features in the ESSEC text from a grammatical point of view are the dominance of noun phrases and the combination of what are termed 'binary' (×2) and 'ternary' (×3) rhythms in the sentence structure:

ESSEC: binary and ternary rhythms

BINARY . . . *de gestion* (1) *et de direction* (2) *des entreprises* . . .

BINARY . . . *la connaissance* (1) *et la pratique* (2) *des techniques les plus avancées* . . .

TERNARY . . . *le sens des responsabilités* (1), *le souci de la communication* (2), *la passion d'entreprendre* (3) . . . .

The combination of these rhythmic patterns in the text can be used as a 'model of good practice' to be imitated in writing and can be highlighted as a marker of a balanced, classical style which combines effectiveness with simplicity. Simultaneously, the same stylistic features evoke a sense of tradition and privilege which has symbolic value. The text is as much about exclusion as about promotion. Few candidates will be in a position to apply for ESSEC and, of those who apply, fewer still will be admitted. The prospect of a senior managerial position which the school offers is by definition only open to those who already share the culture and background which is being mythologised by the stylistic structure of the text. ESSEC is one of four schools which see themselves as being in the top league of business schools in France and which recruit following a highly competitive two-year preparation post-*baccalauréat*. Unlike most of the *Grandes Ecoles* in other discipline areas, the *Ecoles de Commerce* are privately owned but have to conform to State criteria which are regulated by a special association or '*Chapitre*'. In terms of its value as a pedagogical instrument, ESSEC is therefore both a source of stylistic and linguistic instruction and a social document, and can be studied from both perspectives.

Background and context

Although it has been convenient to present stylistics and discourse analysis as bred of different traditions, the two fields do in fact have common roots. Since the time of the ancient Greeks, text analysis has had a huge influence on the form of written texts. It was also part of the agenda of the original academies in Athens to question the ethical basis of political argument and to use an understanding of the nature of discourse to make citizens more critically aware. The influence of this tradition has been especially strongly felt in France. Textual commentary has been part of an educational cycle which has caused written conventions to reproduce themselves through the ages and – until very recently – to impose closely defined conditions of literacy on citizens' inclusion in a French national community. Young people were – and to some extent still are – required to analyse problems according to a defined discursive format and, if they fail to do so, do not succeed in the educational system. The conventions of written texts impose constraints on members of a linguistic community and it is part of the task of text analysis to explore the relationship between these conventions and the acts of writing and reading. An historical knowledge of the principles of text analysis helps us to develop a more critical understanding of the relationship between written texts and the social and cultural contexts in which they have been produced.

Rhetorical origins and the written standard

The ancestor of modern text analysis is the discipline of 'rhetoric', which originated as a core element of democratic politics and philosophy in classical Greece. The democracies of Greek city states revolved around open discussion and debate and it was customary for citizens to be called upon to defend themselves publicly in cases of civil or criminal litigation. It was therefore essential to become skilful in formal oral communication. Rhetoric – 'the art of speaking well' – was explicitly codified by reputed teachers who founded rival academies offering training in verbal skills. In the best of these schools, the acquisition of verbal virtuosity was not seen only as a necessary social skill but as part of the development of the whole person. The ethical foundations of rhetoric were themselves hotly debated and gave rise to philosophical arguments (which are still with us today) about the nature of virtue and truth and the relationship between reality and representation (cf. Conley 1990; Dixon 1971; Molinié 1993; Pinker 1997).

Only a few written examples of these codifications still exist today. However, those which have survived have had a profound and lasting influence on language learning, composition and techniques of analysis through the ages. The most wide-ranging original Greek source is Aristotle's *The Art of Rhetoric*, a treatise on human nature which sets out a complete theory and description of communication. The process of persuasion is explained in full from the choice of subject matter through the selection and organisation of the material to the psychological factors which have to be taken into account if a message is to be communicated effectively. *The Art of Rhetoric* was more a work of psychology and philosophy than a manual of instruction (Lawson-Tancred 1991), but it served as a point of reference for the subsequent generations of thinkers and teachers who have wished to make the techniques of effective expression and communication more accessible to their pupils.

Four hundred years later, Roman thinkers took the Greeks' writings on rhetoric as models and developed treatises of their own. The best known of these are the works by Cicero and Quintilian, and one complete textbook on rhetoric with an explicitly pedagogical function, the *Rhetorica ad Herennium*, whose author is unknown. Like all attempts to reduce complex social functions to categories which can be readily understood and remembered, the principles on which rhetorical instruction was based were greatly oversimplified and inevitably artificial. But it is precisely for this reason that they have lasted so long. Reduced to its basic elements, the aims and objectives of rhetoric were threefold: *docere*: 'to teach', a principle which entailed the aim of convincing others of the truth; *placere*: 'to please', that is, to give pleasure and interest to those listening; *movere*: 'to move', or appeal to the emotions of the audience. Underlying the whole process was the desire to promote the twin principles of virtue and truth for the greater well-being of the individual learner and of society at large.

There were three main types or genres of rhetorical composition, each being related to a particular ethical principle. The goal of deliberative or political oration was to convince an audience to follow a particular course of action and was underpinned, in theory at least, by the principle of maximising the prospect of happiness for the majority. Demonstrative oratory, the ancestor of the modern personality profile, sought to give a portrait of a particular person, attributing praise or blame as the speaker deemed appropriate. The underlying aim of the demonstrative genre was that of virtue. The audience was to learn a moral lesson from the strengths and weaknesses of the individual concerned which would inform its own future conduct. The third type of oratory was known as judicial or forensic, that is accusation and defence in law underpinned by the principles of social justice and truth.

As with the composition of any written document, the art of constructing and presenting a good speech was divided into five key components:

- the choice of subject matter or motivation which lay behind the message (*inventio*);
- the arrangement or organisation of the material (*dispositio*);
- the selection and the organisation of the language used to express the message (*elocutio*);
- the committing of the text to memory (*memoria*);
- the manner of delivery: the volume and tone of voice, accent, stress, intonation and pace of speech (*pronunciatio*).

In its purest form, effective composition should include an introduction to the main theme or proposition (*exordium*), a development (*narratio*), a confirmation or argument in favour (*confirmatio*), a refutation or argument against (*refutatio*) and, finally, a summing-up or conclusion (*peroratio*). Obviously, it was central to a successful speech that the message be appropriate to the audience for whom the speech was intended and to the context in which it was delivered. With this in mind, rhetorical teaching divided language into three registers or levels – high, medium and low – the important thing being to respect the wishes of the audience and to conform to the relative formality or informality of the occasion. Central to finding the right tone was the measured use of imagery (tropes) and the integration of patterns, rhythms and sounds in the grammatical and phonic organisation of sentences (schemes). These have been handed down to us as figures of speech (including such well-known examples as antithesis, euphemism, hyperbole, irony, metaphor, progression, etc.), which are still taught as stock techniques that can help to give prose style greater resonance, richness and variety.

In France, particularly after the Renaissance, the teaching of rhetoric became a key part of the education of every young aspiring French nobleman (France 1972) and is generally felt to have found its highest expression in the neo-classical tragedies of the mid- to late seventeenth century, notably those of the playwright Jean Racine (1639–1699), and in public orations such as the sermons preached by the Bishop of Meaux, Jacques Bossuet (1627–1704). Concern with conventions extended to more standard forms of communication in society. Towards the end of the seventeenth century, the preoccupation with appropriateness (*bienséance*) had become so great that it was possible for the moralist and social commentator Jean de La Bruyère (1688: 71) to assert that, for properly educated members of society, there was only one 'right' way of saying something in a particular context:

> *Entre toutes les expressions que peuvent rendre une seule de nos pensées, il n'y en a qu'une qui soit la bonne. On ne la rencontre pas toujours en parlant ou en écrivant; il est vrai néanmoins qu'il existe, que tout ce qui ne l'est point est faible, et ne satisfait point un homme d'esprit qui veut se faire entendre.*

This position, which represented the most extreme fusion of idealism and absolutism applied to language, was about as far as the practical implementation of rhetorical principles could go. It depended on norms of conduct, including verbal behaviour, being explicitly codified and tightly controlled. Despite leaving indelible traces on French culture, the absolute prescription of linguistic behaviour was not a principle which, in its most extreme form, could last for very long.

Inevitably, the balanced, formal codes which were characteristic of the hierarchical structures of late seventeenth century France, contained as they were by absolute monarchy and the power of the Catholic Church, eventually gave way to more free-flowing forms of discourse (Deloffre 1970). The balance and control of classical style was later replaced as a model by the fluid but no less rhetorical expression of sentiment linked to an affinity with nature popularised by Jean-Jacques Rousseau (1712–1778). However, the cult of *sensibilité* which eventually became the doctrine of the revolutionary government (Schama 1989) did not in any way imply a lessening in the urge to centralise. After the upheavals of the 1789 Revolution, the leaders of the First Republic engaged in an intensive nation-building project. France had up to this point been a fairly disparate collection of regions. One of the goals of the revolutionaries was to recreate France as the first European republic of the modern era and to instil a new sense of national identity. The centralised national education system sought to impose a common linguistic culture on the country as a whole. As well as taking the writings of the great Roman republican politicians as models of rhetorical composition, it became standard for French writers of philosophy and literature to exemplify the highest forms of linguistic achievement which young citizens of the republic should seek to emulate, a practice which had already become current 150 years earlier amongst the aristocracy and the *haute bourgeoisie* (Brunot 1947: 51). Since the Renaissance, textual commentary has remained one of the lasting cornerstones of French secular education. The speeches of great political orators or leading writers of literature whose texts have become sanctified or 'canonised' are exploited as 'models of good practice' by the state education system, an approach which is exemplified by the following in the introduction to a secondary school manual published as recently as 1995 (Amon and Bomati):

Vocabulaire du Commentaire de Texte: Avant-propos

Qu'est-ce que le 'style'? Une manière d'écrire, une certaine façon d'exploiter les ressources de la langue pour donner de la personnalité à un texte. Mais qu'est-ce que la 'langue'? La langue est à l'écrivain ce que la peinture est au peintre: une matière première. Composée de sons, de formes et de constructions, elle offre une source inépuisable de moyens d'expression. Comme le peintre, l'écrivain choisit et dose, soucieux de donner une forme idéale à sa vision, qu'il calcule au détail près les effets escomptés ou qu'il obéisse à sa seule intuition. De cette combinaison volontaire ou spontanée jaillit une formule magique: le style d'un auteur.

Si les lycéens ne manquent pas une sensibilité littéraire, il faut avouer qu'ils sont cruellement désarmés lorsqu'il s'agit d'identifier, de décrire et d'analyser un fait de style. Le Vocabulaire du commentaire de texte entend combler cette lacune: voici un outil de travail qui permettra aux élèves d'apprécier l'art d'un auteur, puis d'acquérir de solides connaissances techniques pour aborder avec assurance les épreuves de français au baccalauréat. Il présente les principaux moyens d'expression utilisés en littérature, notamment un ensemble de formules héritées de la rhétorique grecque et connues sous le nom de 'figures de style', les règles de versification, les divers types de style, niveaux de langue etc.

As the above extract makes clear, the classical approach to stylistic description depends essentially on the separation between content and form. The idea itself or the subject matter of a text can be formulated in different ways. The art of the writer lies in the manner in which he or she expresses it. As Quintilian, the first-century Roman writer and theoretician of rhetoric, put it: 'style is the dress of thought'. It is seen as an adornment, a way of presenting a given reality. If things and ideas are 'the what' (*inventio*), style is 'the how' (*dispositio* and *elocutio*). Seen from this traditional perspective, style is therefore a matter of informed choice. Words are selected from the stock of vocabulary in the language; different sentence structures, sounds and figures of speech are combined in such a way as to lend a written message beauty and expressive force. These techniques can be learned through conscious imitation and their acquisition is a core component of the traditional humanities curriculum.

However, as was true when the teaching of rhetoric was first promoted in classical times, more recent programmes of literacy training based on the appreciation and imitation of great writers do more than just enfranchise the citizen. As we have seen, they reinforce a sense of group identity by imposing a norm which becomes accepted as the standard code (or *koiné*) for 'educated' members of the speech community. '*Le bon usage*' represents an official consensus which is exemplified with reference to literary models and is held to symbolise a national tradition. To borrow Pierre Bourdieu's metaphor, the acquisition of a certain 'approved' spoken and written idiom represents a form of social capital (Bourdieu 1982). This is no accident. Since the seventeenth century, despite being constantly challenged, the written standard has been seen by the majority of the French population for what it is: the official hallmark of the culture in power. Having originally developed as a means of individual emancipation, the rhetorical tradition has long since become an institutionalised feature of French language and culture which serves not only to educate the individual but also operates as an instrument of control and social exclusion. To write 'in the manner of' the approved writers of the canon who feature on the syllabus of the French *baccalauréat* is not simply a condition of belonging to the national community. It is a symbol of identity which has always been recognised as such by the French government and by the population as a whole – if only by default.

The ESSEC text can clearly be analysed as a rhetorical text. It is designed, as are all advertisements, to persuade the reader to follow a particular course of action, in this case that of applying to a prestigious institution, by linking a positive description of the attributes of the entrepreneurial executive to an assertion that the school will develop these qualities. It qualifies as a demonstrative text which has a deliberative function in that it links persuasion to the portrait of an idealised model. Different aspects of the text fulfil the three principal goals of rhetoric: *docere*, *placere*, *movere*. The use and repetition of high-sounding expressions ('*excellence . . . passion . . . renommée*'), incorporated into simple sentences, informs the reader of the school's reputation; the coherence and symmetry of the text, reinforced by the sound patterns, could be said to arouse pleasure, while together with '*exige . . . exigence*' the words carry evident emotional force. Equally, the structure of the text, while not exhibiting all the five rhetorical subcategories (*refutatio* is missing), can be seen to have a clearly signalled start (*exordium*) in the headline, a central description (*narratio*) and a strong, confirmatory conclusion (*confirmatio/peroratio*) in the two subheaders: '*L'excellence dans la formation; la pas-sion d'entreprendre*'.

Rhetoric is often decried today. It is used pejoratively to refer to language which is unnecessarily overblown or to the use of complex forms of expression which disguise shallowness of content. However, this is to misunderstand a discipline which has always had far-reaching social and moral objectives. Despite appearances to the contrary, rhetoric was not simply a formula. It was more a flexible guide to effective communication in which the ethical and pedagogical functions were paramount. In their wider sense, rhetorical principles are not simply applied to exercises in speechifying or in written composition. They can be seen to be present in written and spoken messages of all kinds and have long been used as tools in reading: to enhance appreciation of the expressive qualities of texts produced by others, and also, more recently – as in this book – to sharpen awareness of their social significance.

Structuralism, functionalism and the analysis of written style

Rhetoric is essentially a model of performance designed for an individual seeking to produce language for a given end in a given social situation. It is hardly surprising that, since rhetorical principles have always been taught by the major educational institutions, these principles should have become identified with the official norm or 'standard' against which other forms of expression are seen as vulgar or inappropriate. In a narrow sense, rhetoric is often seen as a form of institutional control promoting conformity to a dominant culture rather than a type of education which embraces the values and behaviours of diverse social groups. It has also been criticised for placing undue emphasis on aesthetic value or beauty of expression. In exploiting the figurative potential of the language, the individual speaker or writer is more likely to be persuasive if he or she uses expressions which are 'well-formed'; that is to say, agreeable to listen to, balanced and harmonious, a principle all too easily subject to regulation by social forces which favour stability and central control over dynamism and plurality of expression.

While the traditional interests of rhetoric have often been represented as essentially developmental and politically motivated, the same cannot be said of twentieth-century theorists whose objective has been to develop a more detached, scientifically grounded approach to style. Roman Jakobson (1896–1982) is one of the major linguists who explained language and linguistic processes in terms of internally coherent formal structures. From his earliest days as a student in Moscow before World War I, Jakobson and his fellow founder members of the 'Moscow Linguistics Circle' were preoccupied by the relationship between the structure of language and the formal organisation of poetry and folklore. He and the group which became known as the Russian formalists saw literary (or 'poetic') language as self-referring, detached from the 'real world' and distinct from other forms of discourse. If the observation of structures in matter itself was the task of pure science, the goal of linguistics was to identify the patterns underlying the formulation of sounds, words and sentences as inter-related networks which could be taken as external manifestations of the way in which the human mind worked.

In applying formalist principles to literary language, Jakobson claimed to be giving an objective account of the qualities which gave poetic writing aesthetic value. He was consciously reacting against hypothetical interpretations of litera-ture based on information about the writers' life. In the spirit of abstraction which marked the modernist era, he was reducing poetry to its formal essentials, seeking to identify recurrent patterns of grammatical structures, the repetition of rhythms and sounds, symmetries and asymmetries which formed a symbolic framework reflecting the thematic structures of the piece of language under review. A particu-lar sequence of word order might be repeated and the resulting comparison or contrast would point towards the wider meanings at work within the piece.

Jakobson's ideas on 'poetics' (the application of stylistic analysis to literary language) evolved over more than forty-five years, while his more general pre-occupation with structure remained the defining feature of his long and dis-tinguished career as a researcher and teacher. His relentless enquiries into the formal systems which underpinned the expression of thought in language covered every field of linguistic research including phonology, language acquisition, loss of language function due to physical damage (traumatic aphasia), grammar and trans-lation. It was through his desire to integrate a theory of structure into a model of communication that Jakobson turned his attention to the notion of function. He wanted to apply principles which had so far been developed through the analysis of poetic language within a wider, more practical social context, to show how 'poetic' language and language of other types related to each other within a communicative setting. His ideas found definitive expression in a seminal paper published in 1960, 'Closing statement: linguistics and poetics'. In this article, he returned to the earlier thesis of the Russian formalists that poetic language was fundamentally distinct from 'everyday' communication. In poetry, the main emphasis was on the linguistic sign itself rather than on objects in the real world, whereas in 'standard' communication, the main purpose was to refer to tangible objects, to express identifiable emotions or to get other people to do things. In fact, although it was not his main intention, his paper demonstrated how simplistic this distinction was. He revealed how unusual it is for a text to focus on one function only – and therefore, by extension, how artificial the separation between literary and nonliterary discourse really is.

Jakobson used the term 'function' to describe the particular 'point of emphasis' of the message. His model was two-dimensional. At the two extremities of the horizontal axis were the 'sender/addresser' and the 'receiver/addressee'.

Cutting across this plane, the vertical axis opposed the 'context' in which the communication took place and the 'code' which was appropriate to it. In the middle, at the intersection of the two axes, Jakobson located the twin notions of the message itself and the maintenance of contact between the interlocutors. A different function was identified for each of the different points of emphasis in the model. Following Bühler (1934), the emphasis on the sender/addresser was termed 'emotive'; on the receiver/addressee, 'conative'; on the context, 'referential'; on the code, 'metalingual'. Where the focus was on maintaining the contact between speakers, the function concerned was termed phatic, while the poetic function described the type of language where the emphasis was on 'the message for its own sake', i.e. language which had no other point of reference other than itself.

The functions of language
Roman Jakobson (1960)

CONTEXT
referential

MESSAGE
poetic

SENDER   RECEIVER
emotive   conative

CONTACT
phatic

CODE
metalinguistic

Apart from its simplicity, what made Jakobson's model so powerful as an instrument of clarification was the fact that, although it clearly identified what was 'special' about poetic language, it placed all verbal messages of whatever type within a communicative framework. It was very unlikely that a message would fulfil one function to the exclusion of all others. Any text could engage the poetic function to the extent that it had a coherent and identifiable internal structure. Its critical defining feature was that certain elements corresponded to other elements within the same text with which they shared grammatical, rhythmic or phonic features.

The multifunctional nature of text can be demonstrated by analysing the ESSEC text according to Jakobson's terms of reference. Our rhetorical approach to the text has shown that its primary objective was to persuade readers to apply to the school – a conative function. However, the actual language of the text is largely referential, being a description of the qualities of the ideal manager and linking these to the qualities which the school claims to develop in the student. The text does not address prospective students directly, ordering them to apply to the school or even suggesting that they do so. Grammatical structures such as the imperative, which normally articulate the conative function, are absent. However, the element of persuasion is implicit and strongly felt.

While the referential and conative functions appear to be the prime motivating forces behind the ESSEC text, its poetic qualities, as we have seen, cannot be denied. The symmetry of the ESSEC text, for example, is clearly self-referring. The sibilance of the /s/ sound followed by the palatal /k/ framed by the repeated half-close /e/ in the title 'ESSEC' are echoed in the word *'excellence,'* where /k/ and /s/ are inverted and brought together in a double consonant. An immediate association is created in the mind of the reader between the name of the school and the idea of excellence. The relationship between the two within the same message exemplifies the poetic function, yet its underlying objective is conative. If taken literally, Jakobson's definition of the poetic function – 'the message for its own sake' – is too pure. Even within a poem which claims to be nothing else, it is impossible to interpret the contextual meaning of words without taking some account of their meaning within the normal conventions of the language. The title of the poem *Zone* by Guillaume Apollinaire (1880–1918) lends itself to multiple interpretations which can be derived from the poem itself, but the reference to the strip of land between the circumference of the city of Paris and the outer suburbs is a fact of conventional meaning which cannot be ignored.

The influence of Jakobson's 1960 paper was considerable. Yet, despite its formal completeness, it left a number of practical issues unexplained. In particular, it pointed to the need for stylistic analysis to situate written messages within their social context. His model presented texts as the outcome of individuals' generating language in a 'closed' communicative situation, rather than as 'events' which were products of the wider social environment. But to analyse text from a socially grounded perspective demanded a fuller and more detailed explanation than then existed of the link between social relationships and linguistic form. The task of developing a theory of function which placed communication in its cultural context was left to a more practical school of linguistics, Anglo-Saxon in origin, of which Michael Halliday has become the best known proponent.

Halliday and functional linguistics

Much of Halliday's seminal work was produced at a time when the prevailing linguistic model was the formal, psychological model of language developed by the celebrated American linguist and political thinker Noam Chomsky (1957; 1965). This formal model posited an innate, internal mechanism for acquiring language which was universally present in human beings at birth and which could be represented in terms of mathematical rules. These rules which took the form of a new type of grammar served to describe how simple Subject – Verb – Object sentences were 'generated' and to explain how 'simple' sentences could be combined or 'transformed' to produce longer, more complex structures. However, although immensely powerful as a means of describing grammatical structure, Chomsky's model was less well-suited to explaining the relationship between linguistic form and the meaning of messages which, as many linguists and philosophers of language argued, depended not just on the choice of words and the structure of the language itself, but also on the intention of the speaker/writer and the social context in which the communication took place (Leech 1983).

Halliday's approach was to base grammatical descriptions on the functions which the language user was trying to fulfil. Using Bühler as a reference point, he began by observing how his own child acquired language and then went on to develop a descriptive model which could be more widely applied (Halliday 1975). Arguing that children initially develop language in order to fulfil particular needs or desires, he identified a limited set of objectives or 'functions' with which different utterances could be associated. Halliday named seven basic functions that could be seen as the basis for child language, and to which any utterance by a child of a certain age could be 'attached'. His approach worked well for young children, whose functional needs and command of language were relatively limited. However, it was ill-adapted to cope with the complexities of adult discourse, where the function of a particular utterance and the form of the message were less likely to be directly linked. As we have seen when considering Jakobson's model and in our analysis of the ESSEC text, most messages incorporate a number of functions. Halliday reduced this number to three higher-level (or meta-) functions which, he claimed, all adult discourse simultaneously fulfilled.

First, language was representing the world; referring to such things as physical objects and their attributes, processes and thoughts. This representational function is the one that we would most usually ascribe to language, and is called by Halliday the ideational function. It overlaps more or less completely with Jakobson's (and Bühler's) term 'referential'. Language is also constructing and representing relationships between people; defining participants' social roles and the terms of their interactions, representing participants' beliefs and commitments, influencing their states of mind and causing them to respond through 'speech acts' such as commands and questions. This function Halliday calls the interpersonal function, which effectively represents a fusion of Jakobson's emotive and conative categories. Finally, language has a textual function. This refers to the way texts are actually put together as texts, i.e. the grammatical means used to make a text make sense. This function could be said to cover the notion 'poetic' as employed by Jakobson, but Halliday gives it a more social edge, implying that texts are structured in a particular way not for aesthetic or structural reasons, but in order to make the message effective as an act of communication.

Halliday's functional approach provided a significantly new perspective on text analysis. Rather than defining 'context' in abstract terms and style as a property of the 'poetic' function, he sought to account for the way in which linguistic functions were variably related to the reality of the communicative situation. He began by differentiating between two levels at which the notion of context might be applied. The first was what he called the context of situation. A 'situation' was an individual instance of communication which represented the practical realisation in language of a much wider system of meanings shared by the members of a speech community or culture.

> Let us assume that the social system (or the 'culture') can be represented as a construction of meanings – as a semiotic system. The meanings that constitute the social system are exchanged through a variety of modes or channels, of which language is one; but not, of course, the only one – there are many other semiotic modes besides. Given this social-semiotic perspective, a *social context* (or 'situation', in the terms of situation theory) is a temporary construct or instantiation of meanings from the social system.
>
> (Halliday 1978:189)

For Halliday, the 'context of situation' of a text includes three elements. First, what is actually going on; that is, the external features of the context to which the text is referring and of which it is necessarily a part since it interacts with it and will generally cause it to change. This Halliday calls the 'field'. Second, the notion of context implies participants who are involved in one way or other in the act of communication. The participants or 'actors' may be directly engaged in the communicative process as producers of the message or as receivers, actual or implied. Alternatively, the participants may be products of the text itself – either as real people to whom the text refers or as fictional creations who serve to illustrate or embody the message by presenting it in 'human' terms. Halliday refers to this dimension or 'component' of the social context as the 'tenor'. Third, it is necessary to define and describe the form which the language takes in order to communicate the message, covering such things as the medium through which language is produced, the type and format of the text, and its relative importance in the situation. This is described as the 'mode':

> A social context is a semiotic structure which we may interpret in terms of three variables: a 'field' of social processes (what is going on), a 'tenor' of social relationships (who is taking part) and a 'mode' of symbolic interaction (how are the meanings exchanged) . . . The linguistic system, in other words, is organised in such a way that the social context is predictive of the text. This is what makes it possible for a member to make the necessary

predictions about the meanings that are being exchanged in any situation which s/he encounters.

(Halliday 1978:189)

Halliday's argument is similar in principle to that of Michel Foucault. According to the terms of Halliday's approach, no text, spoken or written, can be analysed as an independent entity. Texts are events. They are the direct products of contexts and cannot be accounted for separately from them. Although language can be described as a system in its own right, it is realised in situations which are themselves structured by the social conventions or institutions of which they are part. These conventions in turn constitute a wider semiotic framework or context, which Halliday refers to as the context of culture. Thus, acts of communication can be perceived as the product of four dynamically interrelated dimensions:

> context of culture
> context of situation
> function
> form.

From the moment of birth, all four dimensions contribute to the way in which meaning in society is constructed and represented in language.

Table 1 Halliday's functional approach

Context of culture *the culture as a semiotic system*	Context of situation *an instantiation of meanings from the social system*	Function *a mode of meaning; a component of the semantic system*	Form *the linguistic system – the structure of the language itself*
shared values and experiences, ways of seeing social conventions	field: 'reference, logic and social process – what is going on'	the ideational function	transitivity, nouns/pronouns used for reference, connectors and word order adjectives, etc.
conventions governing interpersonal communication: politeness formulae, directness/ indirectness, etc.	tenor: 'social relationship – who is taking part'	the interpersonal function	mood (imperative, interrogative, declarative, subjunctive, conditional, etc.), semantic value of words and images, etc.
dialect, register, code, form and structure of discourse	mode: 'the medium of communication – how are meanings exchanged'	the textual function	repetition, linking demonstratives, opening and closing of discourse, etc.

As the above table makes clear, in Halliday's model the three aspects of context can be mapped on to the three grammatical metafunctions. The ideational function realises the field of the social situation; the interpersonal function realises the tenor; and the textual function realises the mode. Language and language production are intimately related to the social context, in a way which is manifested in the actual grammar of the language. Halliday's theory of language is therefore based not on the formal, psychological or individual aspects of language production, but on its social nature. As he put it, 'language is a part of the social system, and there is no need to interpose a psychological level of interpretation' (1978: 39). So, although he does not dismiss person-centred explanations of language as wrong, he does suggest that they are unnecessary for the purposes of interpreting 'language in communication' or 'discourse'.

With reference to the ESSEC text, the role which elitist schools play within the French educational system and the economy as a whole, the context of culture, has already been discussed. The context of situation, too, is clear: a prestigious institution advertising in a national student publication, a fact which, given the quality of the school, is a little unexpected and needs to be taken into account. All these points relate to the field of the text. Its tenor concerns the relationship between the institution and the body of prospective applicants. As we have seen, the first clause of the main part of the text:

> *Se préparer aux fonctions de gestion et de direction des entreprises exige la connaissance et la pratique des techniques les plus avancées dans ces domaines. Et aussi une pédagogie que développe le sens des responsabilités, le souci de la communication, la passion d'entreprendre . . .*

is a description of the qualities which the prospective manager needs to develop. The second, '*La renommée de l'ESSEC se fonde sur ces deux exigences*', is a statement which confirms the reputation of the school. Both statements identify the terms of a relationship through verbs which state categorically 'this *is* so' rather than 'this *may be* so'. Assertions are presented as certainties and thereby construct a particular truth, at an ideational level. This aspect of the text is reinforced by the use of Subject–Verb–Object structures and by the use of the reflexive verb '*se préparer*', which depersonalises the truth value of the assertion and lends it a more general status. Thus it appears that the grammatical dynamics of the text make particular use of relational processes in order to construct certainties about the school rather than to enter into a dialogue with the reader. From an interpersonal point of view, it takes for granted that the reader already has a certain view of what the school stands for and will not seek to question this assumption. The construction of certainty is being used as a persuasive strategy. As far as the mode is concerned, the text, a written advertisement, makes full use of the cohesive potential of written style. The essential drives behind the message are purposefully and explicitly reinforced by the balance of the text. This is evident in the use of *ces* in the expression '*ces deux exigences*', which both refers back to the previous objects of *exiger* (the qualities which are being demanded) and forward to the two sub-headings. Thus, the textual function strengthens the various dichotomies in the text: between school and pupil, technical training and human development, rationality and emotion.

Foucault: discourse and power

Michael Halliday is a linguist in the Anglo-Saxon tradition who has developed his theories of discourse from his observation of language in use. Starting from a standpoint which is essentially practical and grounded in reality, he has sought throughout his work to elucidate the relationship between the structure of language and the patterns of social interaction. In his analysis of the relationship between language and social processes, the French philosopher Michel Foucault had wider, more abstract ambitions. He was less preoccupied by the structure of language as such, than by the principles which governed the relationships between groups in society. In *L'Archéologie du Savoir* (1969) and *L'Ordre du Discours* (1971), he argued that there are implicit rules governing the structure of language in text, or what he termed 'discourse', which are directly related to the way in which power is exercised in society. In any given field of communication, these rules underpinned what Foucault called 'discursive formations'. Discursive formations consist of conventions which govern a speaker or writer's choice of topic ('*objet*'), the form or structures in which it is represented ('*modalités d'énonciation*') and the conceptual framework ('*concept*' and '*choix thématique*') within which the treatment of the topic is set.

The implicit rules which govern the production of discourse serve to reproduce the particular configurations of power relations that define a given field of knowledge. Often, knowledge is produced in forms that do not overtly challenge the theories and modes of presentation of the discourse in power. But discursive formations interact and overlap and this dynamic process causes their structures to change. The way in which knowledge is processed and presented is determined by social and economic forces. These forces are not simply abstract and extraneous. They are present within discourse. Moreover, since discourse is central to the construction and maintenance of power relations, it is inevitable that institutions emerge within society to control and channel its production. Thus, the power of institutions is not just sustained through discourse, it resides in the discourse itself. In *L'Ordre du Discours*, his celebrated inaugural lecture to the *Collège de France* delivered in December 1970, Foucault spoke about the means used by institutions to control the power of discourse. These include conventions such as the exclusion of particular objects from particular discourses, prohibitions on speaking about particular things (notably in the realms of sexuality and politics) and implicit agreement between writers and readers as to what constitutes truth.

In creating texts, subjects are constrained in the range of choices they can make. Equally, different forms of discourse impose conditions on readers and listeners which limit the way in which they can be understood. The exercise of power through the rules of discursive formation should not therefore be understood in the traditional sense of one person or institution deliberately exercising power over another. Foucault's point was that the structures of discourse force individuals and groups to adopt certain positions towards each other within a complex web of social relations. It follows that in order to understand society it is necessary to study discourse, to understand the implicit rules governing different discursive formations and so to gain insights into the relationships between them. In *L'Archéologie du Savoir*, Foucault suggested how this should be done. He was anxious to propose an analysis of the social forces present in discourse which would take account of its inconsistencies and discontinuities. The rules of discursive formation could not be uncovered by a sweeping search for unity that ignored the uneven, overlapping nature of discursive events. Instead, a close-grained examination of individual features was necessary.

The ESSEC text, for example, realises at least two discursive formations: that of the world of advertising and that of the *Grande Ecole*. To these can be added the discourse of management associated with a 'culture of enterprise' (Keat and Abercrombie 1991). The first two discourses can be seen to conflict. There is a contradiction between the general function of the text as advertisement and the interpersonal features of the language. In advertising, the producer of an advertisement is trying to appeal to consumers and to influence their choices. Implicitly, it is the consumers who are powerful, since they can choose to accept or reject the product on offer. However, in appearing to offer choice, producers are seeking at the same time to exercise power and control. According to the rules of a discourse of advertising, the school is constructed as a product which is being offered to students in competition with the range of other such products. Seemingly, it is the prospective student who has the power to choose. In the educational discourse of the *Grande Ecole*, however, it is the *school* which has the power of selection, since the applicants are obliged to enter a competition from which only a very few will emerge as successful. At the same time, this conflict of discourses is representative of a wider social tension between, on the one hand, education as a public service whose delivery is based on an implicit moral contract between the citizen and the State, and, on the other, a private good which is open to 'free' competition.

As has already been pointed out, discursive formations do not simply condition the language which can be used to talk about particular objects; they actually produce the objects themselves. The two discourses at work in the ESSEC text generate a new social persona: the 'student as consumer' who, having chosen an institution, can be led to expect a certain quality of service, and the 'student as applicant' who has to pass a severely competitive examination to get in. The privatisation or commodification of educational provision necessarily produces this paradox (Fairclough 1995). The state-provided service becomes a good offered within a public marketplace. The provision having been purchased, the balance of power shifts to the student consumer, who is then in a position to demand value for money; namely, to be transformed into the executive whose properties the advertisement describes. The discourse of the text thereby reinforces the further persona of 'student as potential manager', a specific 'manager object' whose character is so constructed within the discursive formation of a wider enterprise culture that it is assumed by the public at large to have the features described by the ESSEC text: '*le sens des responsabilités, le souci de la communication, la passion d'entreprendre*'.

Clearly, this is a formulation of language and power that differs from rhetorical approaches which were essentially centered on the subject as potential writer. There, citizens were seen as free to construct spoken and written discourse from the resources of language open to them, provided that they had a certain level of education. In the Foucauldian framework, different subjects are differently positioned in networks of power relations and therefore have access to different discourses. The idea that there may be one set of rules as in rhetoric, however complex and far-reaching, simply does not apply. For Foucault, a theory of discourse and a theory of society are completely inseparable, with discourse being the malleable material which moulds and gives a semblance of stability to the structures of institutions and human relationships.

Critical linguistics: language and ideology

Once Michel Foucault's central thesis has been accepted, it is impossible to be indifferent to the social and political consequences of any discourse. In *Language and Control*, Fowler et al. (1979) demonstrated that, through text analysis, it was possible to make explicit the ideologies encoded in texts, particularly those taken from public discourse. Since then, critical linguistic analyses have sought to expose the manner in which texts support socially damaging ideologies such as racism, sexism, nationalism or the oppression of minority groups. This critical approach to language has an emancipatory goal. By making explicit the constraining role played by language in processes of socialisation, critical analysis can render transparent ideologies which have previously been hidden in the discourses of texts, and thereby raise social awareness.

Drawing on the work of Halliday, Foucault and earlier social philosophers of language such as Bakhtin (1895–1975) and Gramsci (1891–1937), Norman Fairclough (1989, 1992, 1995, 2000) has sought to combine linguistic and socially grounded approaches to the analysis of discourse. He links what he terms a 'multi-dimensional' approach to the functional approach adopted by Halliday. His insistence on the need to be 'critical' is a call for discourse analysis to expose the multiple forces involved in social and discursive change and for the analyst to intervene in these processes. In this sense, the critical discourse analyst has an important social and educational role to play in combating relations of inequality which are both material and discursive.

We have seen above how rhetoric is not merely a tool for linguistic analysis but also has a pedagogic role. For Fairclough and others, the critical analysis of discourse outlined above has clear implications, which impact on the educational system as a whole. In terms similar to those of the original rhetoricians, he argues that it is vital for the citizens of a democracy to gain an insight into the relationship between language and power. This political and educational priority is as important as that of providing citizens with their own set of expressive instruments. Following Gramsci, Fairclough stresses that, in modern democracies, power is largely exercised on a discursive level, since 'it is mainly in discourse that consent is achieved, ideologies are transmitted, and practices, meanings, values and identities are taught and learned' (1995: 219). It is essential, therefore, that mature citizens have a proper understanding of the way in which these discursive processes operate. The critical analysis of text is one of the most effective ways in which this insight and understanding are to be achieved.

Stylistics and discourse analysis: the basis for a new approach

In the above discussion we have introduced two broad categories of approach to text analysis. The first, historically rooted in the discipline of rhetoric, developed originally as a way of systematising the 'art of speaking well' in ancient Greece and Rome, and went on to have a central place in the development of the modern French educational system. A central pillar of this system was '*explication de texte*', the exercise of analysing the rhetorical features of texts written by philosophers and writers in the French literary canon who were thought to be worthy of imitation. '*La stylistique*', which originated from this approach, attempted to capture the resources of the French language in use so as to enable learners to use them more effectively. Within this paradigm, language has been seen as a resource available to any individual, and style viewed as an individual aesthetic choice. Individuals can be empowered through a process of education to develop their capacities for autonomous expression.

The second paradigm has presented language as being embedded in social relationships. For Foucault and for the critical linguists who have come after him, language is a form of social practice, and the use of language is subject both to constraints and possibilities. Individuals using language are social beings. The discourses to which they have been exposed and the social situations in which they find themselves determine the range of discursive possibilities available to them. In this paradigm, style derives not merely from individuals choosing to 'dress' their thought in particular ways. Instead, all linguistic choices are constrained by society and also shape it, both at the level of an immediate context of situation and at the wider institutional, ideological and cultural levels. As a consequence of its social grounding, the critical linguistic approach deals largely with contemporary, everyday texts which have little or no pretensions to greatness: management training leaflets, university prospectuses, conversations. Analysis of such texts demonstrates how they reproduce or resist social structures and ideologies, and reveals their role in maintaining configurations of power relationships.

While both approaches see text analysis as having an emancipatory role, each is founded on a distinct theoretical conception of 'the individual'. The first posits an autonomous agent whose integrity and social identity can be developed through an education based on the power of self-expression. For the second, individuals only exist by virtue of their position in society. They are constructed through progressive exposure to social structures and interpersonal relationships, which are institutionalised and mediated through discursive practice. They are simultaneously *made subject to* constraining forces and *produced* as subjects with a capacity for action.

However, the two positions are not as different as might appear. As we have seen, the art of rhetoric is far from being simply an educational instrument. It is present in advertising as much as in political speeches and is as much the product of institutions as of individuals. It is a manipulative as well as a liberating force. Equally, it is perfectly possible to reconcile the power of discourse to 'construct' individuals with their own capacities to accept or reject the 'position' which the discourse invites them to take up. There are two main arguments which support this point of view. First, while individuals are constrained by their positioning with respect to particular discourses, these discourses are always multiple. Although in some fields there is often one dominant or 'primary' discourse, there are always alternative 'resistant' discourses available in the same field which construct the world differently. This contestation and resistance leads to new and original texts as existing discourses are reconciled in new ways. Second, readers come to texts with their own knowledge and experience of discourses, and can reconstruct texts themselves with respect to their own systems of meanings. As Kress puts it:

> Readers need not comply with the demands of a reading position constructed for them. The options range from not being the reader at all, to a distanced, critical reading, where the reader refuses to enter the reading position constructed in the text and thereby reconstructs the text in a significantly different form in reading it. . . . Clearly, the best reader will be a critical, resistant reader, one who sees the constructedness of the text and of the reading position and who can, at the same time, reconstruct the text in a manner useful to himself or herself.
>
> (Kress 1989: 40)

This statement accurately summarises the perspective which this book is seeking to develop. The process of 'understanding' text not only instils in readers the capacity for enfranchisement through critical awareness, but also invests in them the power to achieve fulfilment through a construction of self which is linked to a better society. In this sense, the philosophical and political objectives of critical discourse analysis and rhetorical training, although ideologically distinct, are, in practice, complementary and mutually inclusive. They are both historically specific approaches to the analysis of language, rooted in very different world-views, but, although they come at the same problem from different angles, they do not rule each other out. The 'critical' approach – as its name suggests – has to do with informed understanding and awareness of the way social forces operate through text. Stylistics aims to impart to individuals the power to generate language which will change them and others. The goal of both is emancipation. Critical readers should make creative writers as well as informed citizens. An approach to text analysis which combines a number of traditions offers students of foreign languages the opportunity to gain a deeper insight into a target culture, whilst at the same time understanding better how the language works as an instrument.

Incommensurable though the differences between stylistics and critical discourse analysis may appear, it is perfectly possible to see the individual both as a socially situated and constrained subject and as a creative and original human being. It is the interaction of these two forces that causes the continuity of social structures to be accompanied by change. Individuals have unique discursive histories, and therefore have different relationships with the multiplicity of discursive formations within which they have been positioned. They also have the capacity to make choices within and between discourses. In a Sartrian sense, they are quite literally '*en situation*'. As Kress states, 'A theory which makes no allowance for the social determination of linguistic practice is obviously deficient; at the same time a theory which ignores individual difference in linguistic practice – a matter equally apparent to any observer – is also deficient' (1989: 12). Halliday puts it somewhat differently: 'At every level, the text instantiates the system; and this is . . . a two-way process, since each instance disturbs the probabilities of the system and hence destroys and recreates it – almost identically, but not quite' (1987: ix). For Halliday, the process is a systemic one, which can be expressed in terms of 'probabilities'. Although 'disturbances' result from individual initiative, he does not present these as radical processes but as minute, virtually invisible, transformations. Fairclough, however, goes further: 'Change involves forms of transgression, crossing boundaries, such as putting together existing conventions in new combinations, or drawing upon conventions in situations which usually preclude them' (1992: 96). As he points out, trangression and originality are not the exclusive properties of individuals. Texts produced by institutional agencies may be just as creative and capable of causing the structure of discursive formations to change.

Whether change be initiated by individuals or institutions, Foucault's personal project was to demonstrate that human imagination should strive to exceed the power of society to control and direct it. Innumerable participants in daily discourses redefine conventions and establish the bases for new discursive formations. All individuals and social agencies are in a dynamic relationship with the discourses which have framed their ways of thinking. Although it is not given to the majority of citizens to lay the grounds for radically different forms of expression, the power of language provides them with that potential, or at least with an instrument which, through education, can be used, (more or less freely), to counteract ideologies or to collude with them, to form personal projects for good or ill and to pursue their realisation.

ESSEC: an advert for the *École Supérieure des Sciences Economiques et Commerciales*, from *L'Etudiant: Le Guide des Métiers*, November 1986, p. 167.

ESSEC

Se préparer aux fonctions de gestion et de direction des entreprises exige la connaissance et la pratique des techniques les plus avancées dans ces domaines. Et aussi une pédagogie qui développe le sens des responsabilités, le souci de la communication, la passion d'entreprendre. La renommée de l'ESSEC se fonde sur ces deux exigences.

L'excellence dans la formation

La passion d'entreprendre

Groupe
[logo]
ESSEC

École Supérieure des Sciences Économiques et Commerciales, Établissement
Supérieur Privé reconnu par l'État
Avenue de la Grande École — B.P. 105 — 95021 CERGY-PONTOISE
CEDEX — Tél. : (1) 30.38.38.00

For the original format, see page 6.

Approaching the text

Robert Crawshaw and Karin Tusting

In the previous chapter we explored the theoretical background to an approach to text analysis. Text was seen neither as the product of an individual subject nor as the outcome of a definable set of social determinants but as the dynamic combination of a multiplicity of constraints and creative forces. The constraints include the grammatical form of the language itself, the conventions surrounding the context within which text is produced and which determine its tone or register, the norms which define the genre or type to which a text belongs, the expectations which a text of that type can be expected to generate within its readers, and so on. The creative forces comprise the agency of an author or social collectivity. Whatever agencies have contributed to the text's composition, it will inevitably be located in time and place and will use real or fictional characters to convey a message. By definition, it will draw on the resources of the language. Using these to confirm or question the genre within which it is composed and to enhance its effectiveness as a message, it may contain images and metaphors, long or short sentences, and direct and indirect speech. It may exploit effects of sound and rhythm and may at times display forms which are so deviant as to be at first almost incomprehensible. In a close reading of any text, all these factors need to be acknowledged and made explicit.

In this chapter, our focus shifts from an objective review of the interrelationship between author, context, text and reader to a more didactic analysis of the reading process. Our task now is to attempt to translate our understanding of what text is into a practical technique for making explicit the outcomes of reading and interpretation in a way which draws together the different threads we have just explored. We want to learn not simply how to 'read' but to know how to describe what we have read. This implies being aware of the relationship between the text concerned and others of its kind, appreciating its language and inferring its effects on its readership. We can thereby evaluate its contribution to linguistic and cultural change.

There is, of course, no one 'right' way to read a text. There are as many readings as there are readers. Each of us brings our own background, intellect, culture and assumptions to the ways we see and understand. Moreover, every reading replaces the one which went before. Each time we read a text, even a short extract, we see something different. Just as readings vary, so too do techniques of analysis. As the multiple readings of the ESSEC text in the previous chapter demonstrate, there is no infallible 'method' that can be followed to 'produce' an insightful and informative textual commentary and, as authors, it is not our intention to present one.

Having said this, our project is educational. We wish to provide close readers of French texts with an introductory framework which. will give them the best opportunity to express their insights freely and fully. In presenting a set of methodological guidelines, we have aimed to combine methods derived from traditional stylistic and rhetorical analysis with the language and insights generated by a more critical, social approach to the interpretation of written text. The guidelines that follow should not be read as a rigid framework to be imposed on the analysis of any and every text. The order in which we present individual features is not the only possible one, and the boundaries between different categories are not watertight. A close reading of the commentaries that follow will show that each analysis addresses different issues in different ways.

Situating the text

Text and context

Whatever the input of individuals, a text is by definition a social artefact. It springs from a social context and has been written with certain social goals in mind. Analysts have to situate the text within the context of the culture from which it is drawn. What they do not know, they need to guess, or infer. As a cultural artefact, the text reflects the culture of which it is part. The first questions to ask of a text are: Where does it come from? What type of text is it? Can it be grouped together with other texts of a similar character? Does this grouping have a name?

Identifying the text

Simply to identify the type or genre of a text is a trigger that releases information about the conditions within which it was produced and the kinds of interpretation to which it may give rise. Compare, for example, a hypothetical restaurant review in a magazine with an account of a visit to the same restaurant in a private letter to a friend. The magazine article will have been written for an audience for the most part personally unknown to the writer. The author of a personal letter, on the other hand, is addressing a known audience: a single person with whom he or she has shared memories and associations. Both texts will be seeking to inform and entertain. However, the review will follow the pattern of a public statement, while the form and message of the letter will be private and personal. It will be less governed by codes and conventions, even though some (at least) may apply. Clearly, these differences will affect almost every aspect of the text: the way it is structured, the forms of address, the use of tense, the choice of words and images, the level of formality, and so on. Simply to identify the genre to which each belongs offers the analyst an 'angle' or position from which the relationship between 'writer, reader and character' can be made explicit. It lends a perspective from which the close analysis of the language can be made meaningful.

Defining the context

Contexts change and develop over time, and the form of texts alters accordingly. All texts are produced and interpreted within a social situation involving agencies and institutions, which are by definition part of a wider culture. It is important if possible to identify approximately when, where and how a text was produced. Whether the text is an extract from a more extended sequence or apparently stands alone, it will relate to other texts of a similar genre, either ones which have gone before or others published at more or less the same time with which it can be compared and contrasted. As we saw in the previous chapter, Halliday makes a distinction between the wider points of reference shared by a linguistic community – the context of culture, and the individual circumstances in which a text was produced and received – the context of situation. Similarly, in *L'Archéologie du Savoir* (1969), Foucault invites critical readers to see individual texts as elements within a wider discursive system which they undermine, reinforce or change through the way in which they formulate meanings. It is unrealistic for an individual to claim to have penetrated a complete discursive system. Halliday's 'context of culture' and Foucault's 'orders of discourse' are abstractions which can only be defined in global terms. As partially informed readers, the best we can do is to make inferences about specific aspects of the context of culture from a close examination of the elements within the text. On the basis of what we know about the system, we can imagine what function or position the text has within it.

Subject matter, relationships and structure

Having 'located' or 'positioned' the text within a context, the analyst can make some closer generalisations about it. Halliday (1987) asks three basic questions. Within his own terms of reference, he relates each to a particular metafunction and, as pointers, all are useful for anyone who is looking for a way into text analysis:

What is going on?
Who is taking part?
How are meanings communicated?

What is going on?

The obvious starting point is to say what the text is about. What are its main topics, or subject matter? Words normally form clusters of meaning in texts, described as lexical fields. In gastronomic review, for example, these might be food, tradition, regional characteristics, travel and architectural setting. Where and when do the events described in the text take place? How is the text located in space and time? Is the setting real or imagined? Does it change as the text progresses and, if so, what is the relationship between the different settings presented? What span of time does the text cover? How does it shift between past, present and future? How does this relate to the genre and the text's overall message?

Who is taking part?

Texts do not simply exist. They have been produced by an individual or a group of people and have an intended audience. All texts position readers in some way. In defining a woman as a housewife or a man as an affluent businessman, advertisements for washing powder or fast cars situate them as consumers. Similarly, in 'traditional' novels, the author uses a range of techniques to make readers believe what they are reading to be 'true' in the sense that they are prepared to accept that the events and feelings described 'could have taken place'. We may be oblivious to these processes because they appear 'natural' to us. An analysis of the devices used to position writer, reader and character in text denaturalises them. It leads to a better understanding of some of the assumptions which define the context of culture, and provides an insight into certain of the rules of discursive formation to which Michel Foucault (1969) refers.

The relationship between writer and reader will depend on what the text is trying to do. With reference to Jakobson's taxonomy of functions (1960), is the main emphasis in the text on describing things, expressing feelings, persuading others to accept a particular point of view, explaining difficult terminology, creating a well-formed message, evoking an atmosphere . . . or all of these things at the same time? The likelihood is that one of them at least will be more dominant than the others. Certain markers in the text – the title, the opening and closure, certain key words and images – will normally indicate what the primary function of the text is. The text will not only define the relationship between writer and reader. It will normally involve real or imaginary characters, who will themselves be positioned in relation to the reader and each other. In advertisements, reports, business correspondence, political speeches and feature articles, as in fiction, characters are given specific roles which condition the point of view that implied readers adopt towards them.

The relationships between characters within the text and that between the text and its implied readership are also conditioned by the tone of the discourse. Tone is generally conveyed by the formality or familiarity of the language used, the register of the text. Register is often not uniform. It varies according to which character is speaking or being represented, and register-mixing is often used as a device to establish a closer relationship between the text and the intended reader. Equally, excessive formality may be used to distance readers from a particular character, or to place the producer of the text in a position of authority.

How are meanings communicated?

Halliday's third metafunction, 'the textual function', describes the combination of linguistic features by means of which a text hangs together or achieves coherence. Coherence normally depends on the progression of ideas. What narrative thread or 'argument' does the text follow? Does this fall into natural sections? What are the similarities and differences between them? How are the turning points between the sections marked? Are there any unexpected twists? How does the text open and close? The combination of linguistic features by means of which a text achieves coherence is known as cohesion. It most commonly includes the repetition of words at the beginning or end of sentences (anaphora/cataphora), the reiteration of grammatical structures (parallelism), the devices by means of which sentences and paragraphs are linked, and also the length and structure of the sentences themselves which may be more or less regular and complete. Unexpected changes in direction are usually marked by features which stand out from the remainder of the text (foregrounding) because they break the rhythm, introduce a new type of word and in some way deviate from the pattern which the text itself has set up. Meaning can only be achieved through the coherent combination of cohesion and deviation. It is by virtue of the way in which the different parts of the text relate to each other that we can say that it 'makes sense'. Form is not separate from content; the 'how' is part of the 'what'. It is the language of the text which defines its relationship with its environment and which articulates how society represents itself.

Analysing the text

The main object of text analysis is to apply the three questions considered above to the language of the text. All three dimensions – What . . . ? Between whom . . . ? How . . . ? – interact within the text and operate simultaneously, engaging a range of stylistic features. As in the first chapter, we have taken a particular text as a reference point for many of the features we identify. It is an extract from an introductory 'synopsis' which straddles the divide between fictional and non-fictional language. It is factually summarising the script of a famous film for a prospective readership of the scenario. And yet, at the same time, it demonstrates aspects of its author's highly distinctive style which are found elsewhere in her works of literary fiction. The classic film, *Hiroshima mon Amour*, produced in 1957, is both a highly aesthetic text and a political and moral statement. It concerns a chance meeting at the site of the first offensive nuclear explosion between a young French woman and a Japanese man on the occasion of a film about world peace in which the woman is playing a minor role. Their brief affair, observed over a twenty-four-hour period, is intercut with shocking images of the explosion and its aftermath, and also with flashbacks to the woman's earlier passionate love for a German soldier during the occupation of Nevers (her home town). The flashbacks recapture her grief at his random shooting and her public humiliation. Her head is shaved, she is paraded through the streets and finally hidden in a cellar by her mother before escaping to the anonymity of Paris. The two historical events fuse in her mind and the identities of her former lover, the Japanese man and the names 'Nevers 'and 'Hiroshima', become interchangeable as they wander through the city during the night before her return to France. The film, directed by Alain Resnais, explores the universality of love and human suffering, and the combination of image and prose makes a plea for tolerance and peace in an era of nuclear protest.

Positioning writer, reader and character

The presentation of character

The most obvious grammatical elements involved in constructing the relationships between writer and reader are proper names (Marguerite Duras, Jean Tingaud), common nouns (*l'écrivain, le chef*) and pronouns (*elle, il* and so on). The presence or absence of the writer in the text is central. Frequently, writers – or narrators – are present in texts through the use of the pronouns *je* or *nous* and, occasionally, *on*. *Je* constructs the narrator as an individual personality. What sort of personality does this imply? Is it intended to establish a relationship with the reader and if so of what kind? If writers use *nous*, are they really speaking with a group voice? Who is included in the group? Is it an institution or is the reference much vaguer – as it might be, for instance, in a piece of literary criticism where the *nous* may simply be a more formal way of referring to *je*? Does the *nous* include the reader as well? The use of *on* is particularly subtle. It can relate to the writer or narrator as an individual, to writer and reader, to a specific group of people, or to public opinion at large. It is frequent in fiction for the writer not to appear through the use of pronouns at all. This does not necessarily mean that there are no traces of an authorial voice in the text, simply that it has been embedded in a different way.

Nous sommes dans l'été 1957, en août, à Hiroshima . . .

SYNOPSIS

Nous sommes dans l'été 1957, en août, à Hiroshima.

Une femme française, d'une trentaine d'années, est dans cette ville. Elle y est venue pour jouer dans un film sur la Paix.

L'histoire commence la veille du retour en France de cette Française. Le film dans lequel elle joue est en effet terminé. Il n'en reste qu'une séquence à tourner.

C'est la veille de son retour en France que cette Française, qui ne sera jamais nommée dans le film — cette femme anonyme — rencontrera un Japonais (ingénieur, ou architecte) et qu'ils auront ensemble une histoire d'amour très courte.

Les conditions de leur rencontre ne seront pas éclaircies dans le film. Car ce n'est pas là la question. On se rencontre partout dans le monde. Ce qui importe, c'est ce qui s'ensuit de ces rencontres quotidiennes.

Ce couple de fortune, on ne le voit pas au début du film. Ni elle. Ni lui. On voit en leur lieu et place des corps mutilés — à hauteur de la tête et des hanches — remuants — en proie soit à l'amour, soit à l'agonie — et recouverts successivement des cendres, des rosées, de la mort atomique — et des sueurs de l'amour accompli.

Ce n'est que peu à peu que de ces corps informes, anonymes, sortiront leurs corps à eux.

Ils sont couchés dans une chambre d'hôtel. Ils sont nus. Corps lisses. Intacts.

De quoi parlent-ils? Justement de HIRO-SHIMA.

Elle lui dit qu'elle a tout vu à HIROSHIMA. On voit ce qu'elle a vu. C'est horrible. Cependant que sa voix à lui, négatrice, taxera les images de mensongères et qu'il répétera, impersonnel, insupportable, qu'elle n'a rien vu à HIROSHIMA.

Leur premier propos sera donc allégorique. *Ce sera, en somme, un propos d'opéra.* Impossible de parler de HIROSHIMA. Tout ce qu'on peut faire c'est de parler de l'impossibilité de parler de HIROSHIMA. La *connaissance de Hiroshima* étant a priori posée comme un leurre exemplaire de l'esprit.

Source: Duras, M. (1960) 'Synopsis', *Hiroshima mon Amour*, Paris: Gallimard, pp. 9–10. ©Editions Gallimard.

'*Nous*' here is both figuratively authorial and inclusive of the readership. It is clearly designed to make readers identify with the events to be described. The present tense transports us uncompromisingly to the time and place referred to. Later in the extract, the pronoun shifts to '*on*'. Here, the group which included author and readership has been extended to include the generality of humankind: '*On se rencontre partout dans le monde*'. A few lines later, the use of the pronoun shifts again to mean the viewers of the film, expressed impersonally: '*Ce couple de fortune, on ne ne le voit pas au début du film . . . On voit en leur lieu et place des corps mutilés . . . On voit ce qu'elle a vu . . .* '. Finally, '*on*' returns to the author as bearing witness to human events. She presents her dilemma as that facing anyone who wishes to give an account of a massive moral catastrophe. It cannot be done: '*Impossible de parler de HIROSHIMA. Tout ce qu'on peut faire, c'est de parler de l'impossibilité de parler de HIROSHIMA.*' Through the use of pronouns, the text forcefully positions us as readers and potential viewers of the film in relation to Duras as author and to human beings throughout the world.

In certain texts, the reader may be addressed directly. Where this occurs, there is an obvious difference in status according to whether the reader is addressed as *tu* or *vous*. In either case, the exact identity of the person being addressed may well be unclear. Apollinaire's poem *Zone* (1912) begins with the line:

> *A la fin tu es las de ce monde ancien.*

'*Tu*' might refer to the reader, a third party, the writer as self or – most probably – all three simultaneously. What exactly is the relationship of familiarity being invoked and what purposes does it serve? In the case of *vous*, how many people are included? Is it anyone at all, or are there other traces in the text which restrict the range of people to whom it might apply? The relationships between the characters in the text and the pronouns used to refer to them are often not constant. As we have seen with *on* above, they are frequently – and deliberately – made to change or 'slip' from one part of the text to another.

It is very rare for writer and reader to be the only characters referred to in a text. Through different types of noun phrases, characters can be constructed as having particular points of view and beliefs and as acting in specific ways. There are many different ways in which character can be given 'depth'. A standard journalistic cliché is to introduce a character by name and then to add personal details (compare 'A man drowned' with 'John Smith, 37, father of two, drowned yesterday' . . .). In literary as in media texts, standard strategies such as this are used to make characters more or less sympathetic or easy to identify with.

> *Une femme française, d'une trentaine d'années . . . Cette Française, qui ne sera jamais nommée dans le film – cette femme anonyme – rencontrera un Japonais (ingénieur, ou architecte) . . .*

Clearly Duras is making every effort to depersonalise the two characters and to present them as universal types who are nevertheless recognisable as having national and professional characteristics. Their national features are important because of the historical events depicted, not because of their personalities as individuals. They symbolise West and East and the hope for a new world order in a context where it is impossible to forget the past. Their individual experience is subsumed in the mass suffering of atomic war. They are simply a '*couple de fortune*'. Their symbolic genders are underlined by the pronouns, which emphasise that the opening shots of the film are not of them but of the mutilated victims: '*Ni elle. Ni lui. . . . de ces corps informes, anonymes, sortiront leurs corps à eux.*'

Modes of speech and points of view

Apart from using nouns and pronouns to create a world of the text, texts are also positioned interpersonally through the directness or indirectness of the language. Does the author speak directly to the reader? Are points of view represented through direct, reported, indirect or free indirect speech? Whose voice is being used? What effects are derived from changes of voice?

Consider how the positions of 'author' and 'character' change in the following statements:

'International terrorism will be crushed wherever it is found.'

(Direct Speech)

'International terrorism', said the President, 'will be crushed wherever it is found.'

(Reported Speech)

The President said that international terrorism would be crushed wherever it was found.

(Indirect Speech)

International terrorism would be crushed wherever it was found.

(Free Indirect Speech)

Obviously, both author (the reporter) and character (the President) are present in all four sentences. The 'voice' shifts from one to the other, according to the mode in which the President's statement is presented.

L'histoire commence la veille du retour en France de cette Française. Le film dans lequel elle tourne est en effet terminé. Il n'en reste qu'une séquence à tourner.

The use of the present tense makes this a direct series of statements addressed to the reader by the author of the summary introduction, Marguerite Duras. They have a ring of factual reality about them, even though they are obviously the product of her imagination. It is an *histoire* told in her voice. Once again, the reader is drawn in and the affirmative form changes to become an interrogative as the reader is addressed rhetorically and, in a sense, more directly still:

> *De quoi parlent-ils? Justement de* HIROSHIMA.

The mode then changes again to indirect speech:

> *Elle lui dit qu'elle a tout vu à* HIROSHIMA . . .

The form of the synopsis demands that the author integrate the dialogue of the characters into the prose such that she is able both to represent what the characters said and to comment on it. Her voice and that of the characters in the film become fused.

Mood

A vital aspect of psychological positioning is mood. 'Mood' is a technical term which is used to define the attitude or state of mind of the speaker/writer towards a particular statement. Different moods follow their own grammatical patterns or conjugations and it has become accepted as normal usage that, after certain expressions, a particular mood should be used. Thus, according to standard grammatical conventions, verbs expressing feelings of uncertainty or fear, adverbial phrases such as *avant que*, etc. govern the subjunctive and so on. There are four main moods in French: the indicative, the subjunctive, the conditional and the imperative. Of the four, the indicative is the most common and describes things as they are assumed to be. As its name suggests, it indicates, affirms and points out. The subjunctive expresses the underlying feeling of the subject. It describes events from an imagined point of view, either prospectively – what the situation would be if they happened – or retrospectively – what things would have been like if they had not. The conditional expresses anticipation or supposition of what will or could or might happen or have happened under particular circumstances. It is therefore debatable whether it qualifies as a tense or a mood and this depends very much on the context in which it is used.

Tense and mood affect positioning as much as do features such as pronouns insofar as they condition the attitude of the writer towards the implied reader and that of characters towards each other. The use of the future tense by Duras in the synopsis of *Hiroshima mon Amour* does not simply convey information about time. It makes a statement about what *must* take place because this is the particular vision which she is wishing to communicate to the reader and prospective viewer. There is an insistent, urgent tone about the language conveyed by the future tense and subsequently emphasised by the use of italics: '*Ce* <u>*sera*</u>*, en somme, un propos d'opéra ... La connaissance de Hiroshima étant à priori posée ...*', etc. Inevitably, the tone conveyed by the mood of the verbs will be supported by other stylistic features, including, for example, adjectives or adverbs, which actually describe the manner or attitude of characters as they speak and act ('*anonyme*', '*lisses*', '*intacts*', '*négatrice*', '*impersonnel*', '*insupportable*'). Mood is not therefore used in isolation any more than any other stylistic element, but contributes (together with the other elements) to the collective effect which defines the meaning of the text as a whole.

Positioning in time and space

Deixis and presupposition

Deixis means the identification of something with reference to the position of writer and reader. It refers to structures which have a 'pointing' function, which locate objects and people in space and time and in relation to other elements in the text. Deixis can be spatial; for example *cette table-ci* and *cette table-là* refer to two different tables, one nearer the writer, and one further away. It can be temporal; *aujourd'hui* and *hier* depend for their meaning on the writer's position in time. It can be possessive; *mon manteau* and *ton manteau* refer to two different coats, the coat situated as 'mine' from the point of view of the writer, and that situated as 'yours'.

Deictic reference is a powerful means of positioning the reader. It constructs a 'world of the text' which the reader has to accept as 'true' in order to make sense of the passage. The use of deictics presupposes that the reader and writer are positioned in a particular way. Even such an apparently obvious element as the definite article 'the' implies that author and reader share the same perception of the object. A sentence in a newspaper – 'the rioting demonstrators attacked the police' – presupposes that a particular group of people were indeed rioting and effectively constructs their identity as such. To read a text carefully and to work out what information is presupposed gives further insight into the way in which the producer of the text is constructing the world and indicates the knowledge and beliefs which the reader is assumed to have.

> *Une femme française, d'une trentaine d'années, est dans cette ville ...*

The woman is unspecified but from now on, like Hiroshima ('<u>*cette ville*</u>') she is a known quantity ('<u>*cette*</u> *Française*'), a specific individual, even though nothing is known about her personality. The repetition of '*cette*' reinforces the presence within the text of the character and the city. Its deictic force draws the reader in, and insistently presses home the point: '<u>*cette*</u> *Française* ... <u>*cette*</u> *femme anonyme*', obliging the reader to share the author's perspective on the centrality of the character and what she represents. Thus, in this extract, repetition and uses of the demonstrative adjective both have deictic force. They establish a reality which the reader is invited to share.

Tense and aspect

The 'world of the text' includes the use of pronouns to refer to writer, reader and character; the use of presuppositions to construct the knowledge necessary to understand the text; and the use of deictic references to position writer, reader and character in psychological space. Other resources of the language, however, are equally important in positioning, particularly positioning in time, where verb tense is of course the most crucial element and must always be carefully considered together with aspect which relates to the duration or progressive character of a particular event or process. Verb usage in French is extremely flexible and is becoming more so as the boundaries between different types of text are broken down. Standard rules, such as the principle that the perfect tense (*passé composé* – *j'ai parlé* etc.) should not be used in the same paragraph as the past historic tense (*passé historique* or *passé simple* – *je parlai*, etc.), are frequently broken in written language in order to achieve a particular effect.

Tense defines the moment when events are represented as taking place relative to each other. Aspect defines how long events or processes last. Aspect may be expressed through a tense, such as through the difference between the imperfect and the past historic, or by means of an adverbial phrase such as *longtemps, en train de, brusquement*, etc. It may even be communicated through the meaning of the verbs used. For instance, *flâner, hésiter, traîner* describe actions which take longer than *sauter, jeter* or *saisir*. The use of aspect often provides contrast. Typically, a series of rapid events takes place against a more or less constant or unchanging background.

> *Nous sommes dans l'été 1957, en août, à Hiroshima . . .*

Even at the time when the scenario was written, the events are clearly in the past. '*Nous sommes*' is an imagined present. It is a present which is both immediate – highly specific in the moment referred to – and extended in duration, in that all the events to be described in the scenario take place in August 1957. The sequence of the events themselves is more closely located in time with the clause '*L'histoire commence . . .* ' , since the opening of the story is followed by a series of future tenses. Virtual events – '*rencontrera . . . auront*' – are represented as actually happening by being located in an imagined future. This effect would be lost in English, where the present tense would normally be used. The description relates to an implied reader who has not yet seen the film for whom the meeting between the French woman and the Japanese man and their brief affair are presented as really taking place – a double illusion, since in fact their meeting is not shown in the film. The sequence of events is imaginary; yet, through the combined use of present and future tenses, is represented as real by positioning readers at the fictional point in time where the story begins from which they look forward to events which 'will' occur.

In locating text chronologically, a distinction has therefore to be made between absolute and relative time; that is, time measured against the actual moment at which the reader reads the text as opposed to the time when it is assumed that the text has been written. In the Duras extract, we know that the date at which the text was written was not August 1957 but some time after that month, since the synopsis will have been written after the scenario itself and probably after the film was made. The location of events within the block of time covered by the month of August is strictly relative. As readers, we suspend our disbelief in order to enter the 'timeworld' which the text creates for us.

Words, images and meaning

Word meaning and lexical fields

As we have already seen, the choice of words – lexical items – is the feature which is perhaps most closely related to 'what the text is about'. Words do not have a one-to-one relationship with the objects and concepts with which they are linked. *Mouton* evokes essentially the same response in native speakers of French as 'sheep' does in speakers of English, and yet the words are different. In addition, in French, *mouton* refers both to the animal and to the meat which comes from it, while in English two words are used. So, apart from the words being distinct in themselves, the value of *mouton* and 'sheep' is different in the two languages. Words acquire meaning through their position within a system and not from any preordained link with the physical or mental world. The meaning of words derives from their relationships with other words and from the conventions derived from usage that associates individual words with particular sense responses. In his revolutionary series of lectures on linguistics, *Cours de Linguistique Générale* (1916/ 1973), the Swiss linguist Ferdinand de Saussure (1857–1913) uses the example of the three French words *redouter*, *craindre* and *avoir peur*, all of which mean 'to be afraid'. If only one of these words existed, all the values and connotations associated with being afraid would attach to that one. As it is, the existence of three variants means that each has a slightly different value.

However, although value is systematically defined, this does not imply that the system is static and that the values of words are fixed. On the contrary, word meaning is constantly open to originality and change. As we have seen, texts both instantiate the linguistic and discursive systems of which they are part and, at the same time, question and challenge them. Words can be used by individuals or groups to mean something different from the meanings normally associated with them. The meaning of words can be extended, the properties of one object or idea can be compared to those of another or can be transferred to it. The potential to transfer meaning from one area of meaning to another is evidence that word meaning is not a purely intellectual activity. Words do not only serve to identify rational constructions of objects and concepts – denotations. They also arouse images, associations and feelings – connotations – through their links with different emotional experiences stored in the memories of individuals and groups. One of the most important aspects of cultural formation is the 'regularisation' of associations which attach to particular expressions within a linguistic community. These may be more or less durable according to the relative stability of the social structures and discursive formations of which they are part and according to the effectiveness with which cultural values are transmitted. Connotations act as a point of reference for a certain cultural collectivity within French society and as a reinforcement of that group's identity.

Word meanings therefore come from relationships and not from fixed correspondences. As well as referring to something through agreement between members of a linguistic community, each lexical item has a large number of possible connotations. Some of these are more or less standard within the language; others are original and derive from the word's being placed in an unusual context. The meaning of words is not therefore determined simply by their normal use and their position within the linguistic system but also by their relationship with other words in the immediate context in which they happen to be found. It is the way in which words are put together in a text that defines which meanings and associations are brought into play.

Words relating to a similar area of meaning are referred to as a lexical field. A text constructs lexical relationships within and between different fields by bringing them together within what is known as a semantic space. As we have seen, their use within this space redefines their habitual meaning and regroups words in more or less unusual ways. In any text, several dominant lexical fields can normally be identified and can be linked to the themes or topics which define 'what the text is about'. However, the way in which the words have been used and new meanings created goes beyond simply identifying key words. The juxtaposition of different fields can cause apparent meanings to be contradicted, while dominant imagery and associations can introduce particular force into a text's emotional and aesthetic impact.

It is immediately clear in the synopsis of *Hiroshima mon Amour* that the text concerns the relationship between love, atrocity in war and film-making. The link between love and war has long been a cliché in Western culture but the immediate juxtaposition of images of lovemaking and death agony lends a shocking quality to the contrast and causes the relationship between the two types of event to be seen in symbolic rather than literal terms. Hiroshima is not presented as a real location but as an idea represented in small capital letters – HIROSHIMA – whose emotional significance as a place identified with war and death is universally communicated through its association with an anonymous love affair. As the title itself suggests, the connotations of the words feed off each other and acquire metaphorical status through the bringing together of contrasted lexical fields.

Metaphor, metonymy and simile

One of the most fundamental ways in which the symbolic flexibility of words is exploited in written text is through the extension and transfer of meaning from one lexical field to another. In the terminology of traditional rhetoric, stylistic devices of this type were known as tropes. In fact, the application of terms derived from one field to concepts normally located in another is part of the natural way in which word meaning evolves. Thus, over time, vulgar Latin *testa* (an earthenware pot) replaces classical Latin *caput* (head) to give modern French *tête* – with all the connotations that implies: thick, well or badly made, more or less beautiful, full, empty, broken . . . . All tropes relate two elements, normally known as the tenor (X) and vehicle (Y). In the case of simile, X and Y are *compared* (*on naviguait sur une mer qui luisait comme de l'argent*). Where metaphor is concerned, there is no 'like' – *comme* – to signal a direct comparison. Instead, the vehicle is identified with the tenor and is either directly linked to it grammatically or replaces it completely:

> *La douleur (X) comme une lame (Y) lui perça le coeur.*
>
> (simile/comparison);
>
> *Une lame douloureuse lui perça le coeur.*
>
> (metaphor by linking);
>
> *Une lame lui perça le coeur.*
>
> (metaphor by replacement).

By definition, not all elements of tenor and vehicle are common. In order to pinpoint precisely the quality of the figure, it is necessary to bring a third element into play: the ground (Z). The ground of a metaphor consists of the properties which link X and Y. In the case of the example above, it could be described as the sense of heaviness or slowing down of reactions which accompanies feelings of grief and sorrow. In the expression 'human elephant', used figuratively, there might be two possible 'grounds': clumsiness or having a long memory. Metonymy refers to tropes in which vehicle and tenor are already in some sort of physical relationship. This typically involves substituting part for whole (All *hands* on deck!), container for object or substance contained (We went out for a *glass* or two), building or room for the people who normally live or work there (The *house* will rise), author for book (I've been reading *Proust*) and so on.

Tropes are not necessarily limited to a single sentence or paragraph. In traditional narrative, it is conventional for metaphors evoking the same associations to stand for something else throughout a short story or even a cycle of books. Classical fables and parables from the Bible use this technique, known as allegory, to make a moral point. Albert Camus' *La Peste* (1947) is a well-known example of a twentieth-century novel which presents the image of the plague as an allegory both for the Nazi occupation of France during World War II and for the moral choices which confront people in general in their daily lives. As we have seen, the effectiveness of *Hiroshima mon Amour* as summed up in the synopsis depends on a double symbol which is sustained throughout the film. The man and the city *stand for* the suffering which took place there and elsewhere in the world – HIROSHIMA acts as a metonymy for atrocity in war – while the brief love affair between the French woman and the Japanese man is a metaphor for the commonplace and the universal. The two images are portrayed as two sides of the same symbolic coin. They are kept separate in the text of the synopsis so that the reader/viewer is clearly made aware of the different elements of which the trope is made up.

The processes of building images through words are not, of course, peculiar to discourse that is marked as belonging to an 'artistic' or 'literary' genre. Spoken language is rich in colourful images, which are vital sources of humour and solidarity and an endless reminder of the creativity of human imagination. Even in texts which have a seemingly commonplace function, the use of words goes beyond simply denoting reality. Naming is itself a metaphorical process whereby shared feelings and perceptions are translated into acoustic signals. Through their combination in discourse, they contribute to the symbolic operation of culture. Words stand for or represent social processes and it is an important aspect of text analysis to identify how these processes work.

Sentence structure, rhythm and sound

The meanings of individual words are relatively open in the sense that, within the limitations of short- to medium-term memory, they can be associated with each other in different ways across the boundaries of sentences and paragraphs. However, it is the way words are organised into sentences that lends texts meaning and coherence. The repetition of words in similar positions in the sentence (anaphora) and the recurrence of similar sentence structures (parallelism) are sources of cohesion and enhance memorability. Similarly, sudden changes in sentence length capture the reader's attention and are a common way of foregrounding a particular idea. The identification of these features depends on having first noted the structures themselves and, more generally, on appreciating the principles which govern the organisation of sentences in French and their likely effect on the reader.

Simple, compound and complex sentences

Sentences consist of clauses, which in their turn are made up of phrases. A clause is any combination of words which is governed by a verb. A phrase is a word or group of words which constitutes a grammatical category within a clause. There are five main types of phrase which are defined by the element which governs them: noun phrase, verb phrase, adjectival phrase, adverbial phrase, prepositional phrase. The following are examples of clauses made up of phrases:

Jean	*parle*	*français*
noun phrase	verb phrase	noun phrase

Derrière le mur	*les feuilles*	*commençaient à tomber*
prepositional phrase	noun phrase	verb phrase

Labels such as these are only a means to an end. They do not explain what role each phrase plays within the sentence. In the sentence *Le lion chasse l'homme*, *le lion* and *l'homme* are both noun phrases, but they have different functions: the lion is doing the hunting; the man is being hunted. In order to distinguish between these different sentential functions, we need another set of labels.

The most fundamental terms used to refer to sentential functions are: subject (S), verb (V) and complement (Comp). Complements can consist of a variety of components, the most common of which is a direct or indirect object (O). The SV Comp ordering is as basic to the French language as it is to English. All the following sentences for example follow the SVComp model. In each case, the form of the complement is different:

Les terroristes	*ont attaqué*	*la ville*
noun phrase	verb phrase	noun phrase
subject	verb	complement

Le garçon	*est*	*sage*
noun phrase	verb phrase	adjectival phrase
subject	verb	complement

Marguerite Duras	*a été élevée*	*au Vietnam*
noun phrase	verb phrase	prepositional phrase
subject	verb	complement

La lycéenne	*a donné*	*le livre à son frère*
noun phrase	verb phrase	noun phrase +
		prepositional phrase
subject	verb	complement

Each of these types of phrase can be extended through the addition of adverbial or adjectival phrases (*très sage*, *frère aîné*, etc.). Obviously, the more complements are introduced into the sentence, the more freedom the writer has to manipulate the word order in unusual ways.

The above are examples of 'simple sentences', that is, they consist of only one clause. Simple sentences can be placed alongside one another in apposition:

> *Ils sont couchés dans une chambre d'hôtel. Ils sont nus.*
> *Leur premier propos sera donc allégorique. Ce sera, en somme, un propos d'opéra.*

Readers are left to draw their own conclusions as to the relationship between sentences in apposition. In the first case, the second sentence is an additional element of information which develops our knowledge of the fictional scene. The second example is a commentary by the author on the dialogue which the two main characters are having. Here, the second sentence qualifies and expands the idea presented in the first.

Alternatively, clauses can be coordinated in a single sentence, using *et* or *mais* – such sentences are known as 'compound sentences'.

> *Une Française rencontrera un Japonais et ils auront ensemble une histoire d'amour très courte.*

In most extended prose, simple sentences are also combined to form 'complex' structures. This is normally done by embedding one sentence in another to form one or more 'subordinate clauses'. There are many grammatical structures which allow subordination to take place. The most common are relativisation, participialisation, nominalisation, and the use of adverbial clauses of various types: time (*quand* . . .), condition (*si* . . .), cause (*puisque* . . ., *parce que* . . .), concession (*bien que* . . .), qualification (*tandis que* . . .), purpose (*pour que* . . .), and so on.

For example:

> *Cette femme française, qui ne sera jamais nommée dans le film, rencontrera un Japonais.*
>
> (relativisation)
>
> *Le film dans lequel elle joue est en effet terminé.*
>
> (relativisation)

Impossible de parler de Hiroshima, la connaissance de Hiroshima <u>étant</u> a priori posée comme un leurre exemplaire de l'esprit.

(participialisation)

Une femme française, <u>d'une trentaine d'années</u>, est dans cette ville.

(nominalisation)

Les conditions <u>de leur rencontre</u> ne seront pas éclaircies dans le film.

(nominalisation)

Elle y est venue <u>pour jouer</u> dans un film sur la Paix.

(adverbialisation)

It is not the simple fact that a certain structure is present within a text which makes it stylistically significant. It is the way in which sentence structures are combined to form a cohesive context. '*Synopsis*', for example, is marked by simple subject, verb, complement structures. Often the complements (prepositional phrases, adjectives and nouns) are in a series of two or three, in apposition to each other ('*Nous sommes dans l'été, en août, à Hiroshima*'; '*des corps mutilés . . . remuants*'; '*recouverts . . . des cendres, des rosées . . .* '; '*ces corps informes, anonymes . . .* '; '*il répétera, impersonnel, insupportable . . .* ', etc.). As well as reinforcing the insistent, assertive force of the author's voice, this allows the sentence to follow her thought process and positions her as an authoritative interlocutor in relation to the reader, a perspective which is further reflected in the deixis of '*cette*', the emphatic '*en effet*', and the rhetorical question '*De quoi parlent-ils?*'.

Deviations from standard sentence structure

There is no law other than the need to make oneself understood which obliges speakers or writers to adhere to the conventions which govern the order of elements in sentences. In fact, there is considerable variety, particularly in modern French, as the range of written discourses and communication media increase. Deviation from 'standard' sentence structure is a typical feature of certain genres or may be a mark of an individual writer's originality. In certain forms of journalism, for example, it is common to include sentences without verbs, which gives the style a clipped, telegraphic effect and makes the impact of the message more immediate. This elliptical style is most common in headlines:

<u>Pulpeux</u>. Le marché du jus d'orange aiguise les appétits des marques.

(*Le Nouvel Economiste* 1998: 58)

The technique can also be used to lend a conversational tone to the communication of the message, notably by giving the impression that the writer has had an afterthought which he or she wants to share with the reader.

La guerre du jus d'orange fait rage, les opposant aux fabricants locaux. Et pour cause.

(Ibid.)

In journalism, as in fictional prose, the introduction of a short, often verbless sentence can act as a linking device which serves as a transition from one sentence or paragraph to the next:

Le wonder-kid de la région? Il s'appelle Alain Pavard . . .

(Pudlowski 1994)

Alternatively, it can be used for emphasis:

Ce couple de fortune, on ne le voit pas au début du film. Ni elle. Ni lui.
(Duras 1960: 9)
Ils sont couchés dans une chambre d'hôtel. Ils sont nus. Corps lisses. Intacts.
(Duras 1960: 10)

In these cases, although elements have been left out, the normal conventions governing word order have not been infringed. In very many instances, however, for functional or aesthetic reasons, the standard word order of sentences is actually changed.

For example:

1   The subject is displaced (i.e. delayed) to the end of the clause:
     Elle était belle, élégante, courageuse, Hélène.
     The effect is to create an artificially conversational tone whereby the pronoun is placed in the normal subject position, emphasising the person concerned by placing the name last. The same effect of subject displacement is found in certain dialects of English:
     He's a right nuisance, is *George.*
2   Subject (S) and verb (V) are inverted:
     Sera convoqué (V) *tout étudiant* (S) *ayant enfreint au règlement du collège.*
     Subject–verb inversion is a common feature of legal texts or of official language in general, as it is of certain literary texts where the device of changing the word order in order to make the words rhyme or to fit in with the metrical structures of poetry is transferred to prose:

     En effet, assis sur une pile du pont des Glacis, nous attendait (V) *le Grand Meaulnes* (S).
     (Alain Fournier)

Here, the effect of having delayed the subject noun phrase until the end of the sentence heightens the reader's expectations of it and therefore foregrounds it.

3 Double subjects are split:

Le soir, le bombardement (S1) *commençaient, et la peur* (S2).

where the splitting of the subject has the effect of foregrounding *peur*, thereby increasing the atmosphere of menace.

4 Verb complements are placed before the verb:

L'art et la religion en moi (PP) *dévotieusement* (Adv) *s'épousaient.*

(Gide)

In the above example, the effect is to lend an elevated, poetic, slightly ironic tone to the statement, which is increased by placing the prepositional phrase in front of the verb as well as the adverbial complement. A more common form of deviant word order is to place the direct object complement right at the beginning of the sentence and then to refer back to it by means of an object pronoun:

Ce couple de fortune, on ne le voit pas au début du film.

(Duras 1960: 9)

Where there is more than one complement, the writer clearly has a greater range of choice. There are a number of rules which describe the most common sequences followed by different complements. These rules only represent a systematic description of normal practice and are certainly not absolute. However, when they are broken, this contributes to specific stylistic effects and foregrounds particular parts of sentences and complements. They represent a useful guide as to what to look out for when considering word order in French sentences and when seeking to identify repeated deviations which characterise certain types of text:

1 The direct complement should be placed before the indirect complement:
J'ai donné le livre à mon fils.

2 The complement which carries the greatest emphasis is normally placed at the end of the sentence:
Napoléon contemplait de son armée l'inexorable destruction.

3 Shorter complements should be placed before longer ones:
Un sommet américo-cubain a réuni en mars 1998, à Cancun, une cinquantaine de grosses compagnies nord-américaines.

4   Placing complements in an order which breaks one or more of the above
     rules automatically foregrounds them:
     Délivrez-moi de mes amis. Mes ennemis, je m'en charge!

Rhythm and intonation

The relationship between word order, sentence structure and the meaning of text
is far from being simply a grammatical one. Meaning and structure are in part
products of rhythmic and metrical patterns which are built into the language.
Rhythm and metre are the combined outcome of the length of syllables, accent or
stress, and intonation, the rise and fall of the language. These features need not be
expressed openly as in real speech. They work 'inside the head' as the writer
writes and the reader reads. They set up patterns in the mind, bind the text
together and reinforce the relationships between key ideas. They are part of the
content of the text as well as of the functional link between sender and receiver.
Hence, they are a social as well as a linguistic construct, forming networks of
feelings and associations which are inseparable from the meaning of sentences
themselves.

Stress, or 'accent' as it is called in both French and English, is the combined
effect of volume and intonation. These increase the intensity of particular syllables
in the word or phrase. In order to evaluate their impact on sentence structure and
meaning, it is normal to break sentences up into 'breath groups' (*groupes de
souffle*), which generally correspond to the grammatical units of which the sentences are made up. Reading a sentence 'out loud' in your mind immediately
helps to identify what the intonation pattern is likely to be and indicates where the
accent should fall. It makes the reader more aware of the contrasts between long
and short sentences and of the particular effects which the writer may have been
attempting to achieve.

Unlike English, French is a 'syllabic language'. Stress is theoretically even; that
is, each syllable is of the same length. The volume and length of the syllable
depends on its position within the phrase rather than on its meaning, the standard
rule in French being that the main accent falls on the last open vowel in the breath
group. In English, the question:

Have you read any plays by Sartre?

can be made to have a number of quite different meanings simply by changing
the position of the main accent without at the same time having to alter the
vocabulary while in French, for each change of meaning you would need a different form of words.

The standard French sentence is marked by a regular, rapid stress pattern,
which builds up to the last syllable in each group. This point of emphasis is

normally accompanied by a rise in intonation and a more or less immediate continuation to the next group in the series leading to a natural high point. The voice then falls away in a further series of groups, each marked by a final accent, until the last syllable of the last group, which carries the main stress (Mazaleyrat 1974: 11–14). Thus, in most standard written texts, syllabic rhythm builds up a sense of regularity or cohesion through repetition. Depending on the genre or on the originality of the text, this cohesion is more or less frequently interrupted, having the effect of foregrounding the word or phrase. Although grammar and rhythmic structure are normally expected to reinforce each other, the sentence may be constructed so that they are deliberately discordant – for emphasis, irony, humour, to introduce a conversational tone into the language, or to raise questions about the text's underlying meaning.

Apart from the patterning created by the recurrence of syllabic groups, one of the 'standard' features of rhythmic structure in French is that the groups tend to increase in length as the sentence proceeds. This is referred to as the *loi de longueur* or *cadence majeure*:

> *Ce qui importe, / / c'est ce qui s'ensuit de ces rencontres quotidiennes.*
> (Duras 1960:9)

Conventions such as these are not absolute. They simply define options and tendencies. For emphasis, or to introduce a sudden change of tone, the final syllable in the group may be shorter than those which precede, a feature known as *cadence mineure*. *Cadence mineure* may be used as a means of closing the sentence or paragraph, introducing an element of finality (or occasionally doubt) into the foregoing statement:

> *Mais déjà / un autre ouvrier s'était mis à l'oeuvre: / / le seigneur.*
> (Gaxotte 1928 / 1970)

or, less melodramatically:

> *Lorsque les réseaux sont en mauvais état, / / il faut les rénover.*
> (Compagnie des Eaux et de l'Ozone)

Intonation, the rise and fall of the voice, is an integral element of stress. The standard pattern within the French sentence is for the voice to rise at the end of each breath group and then to fall on the last syllable in the sentence or series of groups. The pitch of the voice rises in a sequence of steps to the caesura (the natural pause, marked with // above), and the process is then theoretically reversed in the second part of the series. The progressive rise of the voice is known as the protasis and the stepped drop in pitch after the caesura the apodosis.

It is important as part of the process of reading for the 'inner voice' of the reader to 'sing' the sentence, so that the relationships between the different rhythmic patterns and the grammatical structures become apparent.

<pre>
        rise   rise   half-fall// rise   fall
         /   /   `       /       `
</pre>

Ce couple de fortune, on ne le voit pas au début du film. Ni elle. Ni lui.

(Duras 1960: 9)

The balanced rise and fall of the last two phrases is contrastive and emphatic. It reinforces the point made in the previous sentence and, taken as a whole, marks the transition from the earlier part of the text which has dealt more or less exclusively with the two main characters themselves.

There is a direct link between intonation, cadence and foregrounding. In the following example of *cadence mineure*, again from *Hiroshima mon Amour*, the apodosis is held in suspense as the subject of the sentence is extended in a succession of rising groups until it finally falls on the final brief complement:

> *Ce début, ce défilé officiel des horreurs déjà célébrées de* HIROSHIMA, évoqué dans un
> *lit d'hôtel, cette évocation* sacrilège, *est volontaire.*

(Duras 1960: 10)

By contrast, in the sentence below from *L'Archéologie du Savoir*, the short rhythmic groups of the protasis build up to the extended apodosis in a classic instance of *cadence majeure*:

> *Ni caché, ni visible, le niveau énonciatif est à la limite du langage.*

(Foucault 1969: 147)

Uses of sound

The relationship between sound, meaning and style is complex and indirect. As we have seen, words are not generally interpreted as referring to objects and concepts simply because of the way they sound, but because it has been agreed between members of a speech community that a given combination of sounds corresponds to a shared perceptual response. The sound itself is a secondary factor. Unless they are derived from the same linguistic root, words referring to more or less the same object or concept sound quite different from one language to another. *Hund, dog* and *chien* all have essentially the same meaning. This general observation led Saussure (1916/1973) to describe the relationship between words and their referents as *arbitrary*. Exceptions had to be made for a range of words – such as *pan! chut! clac!* – whose pronunciation replicated the sound to which they referred. In cases such as these, known as onomatopoeia, the relationship between word and referent is not arbitrary or even, strictly speaking, symbolic. Rather it is imitative, or acoustic. The situation is less clear in the case of words which are integrated into the grammar of the language (nouns, verbs, adjectives, etc.), but are clearly evocative of the sounds which they represent – *tinter, chuchoter, murmurer* – and less clear still for words referring to processes or feelings which arouse strong sensations but which are not necessarily audible, such as *gratter, piquer, picoter, crispation, dur* or *tendre*. Here the sound of the word gives rise to associations which are consistent with the qualities of the actions or feelings being described but cannot be said to replicate them directly. An effect is created which is sometimes referred to as sound symbolism. The sound enhances the effect of the word but its central meaning is dependent on convention and, as has been seen, on its relationship with other words.

It is therefore very hazardous when analysing written text to draw direct conclusions as to the influence of sound on meaning. More than in any other area of style, interpretation is likely to be subjective. When combined to form words, individual sounds do not, in themselves, have a one-to-one relationship with experience. As in music, the essential meaning of sounds is derived less from their identification with phenomena in the real world than from their harmonious or disharmonious relationships with other sounds in the same textual environment. Their combination in written text enhances a sense of coherence or fragmentation and, as with rhythm and metre, has an immediate impact on the communicative effectiveness of a message. The most common forms of sound combination are alliteration (the repetition of consonants at the beginning of words) and assonance (the repetition of vowel sounds within words), which normally serve to reinforce links between words. Alternatively, dissonance can be used to foreground a word or phrase. In general, sound patterns create an effect of beauty or harshness which, when taken together with all the other features of style, make a text more or less memorable as a communicative experience.

Relating text to culture

We have broken down the process of analysis into a series of discursive features which should be taken into account in the appreciation of text. But, as must now be clear, it is not the features in themselves which carry significance but the manner in which their combination within the text interacts with the wider cultural context. Our task as stylistic and cultural commentators is to describe or deconstruct the way in which the features of style have been brought together and to consider what they reveal about the culture of which they are part.

An individual writer or a collective agency creates a text within the context of contemporary norms and conventions. These cannot, by definition, be understood in their entirety by any individual, particularly not by a native speaker of another language who may be observing a text at an historical distance. The totality of a discursive system can only be guessed at and approximately described. Through the analysis of particular texts, however, we can gain insight into the wider culture, since, as we have demonstrated in Chapter 1, discourse reflects and conditions the structure of relationships within society. The relationships and the discourses which express them are an integral part of the social process, generating constant tension between change and continuity. It is this dynamic which stylistic analysis should seek to illuminate and, in order to do so, the individual features of discourse have to be taken into account. Part 2 illustrates various ways in which this can be realised in practice.

Marguerite Duras, 'Synopsis', *Hiroshima mon Amour*, Paris: Gallimard, 1960, pp. 9–10.

SYNOPSIS

3 Nous sommes dans l'été 1957, en août, à Hiroshima.

5 Une femme française, d'une trentaine d'années, est dans cette ville. Elle y est
6 venue pour jouer dans un film sur la Paix.

8 L'histoire commence la veille du retour en France de cette Française. Le film dans
9 lequel elle joue est en effet terminé. Il n'en reste qu'une séquence à tourner.

11 C'est la veille de son retour en France que cette Française, qui ne sera jamais
12 nommée dans le film — cette femme anonyme — rencontrera un Japonais (ingén-
13 ieur, ou architecte) et qu'ils auront ensemble une histoire d'amour très courte.

15 Les conditions de leur rencontre ne seront pas éclaircies dans le film. Car ce n'est
16 pas là la question. On se rencontre partout dans le monde. Ce qui importe, c'est
17 ce qui s'ensuit de ces rencontres quotidiennes.

19 Ce couple de fortune, on ne le voit pas au début du film. Ni elle. Ni lui. On voit
20 en leur lieu et place des corps mutilés — à hauteur de la tête et des hanches —
21 remuants — en proie soit à l'amour, soit à l'agonie — et recouverts successive-
22 ment des cendres, des rosées, de la mort atomique — et des sueurs de l'amour
23 accompli.

25 Ce n'est que peu à peu que de ces corps informes, anonymes, sortiront leurs
26 corps à eux.

28 Ils sont couchés dans une chambre d'hôtel. Ils sont nus. Corps lisses. Intacts.

30 De quoi parlent-ils? Justement de HIROSHIMA.

32 Elle lui dit qu'elle a tout vu à HIROSHIMA. On voit ce qu'elle a vu. C'est horrible.
33 Cependant que sa voix à lui, négatrice, taxera les images de mensongères et qu'il
34 répétera, impersonnel, insupportable, qu'elle n'a rien vu à HIROSHIMA.

36 Leur premier propos sera donc allégorique. *Ce sera, en somme, un propos d'opéra.*
37 Impossible de parler de HIROSHIMA. Tout ce qu'on peut faire c'est de parler de
38 l'impossibilité de parler de HIROSHIMA. La *connaissance de Hiroshima* étant a priori
39 posée comme un leurre exemplaire de l'esprit.

For the original format, see page 39.

A methodological framework for text analysis

Robert Crawshaw and Karin Tusting

I. SITUATING THE TEXT (pp. 34–35)

Text and context (p. 34)

Identifying the text	What *publication* or *type of publication* does the text come from? What *genre* does it belong to, and what are the implications of this for the analysis?
Defining the context	What is the *context of culture*? What is the *context of situation*? What are the characteristics of the *discursive formation* within which the text is situated?

Subject matter, relationships and structure (pp. 35–37)

What is going on?	What is the text about? What are its main *topics*? Which *lexical items* set up different *lexical fields* in the text? How is the text *located in space and time*?
Who is taking part?	How are writer, reader and character *positioned*? What is the *function* of the text? How does the *tone* or *register* of the text affect the writer/reader relationship?
How are meanings communicated?	How does the text *hang together (cohere)*? How is *cohesion* achieved? What features are *marked* through *foregrounding*?

II. ANALYSING THE TEXT (pp. 37–38)

Positioning writer, reader and character (p. 38)

The presentation of character	How are *proper names, nouns and pronouns* used to *position* writer, reader and character? What techniques are used to portray character?
Modes of speech and points of view	Are points of view represented by *direct*, *reported*, *indirect* or *free indirect speech* and what effect does this have? Whose *voice* is being used and how does this change?
Mood	How does the *mood* of verbs contribute to the tone of the text and the relationships between writer, reader and character? How does mood interact with other features of the text?

Positioning in time and space (pp. 43–45)

Deixis and presupposition	What relations in space and time are constructed by *deictic structures*? What *presuppositions* are implied? How do these *construct* relations between writer, reader and character within the text?
Tense and aspect	What different *verb tenses* are used and what are the effects of these? How is *aspect* expressed in the text? How is the text *situated* in *relative time*?

Words, images and meaning (pp. 45–48)

Word meaning and lexical fields	How are the *denotations* and *connotations* of different *lexical items* used to set up particular *lexical fields* or *semantic spaces*?
Metaphor, metonymy and simile	What patterns of *simile*, *metaphor* or *metonymy* can be identified in the text? Is the text in general *allegorical*?

Sentence structure, rhythm and sound (pp. 48–57)

Simple, compound and complex sentences	Are sentences *simple* or *complex*? Are there patterns of *embedded* or *subordinate clauses*? Do these patterns form *parallel structures* within the text?
Deviations from standard sentence structure	Is there *ellipsis, displacement* of the subject, *inversion* of subject and verb, *splitting* of double subjects, *verb complements* placed *before the verb*? Are the general rules governing the order of complements broken in any way?
Rhythm and intonation	How do patterns of *sentence length*, *stress* and *intonation* contribute to the overall effect of the text? How do these patterns relate to other features of *coherence*?
Uses of sound	What is the value of *onomatopoeia* or *sound symbolism* within the text? How do patterns of *alliteration* and *assonance* relate to other stylistic features of the text?

III. RELATING TEXT TO CULTURE (pp. 57–58)

	How is the *style* of the text related to its context of *culture*? What is its wider social and cultural *significance*? How and to what extent does the text contribute to *social* and *discursive change*?

Part 2

Text analysis and the interpretation of national identity

Chemins d'eau

Rediscovering a stretch of the Burgundy Canal

David Scott

This passage is the fortieth of the forty-two chapters which constitute Jean Rolin's travelogue *Les Chemins d'eau*. It is critically analysed here as an example of the travel-writing genre, with particular reference to the intertextual and contextual frames within which such texts normally operate. This implies considering the implicitly posited relationship between writer and reader, the status of individual experience within the social community and the degree to which the authenticity of that experience is the product of the author's presentational skills. It therefore involves investigating the way in which rhetoric, narrative plot, humour and irony affect reader response and how passages that appear anecdotal or parenthetical point indirectly to relations of power and authority between reader and writer.

In engaging in such a critique, it is impossible to avoid being implicated myself in the process of establishing 'authority', and it is appropriate that the account that I give of *Chemins d'Eau* be itself interrogated by the reader, since no text, however much it may try to qualify its claims, is exempt from some form of discursive coercion. The use of the present indicative rather than the conditional tense, for example, or the omission of phrases suggesting option or doubt, already presuppose authorial assertion. Even the use of disclaimers or the inscribing of the commentary in the realm of hypothesis can be seen as discursive strategies designed to make the reader acquiesce to a particular assessment or point of view. Critical discourse analysis is therefore proposed here as a process in which text, commentator, and reader as third party, enter into a critical relationship with each other. It should be a relationship in which there is no absolute position of authority, since authority is distributed over the three positions in an uneven and continuously renegotiable way. Thus, individual subjectivity and critical insight enter into a dialogue with the conventions of writing and social practice, in an economy of exchange which is, in theory, infinitely renewable.

A cue for such an approach to Rolin's text is provided by an anecdote at the end of the passage. Having described the little town of Laroche-Migennes and the stretch of the Burgundy Canal that runs south of it, the author ends his day's journey at Ancy-le-Franc. On arriving in the town, he sees a girl with a bicycle engaged in animated conversation with an older man walking his dog. In providing an image which catches momentarily the contrast between the old and the new and evokes the fragility of French provincial traditions, the author pinpoints the complex relationship between the four agents involved: speaker, listener, writer and reader. The speaker is the young female cyclist who declares (*'superbe et péremptoire'*) that the world can end at any moment. Her interlocutor, the man with the dog, appears indifferent to her conviction ('[*Il*] *n'a pas l'air, lui, de s'en faire*'). Yet the author of the text, Jean Rolin, who has himself only caught snatches of the conversation, clearly is interested in the interchange, more interested than one of the participants and, by highlighting the incongruity of the non-communication, draws the attention of the reader to it. This leaves the incompleteness of the conversation open to wider symbolic interpretations which Jean Rolin leaves deliberately unstated. The anecdote thus serves to remind the reader that any discourse situation is always capable of being framed within a larger grid which brings to bear other potential angles or projections. It also encapsulates the suggestive nature of Rolin's style, which is both authoritative yet open-ended in the social interpretation which the reader is allowed to form.

Rolin's approach to travel writing is both that of a journalist who sets out to capture *'clichés'* of the French provincial scene which are directly derived from lived experience, and that of a writer who is aware of the narrative background – or discursive formation – within which all stories of travel are inevitably located. Like all travel writers in the European tradition, from Marco Polo onwards, he seeks to communicate a real experience to the reader, while at the same time appealing to literary and aesthetic references which may problematise the veracity of the phenomena he describes. In so doing, he implicitly acknowledges the impossibility of conveying the 'authentic' in writing from an objective point of view. Marco Polo claims to have seen with his own eyes the dragons that figure in thirteenth-century Chinese mythology. Any detail in written text, however much based in actual experience, may be a fictional ploy; indeed, in an absolute sense, becomes fiction through the processes of its selection, its formulation in language and its relationship with other linguistic representations in the same text.

At the same time, Rolin cannot be unaware of the expectations of his readers, in particular insofar as they relate to the genre of travel writing. As a genre, travel writing is particularly rich in intertextual reference. Often inspired by previous writers, or by voyages which have become part of cultural tradition (*Robinson Crusoe, Treasure Island, Heart of Darkness*), travel writing implies mystery, adventure, surprise, danger and survival. If the full potential of these themes is not developed in a given travel text, fragmentary or parodic hints may be given of them so that the reader's conventional expectations of the genre can be responded to, if not fully satisfied. The features to which Rolin gives particular attention are the itinerary chosen, the pace and rhythm of the journey, the receptivity of the

40

Laroche-Migennes est certainement une des petites villes de France les plus familières de la vitesse, puisque jour et nuit, à tout instant, des convois la traversent à fond de train, sans lui prodiguer d'autres marques d'attention que ces longs et déchirants hurlements, qui, dans le temps, faisaient voyager les imaginations nomades. Or au pied de cette gare que les grands express saluent distraitement, le canal de Bourgogne vient se jeter dans l'Yonne, tirant entre la ville et le chemin de fer un trait d'eau stagnante, presque morte, ombragée sur chaque bord d'une double rangée de platanes, et qui restaure à côté de cette agitation la dimension de la lenteur, du silence, du croupissement. Les gens qui montent ou descendent du train à Migennes – car certains, tout de même, s'arrêtent – doivent l'enjamber sur un pont en dos d'âne interdit à la circulation, même des vélos, et ils ont ainsi le loisir, entre deux précipitations, entre deux hâtes, de prendre la mesure d'un temps moins compté.

Migennes, néanmoins, reste une ville de transition plutôt que de séjour, et le nom du seul hôtel que j'y connaisse – l'Hôtel de la Gare et de l'Escale – indique assez qu'il n'est pas question de s'y éterniser. (Ainsi la disposition des multiples salles à manger de cet établissement, de prime abord assez déconcertante, comme si elle correspondait aux différents stades d'une initiation, traduit-elle simplement le désir de satisfaire simultanément des clients diversement pressés, de l'avaleur en hâte de sandwiches – tel ce cadre affublé de tous les insignes de sa condition, haletant comme s'il venait de traverser dans cet appareil la Cordillère des Andes – au baffreur de jambon à la crème et autres approximations de spécialités régionales.)

La nuit, lorsqu'à travers la double rangée de platanes, le canal reflète les néons de la gare et les lumières fugitives des trains, l'ensemble évoque assez exactement une toile de Delvaux où il ne manquerait que quelques grandes femmes nues et ennuyées.

On ne s'écarte pas de cet univers ferroviaire à suivre le canal, voie d'eau et voie ferrée étant à peu près inséparables jusque dans les parages de Vitteaux. La faune aquatique semble d'ailleurs avoir pris son parti de ce mariage : entre Brienon et Saint-Florentin, sur un lac artificiel béant parmi les terres ocres remuées par le chantier du T.G.V., deux hérons dérivent sur des souches – chacun la sienne – parfaite image de l'anachorétisme. Dans l'eau du canal s'épanouissent de loin en loin d'énormes remous, d'énormes borborygmes, effloraisons gargouillantes de peu vraisemblables explosions sous-marines. Toute la matinée – et encore pendant ma brève halte du midi, à Tonnerre – j'échoue à résoudre cette énigme dont la clef ne me sera donnée qu'à l'écluse d'Argentenay : ces remous, ce sont des carpes qui les produisent, vautrées en surface parmi d'équivoques chevelures aquatiques, des carpes écœurantes, aussi grasses que celles des fossés de Chantilly. Elles pullulent entre Argentenay et Lézinnes, tellement gavées, tellement sûres de leur affaire qu'elles ne prennent même plus la peine de se mettre en plongée à mon approche. Toute la journée placée sous ce double signe de la carpe et du chemin de fer. Le soir, lorsque j'atteins Ancy-le-Franc, une adolescente, comme moi bicycliste, sur l'esplanade du château, dans l'ombre des platanes – car il règne alentour un soleil éclatant bien que sur le point de disparaître – entretient de la mort – la sienne, celle des autres, la mort en général – un homme plus âgé qui promène un chien noir et n'a pas l'air, lui, de s'en faire.

« Mais le monde entier peut mourir à l'instant », déclare-t-elle, superbe et péremptoire, au terme d'une conversation dont je n'ai malheureusement recueilli que des bribes.

Source: Rolin, J. (1996) *Les Chemins d'eau*, Paris: Payot et Rivages, pp. 267–269. ©Editions Jean-Claude Lattès.

traveller/writer to his experience and the textual tradition within which travel writing is conventionally situated.

In choosing in *Chemins d'eau* to follow the canals and inland waterways of France, Jean Rolin is consciously submitting his journey to an itinerary which follows a different logic from that of pilgrimages, tourist trails, monuments and sites. Cutting across the tracks of the TGV and the motorways, the waterways enable Rolin to rediscover forgotten perspectives and neglected corners of the provincial scene. The function of the canals, constructed in France from the seventeenth to the nineteenth centuries, was primarily utilitarian, the waterways being used for the transport of grain, fuel and other important raw materials. Until the advent of motorised barges, most lighters were towed by horses, the 'towpath' along the canal banks being an important feature of waterway topography. The construction and route of the canals were inevitably governed by considerations of gradient and geological formation and were often linked to the courses of navigable rivers. Complicated systems of locks and channels enabled the canals to negotiate differences of level and terrain. As a result, the itineraries offered by the canals do not normally lead to the *châteaux* and cathedrals that have, since the beginning of regional tourism in France in the early nineteenth century, been the focus of tourist interest. The commentary to which the canals give rise is therefore clearly not that of the classic guides to national icons. With the expansion of the railway network in the last century, France's canals have become this century's backwaters, the haunt of fishermen and pleasure craft. While they cannot be described as what Marc Augé (1992) refers to as '*non-lieux*' (the impersonal spaces created by modern communications – airports, motorways, etc.) nor, following the historian Pierre Nora (1984, 1986), as '*lieux de mémoire*', the French waterways, as places, share elements of both categories. Rolin's text causes them to become re-iconised as the locus of a reflection that includes personal, ethno-sociological, historical and cultural dimensions.

A second authenticating feature of waterway travel is the pace at which it is pursued. When Rolin is unable to navigate the canals of France in small barges or boats, he walks or cycles along the towpaths. All three means of transport are slow and admit of immediate stops, as interest, social intercourse or any other motivation requires. The social aspect of this leisurely rhythm of travel is important. Whereas for the standard tourist, the native person himself/herself is either a picturesque part of the scenery or a nuisance, the water traveller is often obliged to enter into discussion with lock-keepers, fishermen and the subjects of other fortuitous encounters. This pace of movement also means that otherwise unnoticed phenomena – the activities of birds and animals, plants and vegetation, smells and tastes – are perceived with a vividness that authenticates and enriches the experience. Travel is lived as a continuum, not as a series of sites, the process itself becoming as rich as the arrival at a given destination. The sights awaiting the explorer of canals are mostly yet to be discovered. They are not known before the journey begins and thus bring the accidents of chance to bear on the project. The way Rolin presents his material is both an invitation to his readers to identify with it and to seek out for themselves the experiences that such an itinerary is likely to produce.

Third, the travel writer's receptivity to his environment is a paramount consideration in communicating the authenticity of travel experience. Since travellers have no particular preconceptions about what they are going to see or experience, they must remain open and alert to all eventualities. Only the experience itself brings the events and sensation that will, retrospectively, be recognised as the rewards of the project. The price to be paid for this is, of course, the potential for tedium, frustration or exhaustion – which is sometimes felt as much by the reader of the travelogue as by the writer as the need to recount all the petty obstacles he or she encounters. Basic activities such as finding food and shelter become major concerns which have largely been abstracted from life in the Western world. The reality and the aesthetic qualities of these need to be recaptured in travel writing for the genre to be successful. The exotic, the humorous and the personal have to combine for the interest of the reader to be aroused and sustained. The advent of modern communications has reduced many of these effects to televisual cliché, yet the current success of travel writing is a reminder that, while the reading public's appetite for vicarious adventure is insatiable, there is also a desire to be amused and reassured by the myth of the simple and the unplanned which represents an alternative to the complex pace of everyday life. In this, travel writing since the eighteenth century responds to an essentially romantic urge for self-discovery and renewal of identity in which the project of providing a record is an intrinsic element of the experience.

While Jean Rolin's account bears witness to the incidental and accidental, it remains a fundamentally textual endeavour, and, as such, is marked by the conventions, references and intertextualities of all travel writing. In addition to his predecessors in the French tradition (Flaubert, Mérimée and, most particularly, Robert Louis Stevenson, whose *La France que j'aime ou Voyage sans âne* becomes in a sense the *vade mecum* of *Chemins d'eau*), Rolin cites many of the standard guides (*Michelin, Le Guide vert*), articles from journals and newspapers (*Ouest France, Le Monde, Toulouse-Midi-Pyrénées*), encyclopedias and dictionaries (*Le Petit Robert, La Grande Encyclopédie*), and even the roneo-typed text of one M. Gachet, lock-keeper at Josselin, on the waterway between Nantes and Brest. In addition, Rolin is sensitive to visual intertexts, admiringly citing the British landscape artist John Constable as well as the *paysagiste*, Hubert Robert. Certain unexpected, surrealist effects more than once lead Rolin to draw a comparison with the paintings of the Belgian artist Paul Delvaux. But the coincidence of text and experience is most fully brought out in the structure of Rolin's book. Taking the form of a journal, it ascribes a short chapter to each day, allowing him to capture the variety, triviality and spontaneity of experience within a series of individual time frames, incorporated into a coherent whole.

The chapter which forms the basis of this analysis is entirely typical of Rolin's approach to regional travel. Its aim is to give an impression of one of the hundreds of '*petites villes de France*' encountered along French waterways, showing its relationship with the canal, the degree to which it has been affected by modern life and the distinctive features it, or the region, has retained. Also recounted are the particular incidents associated with the writer's personal association with the place. Like some tourist guides, the chapter commences with a general remark about the site in question: '*Laroche-Migennes est certainement une des petites villes de France les plus familières de la vitesse . . .*'. The reader is not surprised to see the description rapidly take a more vivid and personal turn. Sounds and images are evoked and the text becomes seasoned with irony and parody as Rolin delves more deeply into his reactions to the scene.

The dominant theme of this short chapter – as of the book as a whole – is that of two speeds or double rhythms of late twentieth-century France. The little town of Laroche-Migennes in Burgundy is situated at the point at which the Burgundy Canal enters the River Yonne and is bisected by the main southbound railway line. It is a place where both rhythms are felt. The township is '*familière de la vitesse*', in that express trains hurtle through, whistles blowing, while, less than a stone's throw away, the waters of the canal stagnate in silence, sheltered by an avenue of plane trees. '*Vitesse*', '*agitation*' and '*déchirants hurlements*' are juxtaposed with '*lenteur*', '*silence*' and '*croupissement*'. With an apt play on words, Rolin describes the stretch of stagnant canal as a '*trait d'eau*' – a metaphorical *trait d'union* or hyphen setting up an apparently grammatical relationship between two otherwise separate worlds ('*univers*'). Further images juxtaposing the two rhythms include the '*pont en dos d'âne*', accessible only to pedestrians, and the restaurant facilities in the '*Hôtel de la Gare et de l'Escale*', which contrast the fast-food snack for the passing executive with the more leisurely indulgence of a regional lunch ('*deux précipitations . . . deux hâtes*'), allowing the reader to be made aware of a less measured form of time: '*un temps moins compté*'.

The contrasting rhythms of modern and traditional life are maintained as Rolin continues his journey along the Burgundy Canal, which follows the railway as far as Vitteaux. The detachment of the two worlds is marked by the unconcern of the aquatic fauna which inhabit the canal (two hermitic herons and the disturbingly sluggish and self-satisfied carp whose gurglings trouble the surface of the water) and the upheaval caused by the construction of the new TGV line. Rolin makes the contrast explicitly symbolic in his phrase '*le double signe de la carpe et du chemin de fer*'. The opposition between the speed of the new and the stasis of a more timeless way of life does not appear to offer grounds for comfort or reassurance. The reflection of the neon lights of the station in the canal produces a hallucinatory effect, which is evoked in terms of one of Paul Delvaux's surrealist railway scenes – a reminder of the unreal juxtaposition of two contrasted worlds in which, for Delvaux, modern urban reality becomes the setting for dreamlike, erotic projections. The overall effect is unsettling. Nothing in this environment seems stable or real. The trains, like fantastic beasts of the wild, let out *'longs et déchirants hurlements'* as they pass through the town. Migennes is a *'ville de transition'*, the *'disposition des multiples salles à manger'* of its hotel is *'de prime abord assez déconcertante'*, and the *'lumières'* of the trains are *'fugitives'*. Finally, there is the strange and unexplained conversation about death between the young woman and the older man to which I have already referred.

At the same time, in portraying the unsettling duality of modern France, Rolin underlines the seeming resistance to change of certain of the traditional features of French landscape and custom. The *'double rangée de platanes'*, which for hundreds of years have provided shade for France's country roads and waterways, has become an icon of French landscape celebrated in French poetry and art of the 20th century and is mentioned no less than three times in this short chapter. The *'pont en dos d'âne'* is a somewhat more vulnerable symbol of rural life, but survives in this passage as the transition which necessarily slows down the fast rhythms of modern life. The herons and the carp, as sleek and complacent as those of Chantilly, appear to thrive despite the proximity of the railway works, yet the picture of the fish *'vautrées en surface'*, *'écœurantes'* and *'gavées'* is not an attractive one.

What allows Rolin to conjoin the reality of the two worlds while commenting on their incongruity is his recourse to comic hyperbole and parody. This enables him to remain the outsider, observing the world with the superior and humorous eye of the travelling artist, obliging the reader to take his point of view and preventing him or her from identifying with either way of life. It is part of the way in which Rolin marks and celebrates the resistance to change of certain aspects of French life while calling into question their pretension to represent reality. The *'spécialités régionales'* are, after all, only *'approximations'* and the slower pace of life is defined with the detachment of abstraction as a *'dimension'* or as *'silence'*, *'lenteur'* and *'croupissement'*. Nevertheless, whereas the traditionally gluttonous, gastronomic tourist is let off lightly as a *'baffreur de jambon à la crème'*, the hapless executive *'affublé de tous les insignes de sa condition'* is described comically as gasping for breath as if he had just crossed the Andes in suit and tie.

Much of the comic distancing in Rolin's style derives from applying fantastical images to the essentially commonplace realities he is observing. The reference to the Andes and the comparison of herons on stumps to anchorites normally found in the mountainous wilds of China or Tibet are ironic links with tales of travel and adventure, both situating Rolin's text within a genre and distancing his narrative from it. Similarly, the enigma of the classic traveller's story is parodied here by the mysterious churning of the canal waters. This turns out to be caused not by some exotic, subaquatic monster, but by the thrashings of overweight carp. So, unlike

Marco Polo's travels, Rolin's visit to the Burgundy Canal is not connoted by mythological dragons but takes place under the sign of the Carp and Railway.

The lexis of the text matches the ironic quality of these shifts in level. The language of factual description relating to time, duration and place ('*temps*', '*mesure*', '*lenteur*', '*hâte*', etc.) soon becomes seasoned with words expressing a more personal assessment, often marked by longer, more hyperbolic forms ('*croupissement*', '*précipitation*', '*éterniser*'). In relation to the physical landscapes, clichéd features such as the '*pont en dos d'âne*' or the repeated '*double rangée de platanes*' give way to the lyricism, hyperbole or even burlesque with which many travel writers choose to enliven their accounts of otherwise relatively banal details. Thus, the thrashing of the carp in the water of the canal, at first referred to generically and detachedly as '*La faune aquatique*', is later described as '*borborygmes*', '*effloraisons gargouillantes*' and '*explosions sous-marines*'. A similar shift is witnessed in the second paragraph, where the simple description of the station hotel becomes the stage on to which the panting junior executive makes his appropriately theatrical entrance – '*affublé . . . insignes . . . appareil*' – the event being framed between dashes as if in a comic strip.

The varying strands of thematic or narrative imperative that constitute the structure of the travel book as a genre – objective description, political or social reflection, personal reaction – are therefore all identifiable in Rolin's style and particularly in the various registers through which the language travels. Most obviously, the use of quotation marks (foregrounded at the closure of the piece), parentheses, dashes, and other signs of embedding, mark the successive layers of reference – factual, personal, fantastical, intertextual – that characterise travel writing. The sentences are extended to allow the author to add a personal remark addressed as an aside as if to the reader, with the demonstratives not only providing a stronger sense of place but also including the reader in the setting and acting as a cohesive device ('*au pied de cette gare que les trains saluent distraitement . . .*', '*- tel ce cadre affublé de tous les insignes de sa condition . . .*', '*ce double signe de la carpe et du chemin de fer, . . .*' etc.). Often these embedded remarks take the form of a justification or qualification introduced by *car* ('*car certains, tout de même, s'arrêtent*', '*car il règne alentour un soleil éclatant bien que sur le point de disparaître*'). These features of sentence structure lend the prose the circuitous style characteristic of spoken language, despite the obvious signals – such as the careful choice of words and the fronting of the adjectives ('*longs et déchirants hurlements*') – that it is in reality a very consciously composed written parody, imbued with mildly disturbing overtones.

These overtones come through most tellingly in the change of register, which occurs in the final part of the last paragraph. The chance meeting with the young woman cyclist under the plane trees at Ancy-le-Franc has multiple functions. First the passage brings the text back from the comic hyperbole to the humdrum and anecdotal – the juxtaposition, typical of travel writing, of the unexpected and the banal. But it is possible that the writer is making another, more telling point: that, even in the most trivial of experiences – a conversation between a cyclist and an old man walking a dog – some underlying and barely apprehended significance may be present. '*Mais le monde entier peut mourir à l'instant,*' the girl proclaims. The statement is a cliché, yet the sublime confidence of the girl and its incongruity – apart from being unexpected, (it is she who says it and not the older man) – restore its authentic value. What is or could be about to die is not clear: perhaps the vestiges of rural France, its tranquil rhythms made more apparent by the frenetic existence which rushes past indifferently so close by. Or perhaps rural France itself offers only a form of slow death in a world where speed has replaced a sense of lived reality, time and place.

In the way in which it plays self-consciously with the styles and conventions of its genre, while at the same time opening itself to the insights of other disciplines, Rolin's text is exemplary of contemporary French writing and cultural expression. Since the 1960s, 'literature', while increasingly aware of its intertextuality, has also become enriched by other areas of intellectual enquiry as the interdiscursive potential of all writing has become consciously recognised and pursued. In the specific case of travel literature, the existing generical markers – epic plot, adventure, documentary record, personal experience – have become complicated by insights from ethnology, semiotics and sociology. These insights have introduced a tension between the quest for scientific analysis and the subjectivity of individual experience. In this respect, travel writing has become a privileged area for experiment, counting amongst its twentieth-century adherents ethnographers, sociologists and semioticians such as Augé (1992), Barthes (1970) and Baudrillard (1986). Yet, at the dawn of the twenty-first century, travel and human experience itself have become commodities. The generic boundaries between feature, promotional journalism, anthropological investigation and personal adventure have become blurred. In its purest form, travel writing, as Lévi-Strauss showed in his *Tristes Tropiques* (1955), is both ethnography and fiction, a genre which offers a privileged insight into the relationship between science and subjectivity. Yet at the other end of the scale it is produced and sold as a 'consumable' in a televisual mass marketplace. Rolin's text is indicative of these tensions in the way it positions itself and exercises authority over the reader. It draws on discourses of analysis, description, literature and anecdote, and, at the same time, through parodic distancing, retains the idiosyncrasy of the '*je*' whose appeal the reader is invited to share.

Jean Rolin, *Les Chemins d'eau*, Paris: Payot et Rivages, 1996, pp. 267–269.

LAROCHE-MIGENNES

Laroche-Migennes est certainement une des petites villes de France les plus familières de la vitesse, puisque jour et nuit, à tout instant, des convois la traversent à fond de train, sans lui prodiguer d'autres marques d'attention que ces longs et déchirants hurlements, qui, dans le temps, faisaient voyager les imaginations nomades. Or au pied de cette gare que les grands express saluent distraitement, le canal de Bourgogne vient se jeter dans l'Yonne, tirant entre la ville et le chemin de fer un trait d'eau stagnante, presque morte, ombragée sur chaque bord d'une double rangée de platanes, et qui restaure à côté de cette agitation la dimension de la lenteur, du silence, du croupissement. Les gens qui montent ou descendent du train à Migennes – car certains, tout de même, s'arrêtent – doivent l'enjamber sur un pont en dos d'âne interdit à la circulation, même des vélos, et ils ont ainsi le loisir, entre deux précipitations, entre deux hâtes, de prendre la mesure d'un temps moins compté.

Migennes, néanmoins, reste une ville de transition plutôt que de séjour, et le nom du seul hôtel que j'y connaisse – l'Hôtel de la Gare et de l'Escale – indique assez qu'il n'est pas question de s'y éterniser. (Ainsi la disposition des multiples salles à manger de cet établissement, de prime abord assez déconcertante, comme si elle correspondait aux différents stades d'une initiation, traduit-elle simplement le désir de satisfaire simultanément des clients diversement pressés, de l'avaleur en hâte de sandwiches – tel ce cadre affublé de tous les insignes de sa condition, haletant comme s'il venait de traverser dans cet appareil la Cordillère des Andes – au baffreur de jambon à la crème et autres approximations de spécialités régionales.)

La nuit, lorsqu'à travers la double rangée de platanes, le canal reflète les néons de la gare et les lumières fugitives des trains, l'ensemble évoque assez exactement une toile de Delvaux où il ne manquerait que quelques grandes femmes nues et ennuyées.

On ne s'écarte pas de cet univers ferroviaire à suivre le canal, voie d'eau et voie ferrée étant à peu près inséparables jusque dans les parages de Vitteaux. La faune aquatique semble d'ailleurs avoir pris son parti de ce mariage : entre Brienon et Saint-Florentin, sur un lac artificiel béant parmi les terres ocres remuées par le chantier du T.G.V., deux hérons dérivent sur des souches – chacun la sienne –

38 parfaite image de l'anachorétisme. Dans l'eau du canal s'épanouissent de loin en
39 loin d'énormes remous, d'énormes borborygmes, effloraisons gargouillantes de
40 peu vraisemblables explosions sous-marines. Toute la matinée – et encore pendant
41 ma brève halte du midi, à Tonnerre – j'échoue à résoudre cette énigme dont la
42 clef ne me sera donnée qu'à l'écluse d'Argentenay : ces remous, ce sont des
43 carpes qui les produisent, vautrées en surface parmi d'équivoques chevelures
44 aquatiques, des carpes écœurantes, aussi grasses que celles des fossés de Chantilly.
45 Elles pullulent entre Argentenay et Lézinnes, tellement gavées, tellement sûres de
46 leur affaire qu'elles ne prennent même plus la peine de se mettre en plongée à
47 mon approche. Toute la journée placée sous ce double signe de la carpe et du
48 chemin de fer. Le soir, lorsque j'atteins Ancy-le-Franc, une adolescente, comme
49 moi bicycliste, sur l'esplanade du château, dans l'ombre des platanes – car il règne
50 alentour un soleil éclatant bien que sur le point de disparaître – entretient de la
51 mort – la sienne, celle des autres, la mort en général – un homme plus âgé qui
52 promène un chien noir et n'a pas l'air, lui, de s'en faire.
53
54 « Mais le monde entier peut mourir à l'instant », déclare-t-elle, superbe et
55 péremptoire, au terme d'une conversation dont je n'ai malheureusement recueilli
56 que des bribes.

For the original format, see page 67.

Reinventing gastronomic heritage

'La Brie, comme autrefois'

Robert Crawshaw

Introduction

Gastronomic writing: historical background

In an era of globalisation and fast food, combined with insecurity in the present and uncertainty about the future, it is not surprising that, in Western Europe at least, food and drink and the description of it should have become a prominent feature of media production. The perception of France as a 'gastronomic culture' is of course not new, and is probably derived as much from its climate and topography as from its cultural heritage. Today, France is still known as the 'country of a thousand cheeses' and the retention of the *commune* as the basic administrative unit, the country's relative underpopulation through the centuries, the uneven pattern of industrialisation and the durability of what Fernand Braudel (1986) called 'the peasant economy' has done much to underpin local traditions and sustain a sense of rural community.

Following the heyday of Louis XIV's Versailles, marked by the publication in 1691 of Massialot's *Le Cuisinier Roïal et Bourgeois*, the development of French gastronomic art was essentially initiated by the Court and the great households of the aristocracy. The principles of gastronomy were only more widely disseminated after the 1789 Revolution as a result of the growth of restaurants and, a century later, through the spread of fashionable hotels (Mennell 1993: 178–179). Nevertheless, the fact that France remained for so long a primarily agricultural economy, based on privately owned smallholdings and backward in its farming methods, has allowed the myth of provincial cuisine to endure as a manifestation of local identity, if not of the peasant way of life. It was the appearance of the *Almanach des Gourmands* between 1803 and 1812 under the editorship of Grimod de la Reynière, and the publication by Brillat-Savarin of *La Physiologie du Goût* (1826), which heralded the launch of a new type of writing (Mennell 1993: 182). A string of more recent manuals have followed in the last 150 years – laying down codes of practice, lauding the physiological merits of particular dishes, embellishing the anecdotes surrounding the most famous chefs and relaunching at regular intervals the principles of a perennially reinvented '*nouvelle cuisine*'.

It is hardly surprising that the popularity of these publications should have coincided with the rise of tourism. The advent of the motor car gave wider access to regional cuisine, and the publication of Michelin's *Guide Rouge* in 1900 lent institutional status to the opportunities for restauration which the automobile tourist might expect. From 1926, the *Guide Rouge* introduced the sign of the star as a mark of quality, which was later extended to the three-star grading system which we know today. Inevitably, Michelin's systematisation of the tourist experience has had the consequence of detaching the status of the object within the system from the quality of the experience itself. Roland Barthes made this point forcibly in 1957 with reference to the *Guide Bleu*, the companion volume to *Le Rouge*. The identification of monuments, buildings and places as 'sites' to be visited reduced their value as lived encounters to bourgeois objects to be 'possessed' as items on an established itinerary. The relationship between buildings and their local communities was abstracted from its authentic environment to form an independent network in the mind of the middle-class traveller.

The *Guide Rouge* has become a national institution in its own right as a guardian of the quality of French cuisine, in Paris and the provinces. Its invisible inspectorate preserve the myth of objectivity and its hierarchy of stars is regarded as an ultimate authority. Yet, although individual specialities are indicated in the references to particular restaurants, the guide's application of uniform standards of adjudication does not allow for representative diversity, and the function of the modern gastronomic review is partly to fill that gap and to evoke in colourful detail the eating places to which the *Guide Rouge* merely refers. The cultural context in which the genre now flourishes is also one in which the eating habits of the French population have undergone rapid and extensive change. In 1957, Barthes commented sardonically on the visual and written texts in the magazine *Elle*, in which weekly photographs of a chosen dish displayed a profusion of coloured coatings whose baroque ornamentation obscured the reality of the food beneath. This trend he condemned as the popularisation of *haute cuisine*, a superficial attempt to recreate the *faux-grandeur* of traditional dishes for general consumption in an era of mass production.

Since the 1960s, France's gastronomic heritage has been under more direct attack from the growth of fast food. Restaurants are visited at least twice as frequently as twenty-five years ago, but this increase is accounted for by changing work patterns rather than by a growing interest in fine cooking. Hamburgers represent 81 per cent of the sales of fast-food chains against 48 per cent in 1988 and an increasing proportion of foodstuffs are produced and sold globally, thus undermining national distinctiveness (Mermet 1996). It is hard to gauge to what extent this revolution in eating habits is affecting the status and reputation of

French gastronomy. The spread of fast-food outlets has led to the closure of numerous *bistrots* (120,000 in ten years). However, small café-restaurants could hardly be described as the mainstay of national culinary standards and it seems that, in the last few years, cooking as an activity has undergone a renaissance in the mind of the public as a consequence of its more intensive coverage in the written and audiovisual media. As a continued development of the type of coverage criticised by Barthes in the 1950s, the description of recipes which combine tradition with convenience is a regular feature of weekly magazines. Their demonstration has also become more popular on television, further confirming his portrayal of cuisine as spectacle.

The genre of gastronomic review

Against a background of changing habits and values, Gilles Pudlowski's column typifies the feature article of the upmarket weekly magazine. *Le Point* is aimed at a professional, middle-class readership with sufficient disposable income to be regular frequenters of restaurants both during the working day and in weekend forays to the provincial countryside. The genre is clearly located in the conflicting traditions of the gastronomic almanac and the tourist guide, and therefore has the complex and overlapping functions of identifying the eating places which it reviews and of evoking through language the quality of the experience which the visitor can be expected to enjoy. It both complements and counteracts the classificatory function of a guide such as *Le Rouge*, since it must restore to the reader a sense of gastronomic authenticity which may otherwise be neutralised or distorted in the manner suggested by Barthes. It is doubtful to what extent the gastronomic feature/review aims primarily to promote. It is improbable that the readership of *Le Point* will systematically refer to Pudlowski's column when selecting restaurants in different parts of France. The function of the text is as much to entertain and describe through the use of expressive language as it is actively to sell a service. Yet all press coverage is a form of promotion. An evocative review is bound to leave a trace in the memory of the reader which a reference to the *Brie* region is liable to trigger off. The critically persuasive function of the text cannot be completely ignored.

Content, structure and tenor

'La Brie, comme autrefois' is a complete piece. It has a racy and familiar tone set immediately by the short opening sentences and the personification of La Brie which follows. The metaphors 'dorlote . . ., aime . . ., flirte' are early signs of the personal and mildly flirtatious atmosphere which pervades the whole passage. The reader is invited to participate in a tour of the *Brie* region, presumably by car, and to savour by proxy the experiences of the author at two restaurants: both of high

TABLES

La Brie, comme autrefois

par Gilles Pudlowski

Paris est à deux pas. Et, pourtant, là est la France profonde, entre Coulommiers et La Ferté. La Brie ménage ses grosses fermes, dorlote ses fromages royaux, aime sa moutarde de Meaux et flirte avec la Champagne.

Dans son fameux « Carnet de croûte », Jean Ferniot rappelle que le vignoble du vin blond commence ici même... dans la cave de l'Auberge de Condé, si riche en belles bouteilles. Le patriarche Emile Tingaud n'est plus là. Mais Pascal, le petit-fils, a repris la tradition. Et l'on se sent bien, dans ce décor cossu, veillé par le maître d'hôtel Lucien, présent depuis un demi-siècle.

Le bonheur de la table, ce n'est pas seulement le fond de l'assiette, mais un accueil souriant, une mise de table soignée, une carte alléchante qui fait la part belle aux produits régionaux. Et voilà ce que l'on trouve dans ce maillon des Relais-Châteaux, où rien ne semble avoir bougé depuis vingt ans, sinon l'allègement nécessaire et la créativité mesurée. Le foie gras mariné au vin de Bouzy, moelleux et rose dans sa gelée fine, le tartare de langouste, le saumon légèrement fumé à la maison sur un lit de pommes roseval, le poulet à l'estragon et le canard à la briarde, c'est-à-dire cuit rosé et pourvu d'une sauce légère à la moutarde en grains de chez Pommery, qui s'accompagne de pommes soufflées, exquises comme un plaisir retrouvé : eh oui, on est bien ici, comme dans le temps, avec un Pol Roger brut sans année, aux arômes nets de brioche chaude et de pain grillé, aux fines bulles, qui vous laissent l'esprit net avant de reprendre la route pour d'autres aventures.

Le « wonder-kid » de la région ? Il s'appelle Alain Pavard, à moins de 30 ans, est inconnu au bataillon des « grands », a fait ses classes non seulement chez Tingaud, mais aussi chez Meneau. à Vézelay. Il a choisi de retourner au pays pour ouvrir une auberge de bord de route. Ô surprise ! même si l'adresse est encore inconnue de la chronique, le bonhomme affiche complet à chaque déjeuner. Il faut dire que son menu du marché à 165 F, offrant, par exemple, gâteau moelleux de saint-jacques sauce gribiche, mi-cuit de saumon à la crème d'épinards, suprême de volaille aux deux purées, feuilleté de brie sur verdure, crème soufflée au citron vert et coulis d'abricot, tous réalisés au petit point, avec des assaisonnements impeccables et des cuissons millimétrées, apparaît comme l'une des plus belles affaires de l'Hexagone. La carte est, certes, plus coûteuse. Mais les produits sont parfaits, les portions, généreuses, l'accueil de la mignonne Mme Pavard, adorable. le cadre de fermette briarde rénovée et fleurie, à croquer. Et les terrines de foie de canard aux asperges, blanc de tur-

29 Août 94
14h25

À L'AUBERGE DE CONDÉ

bot à la crème de céleri – le poisson si frais donne l'impression de gigoter dans l'assiette – et le mille-feuille craquant au chocolat avec coulis d'orange sont du grand art sur le mode du classicisme réinventé. La carte des vins, avec des champagnes de choix, possède du tonus, et l'ensemble donne envie de crier : « Vive la Brie, vive la France comme autrefois ! »

Auberge de Condé. 1. av. de Montmirail, 77260 La Ferté-sous-Jouarre. 60.22.00.07. Menus : 295 F. 345 F. 450 F. Carte : 450 F.
Auberge de la Brie. 14. av. Alphonse-Boulingre. 77860 Couilly-Pont-aux-Dames. 64.63.51.80.

Source: Pudlowski, G. 'La Brie, comme autrefois', *Le Point*, 1 October 1994, no. 1150.

quality but different in character. The '*on*' of '*l'on se sent bien*' implies a shared feeling of contentment and security in the joint rediscovery of traditional values, and the relaxed relationship between author and implied reader is sustained in the second half, where a newly established and relatively undocumented restaurant is explored. The passage falls naturally into two parts. The first describes the *Auberge de Condé*, a restaurant with an apparently long-standing reputation, as the references to Jean Ferniot's '« *Carnet de croûte* »', the '*patriarche Emile Tingaud*' and the half-century that the '*maître d'hôtel, Lucien*' has been in service at the *Auberge* make clear. The second introduces the reader to the '« *wonder-kid* »', Alain Pavard's newly opened roadside inn and the tone changes to suit the different character of the more modern institution.

The structure of the text corresponds naturally to the perspective of the traveller and is carefully articulated accordingly. The first paragraph introduces the region, the gastronomic guide (Jean Ferniot's *Carnet de Croûte*) which has apparently recommended the *Auberge de Condé* to the author, and the traditional character of the *Auberge* itself. The second describes the dishes and leads by way of the continued journey ('. . . *avant de reprendre la route pour d'autres aventures*') to the third and final paragraph to which it is linked by the simple device of the rhetorical question '*le « wonder-kid » de la région ?*'. The latter begins with a brief profile of the new chef, Alain Pavard, continues with a description of the menu, the setting and the atmosphere of the *Auberge de la Brie*, and ends with the spirited exclamation of delight and enthusiasm at the rediscovery of a sense of national identity. Apart from being striking by its cumulative descriptions of dishes, the energy and familiarity of the text are maintained by the exclamations: '*Ô surprise!*', '*vive la France comme autrefois!*' and by phrases of qualification such as '*Il faut dire que . . .*' and '*certes . . .*'. These effects are balanced in their turn by the rhythmic patterning of the sentences which, like other aspects of the passage, deserve closer analysis so that the underlying features of the genre can be better understood.

Close analysis

Lexis

The enumeration of dishes is framed by the proper nouns, which lend the passage a strong sense of place. The title already sets the tone with a direct reference to *La Brie*, a theme which is immediately picked up in the first paragraph by the mention of '*Paris*', '*la France profonde*', '*Coulommiers et La Ferté*', '*Meaux*', '*le Champagne*'. References to Pommery, and to Vézelay where Pavard completed his apprenticeship, to the Hexagone as a whole, lead to the closing exclamation which sends the reader back to the title and links the association with *La Brie* to that of national heritage. Regional features remind the reader of an agricultural tradition – '*grosses fermes'*, *'fermette briarde'* – as do the terms for the food, and the adjectives used to describe it. The use of proper nouns extends to the names of people: Jean Ferniot, *'Le patriarche'* Emile Tingaud, the *'maître d'hôtel'* Pascal, Lucien and the 'new boy' Alain Pavard. This places the emphasis on tradition and old-world familiarity, situates author and reader 'on the inside', and restates, if it were necessary, the strong link between *grands chefs* and the institutions they represent. In this context, the only Anglicism, *'wonder-kid'*, stands out and serves to contrast the second gastronomic experience with the first.

Words such as *'cossu'*, *'bonheur'*, *'accueil souriant'*, *'carte alléchante'*, *'la part belle'*, *'moelleux'* (×2), *'exquises'*, *'plaisir retrouvé'*, *'arômes nets'*, *'fines bulles'* character-ise the description of the first *Auberge*. These differ somewhat in tone from the attributes of the second establishment where quality has had to be more self-consciously sought: *'avec des assaisonnements impeccables et des cuissons millimétrées'*. The diminutive *'fermette . . . rénovée'* invokes the novelty of a restaurant which has had to make its way in accordance with the age and experience of its owners. The *'accueil . . . adorable'* of the *'mignonne Mme Pavard'* is contrasted with the *'accueil souriant'* and the *'mise de table soignée'* of the *Auberge de Condé*. Similarly, the notion of recreating a past style (*'classicisme réinventé'*) is distinct from the *'créativité mesurée'* of the older restaurant, lending a lightness of touch which also surfaces in words such as *'croquer'*, *'gigoter'* and *'tonus'*. From the point of view of word choice, the overall impression can be described as refreshingly direct. Apart from the personification of the first paragraph already referred to, there are virtually no metaphors apart from *'maillon'*, *'bataillon'* and *'cadre . . . à croquer*. Elsewhere, simile takes precedence (*'exquises comme un plaisir retrouvé'*), while the fresh fish *'donne l'impression de gigoter dans l'assiette'*.

Positioning of author and reader: point of view

Mention has already been made of the manner in which Pudlowski creates a sense of place which is linked to the association between author and reader. The text apparently begins in the Brie country on the border with Champagne. The open-ing sentence – *'Paris est à deux pas.'* – means that, psychologically and perceptually, the reader joins the author at the first vantage point in his tour. The contrast between Paris and the provinces is made explicit in the opposition between the two parallel structures. The deictic *'là est La France profonde'* physically points towards a countryside which can be seen in the mind's eye and matches almost exactly the description by Braudel of what could be the same spot:

> *Mais à la recherche du changement brusque vous pouvez encore gagner . . . vers Paris, sur le rebord de la Brie que j'ai déjà signalé (la falaise dite de l'Ile-de-France), les vignobles glorieux avec leurs paysages moutonnés et leurs villages groupés aux maisons de pierre.*
> (Braudel 1986: 50)

The emphasis on physical location is reaffirmed by the '*commence ici même . . .*', which beckons the reader into the *Auberge de Condé* itself, designated as the gateway to the Champagne region. The theme is continued with the '*là*' of line 12, the '*et voilà*' of line 18, the demonstrative '*ce*' of '*ce décor*', '*ce n'est pas seulement le fond de l'assiette*' and '*ce maillon des Relais-Châteaux*', the reiteration of '*ici*' in '*on est bien ici*' and finally the pronoun '*vous*' in '*qui vous laissent l'esprit net*', all of which demands that the reader share the author's experience first hand.

This sense of author and reader's rediscovering together a tradition which has already been in place for a long time ('*un plaisir retrouvé . . .*', '*comme dans le temps . . .*') is evidently distinct from the spirit of discovery which characterises the analysis of the *Auberge de la Brie*. It is as if Pudlowski's stopping at this '*auberge de bord de route . . . encore inconnu de la chronique*' (note the contrast with '*maillon des Relais-Châteaux*') is almost a coincidence, despite being prompted by the reputation of a newly established chef ('*Ô surprise! . . . le bonhomme affiche complet à chaque déjeuner*'.) In the first instance, the reader is participant; in the second, he or she, like the author, is more spectator and judge. The subjects of the second half of the piece are Alain Pavard and the dishes themselves, which assume an almost animate force. The expressions '*donne l'impression*', '*donne envie de crier*' emphasise the spirit of novelty which impresses itself on the visitor. The fact that the author/reader/visitor is gradually constructing an evaluation of the *Auberge de la Brie* is conveyed by the balance between hypo-thetical statement in the form of the '*si*' clause which introduces the recent reputation of Pavard's establishment and the minor qualifications which follow: '*Il faut dire . . .*', '*certes . . .*'. The use of direct speech: affirmations ('*eh oui . . .*'), rhetorical questions ('*Le « wonder kid » de la région ?*'), exclamations ('*Ô surprise!*', '*« Vive la Brie, vive la France comme autrefois ! »*'), cajole the reader into being part of a gradually unfolding experience which leads to a shared and definitive conclusion.

Location in time and place: tense and sentence structure

Chronology is represented by a mixture of present and perfect tenses, appropriate to a text which is evidently aiming to recapture the spirit of the past in the present ('*a repris la tradition*', '*présent depuis un demi-siècle*', '*rien ne semble avoir bougé depuis vingt ans.*'). It is as if the text, like the experience which it recounts, is unfolding in real time yet has a relevance for the reader which transcends the moment. The statements by the author have the status of facts. This is reflected in the number of sentences based on the Subject + Verb + Object or Subject + *être* + Complement constructions around which nouns and adjectives are clustered. Consider, for example, the opening paragraph – '*Paris est à deux pas*' and its inverted form '*là est la France profonde*', a chiasmus which represents precisely the dividing line and the contrast between the capital and the French provinces. This leads to a simple sentence in which four main verbs build on each other in a sequence which reinforces the balance in the line and the relationship between the two pairs of verbs: '*ménage . . . dorlote*' and '*aime . . . flirte*'. A classical sense of sentence structure is combined with a simplicity marked by the frequent use of the conjunctions '*et*' and '*mais*'. One feature after another is presented and described in a sequence of nouns and adjectives leading to a qualitative assessment, again expressed in symmetrical noun phrases: '*l'allègement nécessaire et la créativité mesurée*'. Although the following sentence describing the dishes themselves stands out because of its length, consisting as it does of yet another series of nouns and noun complements, the clause which forms the main point of emphasis, '*eh oui, on est bien ici*' is short and clear and allows the sentence to fall away, referring in passing to the high-quality '*brut*' champagne which accompanies the meal before leading the reader back on to the high road.

Pudlowski's style is marked by a mixture of short and long sentences. Often, the first type is an introductory statement, frequently with *être*, which leads to a qualification introduced by '*mais*' which is followed in turn by a series of three or occasionally four rhythmic groups:

> *Le bonheur de la table, ce n'est pas seulement le fond de l'assiette, mais un accueil souriant, une mise de table soignée, une carte alléchante qui fait la part belle aux produits régionaux.*

> *La carte est, certes, plus coûteuse. Mais les produits sont parfaits, les portions généreuses, l'accueil de la mignonne Mme Pavard, adorable, le cadre de fermette briarde rénovée et fleurie, à croquer.*

In each of the above cases, the classic features of French sentence structure are observed. Rhythmic groups, normally in groups of two (binary) or three (ternary), increase in length as the sentence finishes, giving a balance and musicality to the whole. In the second of the two examples just quoted, the rhythm is deliberately disturbed by the *cadence mineure* of the final infinitive – '*à croquer*' – which is delayed by the insertion of the adjectives '*rénovée et fleurie*'. As already mentioned, metaphors are relatively unusual within the passage and the position of '*à croquer*' at the end of the sentence is a light and mildly humorous touch which typifies the combination of formality and informality in the text as a whole. Elsewhere, the main characteristic of the style is the description of the food itself. Here, Pudlowski deftly manages to fit extended lists of dishes into a standard sentence structure by deferring the main clause in a manner which heightens its prominence, either in the middle of the sentence, as we have seen above, or, as in the description of the menu at the *Auberge de la Brie*, at the end: '. . . *apparaît comme l'une des plus belles affaires de l'Hexagone*'.

Uses of sound

Sound clusters lend euphony and texture to the piece: '*Paris . . . pas . . . pourtant . . . là*', '*vignoble . . . vin*'; '*belles bouteilles*' and there is even a rhyme: '*bien . . . Lucien*'. Similar effects are found later in the text: '*carte . . . coûteuse*', '*produits . . . parfaits*', '*Pavard . . . adorable*', '*champagnes . . . choix*'. However, the essential element of the art of gastronomic writing is obviously to evoke a sense of taste and visual impression, and in this Pudlowski is a master. As already indicated, the technique is evidently to combine the title of the dish with an expressive adjective or more extended clause or complement. Consider the sound clusters in the following phrases: '*Le foie gras mariné au vin de Bouzy, moelleux et rose dans sa gelée fine*', '*pommes roseval*', '*pourvu d'une sauce légère à la moutarde en grains de chez Pommery, qui s'accompagne de pommes soufflées, exquises comme un plaisir retrouvé*'. In the last case in particular, the clustering of /i/ and /z/ linked to the onomatopoeic /sufl/ clearly signals the sentient quality of the language, just as in the phrases '*des assaisonnements impeccables et des cuissons millimétrées*', the coupling of the /s/ sound and the assonance of /i/ combined with the length of the words give an impression of punctilious preparation and of the precision of the final result.

Conclusion: the link between gastronomy and the recreation of national heritage

The stylistic challenge of the genre of gastronomic review is to avoid repetition and the danger of hyperbole which would quickly lead to bathos and cliché. Pudlowski's device of linking his review to a journey, although well-worn, works well. The way in which he merges the countryside of the region and the establishments which he invites us to visit with him is subtle and concise. In the wider cultural context, the piece provides an insight into the relationship between gastronomy and national heritage – at least for a limited sector of the restaurant-going French public. The most striking features of the *Auberge de Condé* are its reassuring quality and its location which, together with its menu, symbolise the perennial character of the Brie/Champagne regions: '*la France profonde*', which is contrasted with the urban environment of the capital. As the title of the passage makes explicit, things have changed, yet it is still possible to rediscover the spirit of continuity in the cuisine of the region. The second case reviewed, the *Auberge de la Brie*, makes this clear. With youthful enthusiasm, expertise and commitment, national heritage can be reconstructed and made to be financially viable. It is not strictly speaking authentic, but '*réinventé*': '*La Brie, comme autrefois*'. The history of French gastronomy has been based on a series of reinventions, not the least of which has been the myth of peasant cuisine and the early twentieth-century institutionalisation of regional recipes. As part of a package, food is not merely an experience; it is also a symbol of identity and a significant element in the national economy. To understand the style of the gastronomic feature is to appreciate one medium through which the image of French national identity is sustained and propagated.

Giles Pudlowski, 'La Brie, comme autrefois', *Le Point*,
1 October 1994, no. 1150.

TABLES

La Brie, comme autrefois

par Gilles Pudlowski

Paris est à deux pas. Et, pourtant, là est la France profonde, entre Coulommiers et
La Ferté. La Brie ménage ses grosses fermes, dorlote ses fromages royaux, aime sa
moutarde de Meaux et flirte avec la Champagne. Dans son fameux « Carnet de
croûte », Jean Ferniot rappelle que le vignoble du vin blond commence ici même
. . . dans la cave de l'Auberge de Condé, si riche en belles bouteilles. Le patriarche Emile Tingaud n'est plus là. Mais Pascal, le petit-fils, a repris la tradition. Et
l'on se sent bien, dans ce décor cossu, veillé par le maître d'hôtel, Lucien, présent
ici depuis un demi-siècle.

Le bonheur de la table, ce n'est pas seulement le fond de l'assiette, mais un accueil
souriant, une mise de table soignée, une carte alléchante qui fait la part belle aux
produits régionaux. Et voilà ce que l'on trouve dans ce maillon des Relais-
Châteaux, où rien ne semble avoir bougé depuis vingt ans, sinon l'allègement
nécessaire et la créativité mesurée. Le foie gras mariné au vin de Bouzy, moelleux
et rose dans sa gelée fine, le tartare de langouste, le saumon légèrement fumé à la
maison sur un lit de pommes roseval, le poulet à l'estragon et le canard à la
briarde, c'est-à-dire cuit rosé et pourvu d'une sauce légère à la moutarde en
grains de chez Pommery, qui s'accompagne de pommes soufflées, exquises
comme un plaisir retrouvé : eh oui, on est bien ici, comme dans le temps, avec un
Pol Roger sans année, aux arômes nets de brioche chaude et de pain grillé, aux
fines bulles, qui vous laissent l'esprit net avant de reprendre la route pour d'autres
aventures.

Le « wonder-kid » de la région? Il s'appelle Alain Pavard, a moins de 30 ans, est
inconnu au bataillon des « grands », a fait des classes non seulement chez Tingaud,
mais aussi chez Meneau, à Vézelay. Il a choisi de retourner au pays pour ouvrir
une auberge de bord de route. Ô surprise ! même si l'adresse est encore inconnue
de la chronique, le bonhomme affiche complet à chaque déjeuner. Il faut dire que
son menu du marché à 165 F, offrant, par exemple, gâteau moelleux de saint-
jacques sauce gribiche, mi-cuit de saumon à la crème d'épinards, suprême de

37 volaille aux deux purées, feuilleté de brie sur verdure, crème soufflée au citron
38 vert et coulis d'abricot, tous réalisés au petit point, avec des assaisonnements
39 impeccables et des cuissons millimétrées, apparaît comme une des plus belles
40 affaires de l'Hexagone. La carte est, certes, plus coûteuse. Mais les produits sont
41 parfaites, les portions généreuses, l'accueil de la mignonne Mme Pavard, adorable,
42 le cadre de fermette briarde rénovée et fleurie, à croquer. Et les terrines de foie
43 de canard aux asperges, blancs de turbot à la crème de céleri – le poisson si frais
44 donne l'impression de gigoter dans l'assiette – et le mille-feuille craquant au
45 chocolat avec coulis d'orange sont du grand art sur le mode du classicisme
46 réinventé. La carte des vins, avec des champagnes de choix, possède du tonus, et
47 l'ensemble donne envie de crier: « Vive la Brie, vive la France comme autrefois ! »
48
49 **Auberge de Condé**, 1, av. de Montmirail, 77260 La Ferté-sous-Jouarre.
50 60.22.00.07. Menus : 295 F, 345 F, 450 F. Carte : 450 F.
51
52 **Auberge de la Brie**, 14, av. Alphonse-Boulingre, 77860 Couilly-Pont-aux-
53 Dames. 64.63.51.80.

For the original format, see page 79.

An original canvas?

Le Malade Imaginaire restored

Robert Crawshaw

Introduction

Context of situation and context of culture

On 16 March 1990, a 'new' version of Molière's last play *Le Malade Imaginaire*, first performed at the *Théâtre du Palais Royal* in February 1673, was to be shown publicly at the *Théâtre Musical de Paris*, Place du Châtelet. Staged by Jean-Marie Villégier and directed by the baroque enthusiast and teacher at the Paris *conservatoire*, William Christie, it was heralded as a novelty, or rather a rediscovery. The production made use of a score which had remained lost in the theatrical archives for over two hundred years. Although fragments of song and dance, in particular the burlesque initiation ceremony at the end of the play, had survived as staple elements of *Le Malade Imaginaire*, these had always been regarded, by producers and critics alike, as secondary to the play's central appeal. Sometimes they were excluded altogether. As with Molière's other classic comedies, criticism had traditionally focused on the depth of the author's moral insights and on the dramatic qualities of his theatrical output.

Molière collaborated in twelve *spectacles* known as *comédies-ballets*, which involved a combination of spoken drama, music, song and dance. Of these, produced at the rate of one per year between 1661 and his death in 1673, only two, *Le Malade Imaginaire* and *Le Bourgeois Gentilhomme*, have attracted lasting popular attention. This may be to some extent because the genre itself was so much of its period, being part of the luxurious paraphernalia of life at Louis XIV's court at Versailles. Apart from the need for its authors to match the spirit of the moment and to conform to the requirements of royal patronage, the genre of the *comédie-ballet* was exclusively the product of the collaboration between Molière and the composers Lully and Charpentier. Despite a few imitations staged in the years following Molière's death, the genre effectively died with them. Even its establishment was partly a matter of chance: the limited troupe of royal dancers needed time to change costume and so required a spoken element to fill in the interludes between the ballets. Thereafter, they were so popular at court that they became a necessary part of royal *divertissements*.

It may be that the greatness of his spoken plays caused critics to regard the *mélange* of the musical genre as an inferior art form. There were even claims that Molière himself wrote *comédies-ballets* mainly in order to curry favour with the monarch and that he did not appreciate them as much as the rest of his production. In any event, it is evident from the text '*La Comédie Musicale du Grand Siècle*' that to have restored the spectacle of *Le Malade Imaginaire* to its 'original' state was regarded by the critics in 1990 as a significant cultural event for the French public. It is intriguing to ask why and to address the question of how the 'review' by Isabelle Garnier positions its readership, and how, as a text, it is situated within its own genre.

Content and positioning

The title

The title of the article is itself revealing. The seventeenth-century genre was known as *comédie-ballet*, the term *comédie musicale* being a latter-day derivative of the popular musical tradition, which flourished in the early eighteenth century because of the restriction on spoken dialogue imposed by the Court. Later, *comédie musicale* found expression in the vaudeville and *opéra comique* of the Paris boulevards and, indirectly, gave rise to the music hall, the American musical, and the hybrid productions of modern writer-composers such as Andrew Lloyd-Webber and Stephen Sondheim. The *comédie-ballet* was a much more exclusive event, which had popularity in the city of Paris because it was a feature of life at Versailles. The spoken part of *Le Malade Imaginaire*, a brilliant satire on the medical profession which deals with the farcical and in some ways tragic obsessions of a bourgeois hypochondriac, seems to be at odds with the ceremonial quality of much of the music. Only some of this has the ironic, burlesque humour of the play, the thirty-five-minute musical prologue being an extended paean of praise for the king, who had just returned from a successful military campaign in Holland. The juxtaposition of the terms '*comédie musicale*' and '*Grand Siècle*' (the capital letters evoking the tradition of greatness which French culture associates with the era of Louis XIV) is a paradox. It invites the reader to apply the same criteria of appreciation to the rediscovered genre of the *comédie-ballet* as to the late twentieth-century musical, and – despite their essential cultural difference – to do so in the name of authenticity.

La comédie musicale du Grand Siècle

L E *Malade imaginaire*, ne dites pas que vous connaissez : personne ne connaît. Il est, pour la première fois depuis sa création en 1673, repris intégralement, tel que Molière l'avait représenté quelques jours avant sa mort.

Depuis des siècles, on en donnait des versions tronquées ou bricolées. Explication : la musique en était perdue. Une heure et demie de musique. Et de danse. Ainsi qu'un mini-opéra intégré dans l'histoire. Ah, ce n'était pas rien, la musique, au temps de Louis XIV !

Tout ce qui, autour de l'Astre, maniait la plume ou l'archet, se mobilisait. En particulier le tandem Molière-Lully, « les deux Jean-Baptiste », dont la fructueuse collaboration sombra dans les intrigues.

L'Italien, ayant pris le pouvoir, devint le gourou de la musique en France. Sa brouille avec Molière eut au moins une conséquence heureuse : ce dernier fit affaire avec le jeune Marc-Antoine Charpentier pour le *Malade imaginaire*.

Il y avait de la comédie musicale dans ce *Malade*-là. Et c'est bien ainsi qu'aujourd'hui l'entend l'équipe du Châtelet. Comme un grand, un très grand spectacle. Royal.

Tous les talents sont réunis : pour la mise en scène, Jean-Marie Villégier et Christophe Galland. Pour la danse, l'ensemble « Ris et Danceries » de Francine Lancelot. Pour les décors : Carlo Tommasi. Pour les costumes : Patrice Cauchetier. Avec une remarquable distribution,

où les comédiens et les chanteurs se mêlent aux comédiens-chanteurs et aux chanteurs-comédiens : Jean Dautremay, Nelly Borgeaud, Denis Manuel, Isabelle Desrochers, Christine Murillo, Denis Léger-Milhau, Howard Crook, Dominique Visse, Jean-François Gardeil, Monique Zanetti...

Et pour la direction musicale de tout ce beau monde ? Vous avez deviné : c'est l'inépuisable William Christie :

– *C'est une magnifique aventure que cette résurrection du* malade imaginaire, *dit-il. Les partitions, retrouvées dans les archives de la Comédie-Française, vont nous permettre de découvrir la dernière œuvre de Molière, telle que celui-ci l'a voulue et jouée. La musique y est omniprésente. Elle éclaire. Elle souligne. Elle renforce l'expression. Elle est le luxe et la philosophie de toute une époque.*

Une époque que William Christie a choisi d'illustrer, avec passion et avec une énergie toujours renouvelée. Il en faut.

– *Le patrimoine musical français est immense. Il reste encore des chefs-d'œuvre à découvrir au fond des bibliothèques, voire dans les greniers.*

Ainsi en est-il pour *le Malade imaginaire* qu'il nous révélera avec sa musique restaurée, comme une toile dépouillée de ses vieux vernis, dans toute sa fraîcheur, dans toute sa splendeur.

ISABELLE GARNIER

● **Châtelet,** *jusqu'au 8 avril. Tél. : 40.28.28.40.*

Source: Garnier, I. 'La Comédie musicale du Grand Siècle', *Figaro Magazine*, 24 April 1990, pp. 40–41. Reproduced with kind permission of Le Figaro-Magazine.

Lexis, metonymy and the recreation of authenticity

In terms of 'what is going on', the text is a conceit in that it makes the process of the 1990 production and those who participated in it interchangeable with the circumstances which applied in 1673. Just as '*ce Malade-là*' (the original version) is described as containing elements of *comédie musicale*, so, conversely, the intention of the Châtelet team is to absorb the principle of royal entertainment into the genre of the modern musical. What in modern terms is a fundamentally popular genre becomes '*un grand, un très grand spectacle*'. The hyperbole of the repeated adjective and the foregrounded ellipsis of '*Royal*' lends it a blatant, almost grotesque prestige. The same principle applies to the participants: actors, musicians, dancers and directors. These are described in the same terms as the artistes who came together ('*se mobilisait*') as part of Louis XIV's entourage. They are referred to here as '*talents*' and '*ce beau monde*' so that, in the language of the reviewer, they become metonymies of the theatrical event which they are claiming to recreate. As we discover from the review which appeared in *Le Monde* of 24 March, the musicians, like the players, were in original costume, while the conductor, William Christie, was dressed in white with a sun ('*L'Astre*'), symbolic of *le Roi Soleil*, emblazoned on his back.

Progression

A cyclical structure

The text describes one way in which France's cultural heritage is being preserved. Its message is not ironic but offers a melodramatic view of the past which can be equated with modern popular values. Its structure reflects a logical progression, which starts with a direct challenge to the reader. Although *Le Malade Imaginaire* is thought to be part of French national heritage and known to all, it is in fact something other: '*personne ne connaît*'. A fresh and fully restored version will be shown to the French public for the first time since 1673. The absence of the musical scores is explained and a thumbnail sketch is provided of the interrelationship between writing and music at the court of Louis XIV. As we have seen, the fourth paragraph makes the key link between the two periods, after which the text is able to introduce the players who have made the new version come to life. The climax of the piece is the introduction of the musical director, William Christie. His statements underline the essential theme of rediscovery on which the whole text is based. The case of *Le Malade Imaginaire* is generalised to include the musical heritage of France as a whole. Comparing the spectacle to a restored picture, the splendour and freshness of the new production is contrasted by implication with the well-worn interpretations of the last two hundred years. The structure of the text is cyclical in terms of the link between the first and the last paragraphs – both deal with the contrast between the traditional and restored versions of *Le Malade Imaginaire*, which is named in both instances – and linear in its progression, having a different focus in each section.

Coherence and cohesion: deixis, anaphora and tense

Considerable care has gone into making this progression seem natural, in particular through the use of deictics, anaphoric links and the clever exploitation of tense. The striking reference in the first line to *Le Malade Imaginaire* itself is picked up by the '*en*' of line 7, the expression '*ce dernier*' helps to bind the third paragraph together, '*ce Malade-là*', the third direct reference to the play, links the third to the fourth paragraph and serves to mark the shift in time from the seventeenth to the twentieth century. The structure of the next two paragraphs hinges on the repetition of '*pour*'. It is this which provides the opportunity to introduce William Christie, whose statement – if indeed it really *is* his – builds up to the strongly foregrounded anaphora: '*Elle . . . Elle . . . Elle . . . Elle . . .*'. The repetition of '*époque*' binds the seventh and eighth paragraphs while, as with the first and second, the pronoun '*en*' is used to link the last two and leads to the parallelism '*dans toute sa fraîcheur, dans toute sa splendeur.*', which offers a balanced close.

The same principle applies to Garnier's use of tense, which is economical and highly effective. Economical, because the fragmented sentence structure reduces the number of verbs in the text as a whole, and effective, because of the range of tenses and the accuracy with which they are used to situate the reader in relation to the subject matter. Already in the first paragraph, the pluperfect '*avait représenté*' distinguishes finely between the moment of Molière's death, which took place on the evening of the third performance, and the production of the opening night. Moreover, the tense locates the reader at an imagined point in time *after* the staging of the restored 1990 version – even though, as we shall see, the article was almost certainly written *before* the restored version was performed.

We encounter at least three different uses of the imperfect in the following paragraphs. The first, after *depuis* ('*Depuis des siècles, on en donnait des versions tronquées ou bricolées*'), is effectively a continuation of the pluperfect ('the versions which *had been* put on'). It thereby emphasises the fact that these productions predated the discovery of the lost musical scores. From the aspectual point of view, the imperfect is iterative; that is, it refers to a series of individual events. In the following sentence, it is stative, i.e. it relates to a general state of affairs – the fact that the music *was* lost. The chronological focus then shifts via another stative ('*était*') from the overarching timespan of two centuries to a much briefer period: '*au temps de Louis XIV!*'. This imperfect provides the link with the next paragraph where the aspect moves from stative ('*maniait*' – 'knew how to use') to progressive ('*se mobilisait*' – 'were getting involved'). These contrast with the sequence of past historic tenses ('*sombra*', '*devint*', '*eut*', '*fit*'), which rapidly sum up the succession of events leading up to the original production of *Le Malade*. The same simple and effective tense changes mark the movement from past to present and from present to future in the following paragraphs. Appropriately, the present perfect is employed in William Christie's statement concerning Molière's intentions ('*l'a voulue*') and the tense finds its echo in the next paragraph ('*a choisi d'illustrer . . .*'). The final two paragraphs look to the future: the potential offered by further research and the immediate promise of the new production.

Genre-mixing and writer–reader relationship: mood, pronouns, sentence structure, sound

The text is not in fact a review. There is no reference to aspects of a live performance which a review would normally contain. The statement by William Christie; '*vont nous permettre de découvrir . . .*'; the future tense of the last paragraph; and the use of the first person plural pronoun ('*qu'il nous révélera . . .*') – all suggest that Isabelle Garnier has not yet seen the production, even as a preview. This gives a literal meaning to the '*personne ne connaît*' of the third line and a special nuance to the clause '*l'entend l'équipe du Châtelet*', which implies that this is how the team behind the new production *would like it to be*. Nobody has yet witnessed the spectacle in its final state, not even the director himself. The text is therefore something of a hybrid, being a preview, an interview/profile *and* a cultural statement. This distinctive status allows the author a certain licence. The reader is addressed directly as an involuntary listener to whom a lesson is about to be taught. The immediate reference to *Le Malade imaginaire* suggests a common point of reference for a significant sector of the French middle class: the majority of the literate French population will be familiar with Molière's last play. The 'fronting' of the opening phrase, the sharp imperative and the omission of the object pronoun '*le*' in '*personne ne connaît*' evoke a conversational tone, clipped and very direct.

The readership is therefore positioned as an interlocutor: the '*vous*' of the third line. We are reminded of this role later in the text by the rhetorical question '*Et pour la direction musicale de tout ce beau monde ?*' and the '*Vous avez deviné . . .*' which follows. As addressees, the foregrounded opening statement puts us on the defensive. We thought we were knowledgeable. We are not. We are about to be enlightened. Either we put the text down or we take up the challenge and read on. The insistent, gossipy, exclamatory, almost hectoring, tone is maintained throughout by the elliptical, telegraphic sentence structure in which the functions of informing, explaining and persuading are present. The presence, and the position, of the implied reader/interlocutor is thereby maintained:

- *Explication: la musique en était perdue.*
- *Une heure et demie de musique.*
- *Et de danse.*
- *Ainsi qu'un mini-opéra intégré dans l'histoire.*
- *Ah, ce n'était pas rien, la musique, au temps de Louis XIV !*

The first four of the above 'sentences' have no verbs. The last deviates from 'standard' word order using the familiar, emphatic device of placing the pronoun first and deferring the subject ('*la musique*'). These clichés impose a tone of jocular connivance on a discourse which contrasts oddly with the supposed majesty of the subject matter. '« *Les deux Jean-Baptiste* »' seems more like a cosy, modern-day comedy act than an attempt to refurbish cultural icons. Such phrases drawn from a familiar idiom are combined with more formal, yet ironic structures such as the fronting of the adjective: '*fructueuse collaboration*', '*remarquable distribution*', '*l'inépuisable William Christie*', '*magnifique aventure*'. Le Grand Siècle is clearly a cliché in French culture yet, as we have seen, the underlying message of the text is that its essential splendour should be taken seriously – more seriously than the 'traditional' reworkings of Molière's classic output ('*ses vieux vernis*'). The tenor of the text apparently undermines the objective.

This distantiation from the object through familiarity and cliché can also be seen in the use of the metaphor '*L'Astre*' which refers to Louis XIV, the depersonalisation of the writers and musicians in the pronominal phrase '*Tout ce qui*' (as opposed to *tous ceux qui* . . .) and the metonymies '*maniait la plume ou l'archet*' – 'the pen or the bow'. A tone of familiarity is sustained in phrases like '*tandem*', '*gourou*', '*fit affaire avec*', '*de la comédie musicale*', the last of which reduces the genre to the status of an ingredient in a dramatic recipe. Ellipsis are used in the fifth paragraph, where all the dramatic participants are named in an extended, heavily foregrounded list. There are only two verbs in the whole paragraph: '*sont*' and '*se mêlent*'. This deliberate fragmentation is combined with an artificially high degree of self-consciousness, evident in the prominent chiasmus '*où les comédiens et les chanteurs se mêlent aux comédiens-chanteurs et aux chanteurs-comédiens*' (a . . . b//b . . . a). It is also found in the repeated '*cadence mineure*' of the sentence rhythms: '. . . *Et de danse*', '. . . *Royal*', '. . . *Il en faut*'. These phrases lend a confident but artificial tone to the text, implying once again that the *Grand Siècle* is not so much being restored as reinvented in twentieth-century terms.

The varied, conversational tenor of Isabelle Garnier's text does not allow the poetic function to dominate. There are, however, discreet examples of alliteration and assonance, normally in pairs, which add to the coherence of the writing and underline its self-conscious quality: '*personne ne connaît*', '*on en donnait*', '*Une heure et demie de musique*', '*ayant pris le pouvoir*', '*fit affaire*', '*choisi d'illustrer*', '*toujours renouvelée*', '*vieux vernis*', '*fraîcheur . . . splendeur*'.

Conclusion

The overall impression left by 'La Comédie Musicale du Grand Siècle' is that of a highly professional, closely written preview, rich in information and variety, whose style is as communicative as its subject matter. This is what makes its cultural message intriguing. The reader is being asked to believe in the authenticity of the new production of a classic text, to rediscover with the audience the past glory of the French monarchy. Yet the author's amused, ironic style detracts from a wholehearted commitment to the rediscovery of heritage. In making the case for what Christie himself calls a 'résurrection', her discourse is out of tune with the subject matter. There is melodrama in the way 'l'inépuisable William Christie' is introduced. The most sincere statement of belief in the effect the production is trying to achieve is expressed through the mouth of Christie himself. We know from the reviews of Christie and Villégier's *Malade* that it was intended to build on the huge success of their earlier production of Lully's opera, *Athys*. Rediscovering the baroque was seriously in fashion. Yet from the style of this article, *comédie-ballet* is less a majestic art form than a case of 'Hollywood goes to Versailles'. The riddle of the text is whether the readership is intended to appreciate the paradox, or whether, for consumers of *Figaro Magazine*, the authenticity of William Christie's inspiration has been reduced to the level of vaudeville.

Isabelle Garnier, 'La Comédie musicale du Grand Siècle',
Figaro Magazine, 24 April 1990, pp. 40–41.

La comédie musicale du Grand Siècle

Le Malade imaginaire, ne dites pas que vous connaissez : personne ne connaît. Il est, pour la première fois depuis sa création en 1673, repris intégralement, tel que Molière l'avait représenté quelques jours avant sa mort.

Depuis des siècles, on en donnait des versions tronquées ou bricolées. Explication : la musique en était perdue. Une heure et demie de musique. Et de danse. Ainsi qu'un mini-opéra intégré dans l'histoire. Ah, ce n'était pas rien, la musique, au temps de Louis XIV !

Tout ce qui, autour de l'Astre, maniait la plume ou l'archet, se mobilisait. En particulier le tandem Molière-Lully, « les deux Jean-Baptiste », dont la fructueuse collaboration sombra dans les intrigues. L'Italien, ayant pris le pouvoir, devint le gourou de la musique en France. Sa brouille avec Molière eut au moins une conséquence heureuse : ce dernier fit affaire avec le jeune Marc-Antoine Charpentier pour *le Malade imaginaire*.

Il y avait de la comédie musicale dans ce *Malade*-là. Et c'est bien ainsi qu'aujourd'-hui l'entend l'équipe du Châtelet. Comme un grand, un très grand spectacle. Royal.

Tous les talents sont réunis : pour la mise en scène, Jean-Marie Villégier et Christophe Galland. Pour la danse, l'ensemble « Ris et Danceries » de Francine Lancelot. Pour les décors : Carlo Tommasi. Pour les costumes : Patrice Cauchetier. Avec une remarquable distribution, où les comédiens et les chanteurs se mêlent aux comédiens-chanteurs et aux chanteurs-comédiens : Jean Dautremay, Nelly Borgeaud, Denis Manuel, Isabelle Desrochers, Christine Murillo, Denis Léger-Milhau, Howard Crook, Dominique Visse, Jean-François Gardeil, Monique Zanetti. . .

Et pour la direction musicale de tout ce beau monde ? Vous avez deviné : c'est l'inépuisable William Christie :

— *C'est une magnifique aventure que cette résurrection du malade imaginaire*, dit-il. *Les partitions, retrouvées dans les archives de la Comédie-Française, vont nous permettre de découvrir la dernière œuvre de Molière, telle que celui-ci l'a voulue et jouée. La musique y*

37 *est omniprésente. Elle éclaire. Elle souligne. Elle renforce l'expression. Elle est le luxe et la*
38 *philosophie de toute une époque.*
39
40 Une époque que William Christie a choisi d'illustrer, avec passion et avec une
41 énergie toujours renouvelée. Il en faut.
42
43 — *Le patrimoine musical français est immense. Il reste encore des chefs-d'œuvre à*
44 *découvrir au fond des bibliothèques, voire dans les greniers.*
45
46 Ainsi en est-il pour *le Malade imaginaire* qu'il nous révélera avec sa musique
47 restaurée, comme une toile dépouillée de ses vieux vernis, dans toute sa fraîcheur,
48 dans toute sa splendeur.
49
50   ISABELLE GARNIER
51 • **Châtelet**, *jusqu'au 8 avril. Tél.: 40.28.28.40.*

For the original format, see page 90.

Your myth, my reality

Authority and positioning in the academic textbook

Karin Tusting

Introduction

This text is taken from the introduction to the book *Le Français dans Tous les Sens*, written by Henriette Walter and published by Laffont in 1988. The book is an introduction to the linguistics of contemporary French, covering the history of the French language, regional and international varieties of French, the structure of the language and the directions in which it is developing. Any work dealing with French language must take into account the important historical role that language has played in the development of French national identity (cf. the opening chapter of this volume). The continued codification and monitoring of the language is evidenced by the existence of such bodies as the *Académie Française*, which awarded Walter's book its *Grand Prix* in 1988. Language is a central subject of debate in French culture. Whether the French that people are speaking is still 'correct', which direction the language is going in, and the extent of the threat of English to the existence of French as an international language – all these issues are dealt with in the body of Walter's work.

While the target audience for the book would probably be those studying French language, either at undergraduate or possibly at *lycée* level, the book does not look like a textbook. It is written in an accessible tone, and would also appear to be aimed at the general lay reader. This combination of erudition and popular appeal lies within the mainstream of French cultural tradition. Since the time of the Enlightenment, intellectuals in France have addressed both those within their own discipline and a more general audience. This book continues this tradition, and this, together with the tone of the text, suggests that the book is written with both an academic (student) audience in mind and a wider audience of educated lay readers.

Whatever the implied audience for this book, it is written with the assumption that the reader knows little or nothing about linguistics. If this really is the first time the reader has read any linguistics, this section has the potential to actually define the discipline for the reader. An academic discipline is, at least in part, constituted textually. There is therefore a dialectical relationship between the discipline and the individual texts which constitute it: any text which is situated within linguistics is also instrumental in shaping what linguistics is. Thus, by definition, all academic discourse engages, explicitly or implicitly, in a dialogue with other texts from the same discipline. Students reading an introductory text may not yet have entered into this textual dialogue; in which case, the text will play a significant role in shaping their conceptions of it (however, these conceptions may change as a result of future interactions).

The text being considered here is not a description of language as object, written in a scientific register in which observation is divorced from human agency. Instead, throughout the text different characters are constructed who act, observe and have emotions. In the first paragraph, there is a description of the attitude which ordinary French people have towards their language. The second and third paragraphs construct an idealised image of 'the professional linguist', which is contrasted with the approach of the 'ordinary people' who feature in the first. In the third and fourth paragraphs, the general approach of the book is outlined – an attempt to imitate the professional linguist and to describe the historical, geographical and structural characteristics of the French language.

Construction of ordinary French people

The first paragraph describes the relationship the French people have with their language, using words and images rich in connotations of emotion and control. The French people hold '*jugements . . . contradictoires*' towards their language. Their response to it is a very active, almost violent one: '*Avec beaucoup de passion, on l'encense, on le corrige, on le plaint, on le réprimande.*' The active verbs here are all associated with some form of verbal correction or punishment. The language is personified, as if it were a child or a living creature over which people see themselves as having power, an association reinforced by the use of the school-room image '*mettre le bonnet d'âne*'.

This gives the impression that people in general have an emotional – rather than a rational – response to their own language, and that this response hides in some way the 'reality' of what French is. This is reinforced by the way in which the paragraph is structured. The binary structure '*tantôt on le donne en exemple pour ce qu'il a été, tantôt on lui met le bonnet d'âne pour ce qu'il est*' underlines the semantic force of '*contradictoires*'. The force of the active verbs referred to above is underlined by the repetition of the same grammatical form, which foregrounds the final judgement on these actions – '*On oublie de le regarder vivre*' – coming as the sixth repetition of the *on* + verb form. Where the first four verbs relate to activities that the French people are engaged in, this fifth clause refers to an important task which they are failing to undertake: passive observation, instead of active critique.

PRÉAMBULE

Le français observé par les linguistes

Le français suscite, de la part des Français, les jugements les plus contradictoires : tantôt on le donne en exemple pour ce qu'il a été, tantôt on lui met le bonnet d'âne pour ce qu'il est. Avec beaucoup de passion, on l'encense, on le corrige, on le plaint, on le réprimande. On oublie de le regarder vivre. Derrière ces attitudes excessives, comment redécouvrir le français tel qu'on le parle. tel qu'on l'écrit, tel qu'on l'aime ?

Pour vraiment observer le français dans sa réalité, examinons-le avec l'œil du linguiste. Ou plutôt servons-nous, comme lui, de nos oreilles. Car le linguiste écoute plus qu'il ne s'exprime. Ne lui reproche-t-on pas de s'intéresser davantage à la façon dont les gens parlent qu'à ce qu'ils disent ? A ses interlocuteurs, que cette attitude gêne parfois, ce professionnel du langage apparaît la plupart du temps comme un personnage déconcertant et même un peu inquiétant : il ne laisse rien échapper de ce que vous dites, il a l'air d'en savoir plus long que vous sur votre propre langue et, pourtant, il paraît toujours ravi de ce qu'il entend. Lorsque vous vous rendez compte que son premier souci n'est pas de voir respecter les formes lexicales ou grammaticales, son attitude en quelque sorte amorale de simple observateur vous déconcerte.

Sans nous laisser impressionner par la sévérité à peine exagérée de ces jugements, c'est bien le point de vue du linguiste que nous adopterons dans cet ouvrage : celui de « l'amateur » de langues (comme on dit qu'on est amateur de musique ou de peinture). Le linguiste s'intéresse à toutes les langues sous tous leurs aspects, et lorsque son examen porte sur une langue particulière, il cherche essentiellement à préciser en quoi cette langue est différente de toutes les autres langues, comment elle fonctionne et comment elle évolue.

Le but de cet ouvrage est donc surtout de montrer par quels traits historiques, géographiques et structuraux se caractérise le français. Mais tant d'idées reçues circulent sur notre langue qu'on ne pourra pas y voir clair si, auparavant, on ne fait pas un sort à quelques-unes d'entre elles, qui ont la vie dure. Citons pêle-mêle : « le français, c'est du gaulois », « le français, c'est du latin », « le patois, c'est du français déformé », ou « le français le plus pur se parle en Touraine ». Dans tout cela, il y a à prendre et à laisser.

Source: Walter, H. (1998) *Le Français dans Tous les Sens*, Pans: Laffont, pp. 13–14. Reproduced with kind permission of S.A. Editions Robert Laffont.

The phrase '*regarder vivre*' suggests that the language is a living thing which can and should be observed in its own right.

This message is reinforced in the next sentence. The repetition of the *on* + verb form is continued in the ternary structure, '*tel qu'on le parle, tel qu'on l'écrit, tel qu'on l'aime*'. It sets up a distinction between emotional response and 'reality', and suggests that the appeal to reality ('*tel que*') is to be valued, while the response of French people is '*excessive*' and to be criticised. The spatial metaphor '*Derrière ces attitudes excessives*', combined with the use of the verb '*redécouvrir*', suggests that the responses of the French described earlier are in some way concealing the truth of what language is.

The opposition is taken up again in the final paragraph, where closure of the section is achieved through repetition and precision of the myths which are supposedly circulating about the French language: '*tant d'idées reçues circulent sur notre langue qu'on ne pourra pas y voir clair si, auparavant, on ne fait pas un sort à quelques-unes d'entre elles*'. The metaphor used (*voir clair*) is one which again suggests that these ideas are in some way concealing reality. The inference is made through reference to the visual, while at the end of the first paragraph the spatial reference '*Derrière*' suggested the same thing. The text constructs a clear opposition between 'myths', associated with ordinary people's ideas about French, and 'truths' about the nature of the language.

Construction of 'the professional linguist'

Thus, the text suggests that French people have an invalid response to their own language and therefore asks what a more valid approach might be. This different approach will be that of 'the linguist', an idealised character constructed in the text to represent the discipline of linguistics as a whole. The use of the pronoun '*on*' rather than '*ils*' to describe the French people includes the writer herself in this community, defined as holding excessive, rather than professional, attitudes towards their language. In the second paragraph, this separation of the writer from the community of professional linguists is reinforced by the way in which the character of 'the ideal linguist' is constructed. The first sentence of the paragraph uses the dead metaphor '*examinons-le avec l'œil du linguiste*' to invite the reader to join the writer in the task of examining French from a linguist's viewpoint. In the second sentence of the paragraph, this dead metaphor is revitalised, constructing '*le linguiste*' as an active character in the text, through the simple expedient of giving him ears: '*Ou plutôt servons-nous, comme lui, de nos oreilles.*' The writer is distanced from this ideal linguist; the repetition of the '*on*' in '*Ne lui reproche-t-on pas de . . .*' continues the inclusive reference to 'ordinary people', as does the use of the imperative '*nous*' form.

In contrast with the emotional attitudes towards French held by the ordinary French speaker of the first paragraph, the 'ideal linguist' is constructed as a rational, scientific observer, unswayed by emotional considerations. While the voluble ordinary people *'encense'*, *'corrige'*, *'plaint'* and *'réprimande'* with *'beaucoup de passion'*, the linguist *'écoute plus qu'il ne s'exprime'*. *'Le linguiste'* is described as a *'professionnel du langage'*, and as having an attitude which is *'en quelque sorte amorale'*, as opposed to the moral *'jugements'* of the general population described in the initial sentence. The reference to the linguist as *'simple observateur'* reinforces this theme of detachment through drawing on a discourse of scientific observation.

The 'ordinary people' of the first paragraph are still referred to in this second part of the text. As one might expect, they are constructed as failing to understand the approach of the linguist, as defined in the text. Their response to the linguist is similar to their response to language itself. They continue to be associated with verbs of criticism: *'[N]e lui reproche-t-on pas de . . .'*, and with emotional responses: those who speak to him are *'gên[és] parfois'* and *'inquiét[és]'*. The gulf between the two is reinforced by the repetition of *'déconcertant'*/ *'déconcerte'*.

Positioning of writer and reader

Despite the fact that the author is herself a professional linguist, in this text a distinction is made between the character of *'le linguiste'* and the voice of the writer. The second paragraph begins with the introduction of an inclusive *nous* form, using the imperatives *'examinons-le'* and *'servons-nous'*. While it is standard to use the *nous* form in French academic writing, the use of the imperative suggests a direct appeal to both reader and writer to engage in the joint task of imitating the professional linguist. However, this relationship between writer and reader shifts as the paragraph goes on. The appeal to the reader continues, but as the paragraph proceeds *nous* is replaced by *vous*: *'il ne laisse rien échapper de ce que vous dites . . .'*, *'Lorsque vous vous rendez compte que . . .'*, *'son attitude . . . vous déconcerte'*. This *'vous'* is identified with the *'interlocuteurs'* of the professional linguist. The text is therefore constructing a relationship of distance between the 'ideal linguist' and those he or she is addressing, from which the writer of the book remains detached. At the beginning of the third paragraph, the *nous* forms reappear, again including reader and writer in the shared task of read/writing the book. This time this task is explicitly identified as 'the imitation of the linguist': *'c'est bien le point de vue du linguiste que nous adopterons dans cet ouvrage . . .'*. To this extent, the writer can be identified with the reader, but not to the extent of sharing a novice's response to the discipline of linguistics.

Conclusions

The text therefore constructs a number of characters: the generalised French population, pronominally referenced with '*on*', the 'ideal linguist', '*il*', the reader and writer engaged in the shared 'task of the book', '*nous*' and the '*interlocuteurs*' of the professional linguist, '*vous*'. The relationship between these characters is subtle and complex. The generalised French population holds emotional and inaccurate opinions about their language, attitudes which are hiding in some way its 'reality'. The linguist behaves in the way appropriate to the professional linguist, engaging in scientific observation detached from emotional response. Readers are invited to join the writer in imitating this behaviour, but do not thereby become professional linguists themselves. The '*interlocuteurs*', a subset of the generalised French community which does not include the writer, are likely to be initially shocked or surprised by this behaviour. The writer, however, remains detached from this response and can therefore lead the reader towards a fuller understanding of the professional linguist's approach.

Two separate communities are therefore constructed. The community of linguists is associated with knowledge, truth, reality; with observing things as they are and removing any obscuring veil. The other community, that of 'the French in general', is associated with '*idées reçues*', '*attitudes excessives*' and confusion on encountering people from the superior community. The text positions the reader as being part of the lower community through the use of the pronouns '*on*' and '*vous*', with the '*lui*' of the professional linguist evidently excluding them. At the same time, '*nous*' situates the writer textually as sharing the task of examining the French language with the reader. However, the underlying implication of the shifts in the text is that the writer must be a professional linguist who, by definition, is part of the superior community of knowledge.

Furthermore, the authority of the writer is betrayed by the way in which the introduction structures the rest of the preface. At the end of this extract the text cites some 'example myths': '« *le français, c'est du gaulois* », « *le français, c'est du latin* », « *le patois, c'est du français déformé* », ou « *le français le plus pur se parle en Touraine* »'. These 'myths' are signalled as coming from the voice of someone other than the writer through the use of quotation marks and the explicit imperative introducing them with '*Citons*'. We can assume from the previous associations that this 'other voice' is that of the French people as a whole. The rest of the *préambule* goes on to be structured around these myths. Variants of them are used as section headings, and in each section the writer explains to what extent each of them is true or false: '*Dans tout cela, il y a à prendre et à laisser*'. Although this section invites the reader to share the writer's task through the imperative '*nous*' forms, the positioning of the different characters suggests that the implicit message to the reader should be read as 'These are *your* myths which *I* as linguist am going to deconstruct for you'.

This text demonstrates the difficulty, or even the impossibility, for an academic author to abdicate authority within the generic and contextual constraints in which he or she is writing, despite the fact that there seems here to be a definite and deliberate attempt to avoid this positioning. It is possible that this reluctance to take on the role of 'the intellectual authority' is part of a generic change which reflects wider social and cultural change. Higher education in France, once reserved for 'the elite', has now been opened to a wider population. An increase in the numbers obtaining the *baccalauréat* has led to expansion in the numbers of university students, which in turn has reduced the mystique that was once associated with the academic world. This extract can therefore be read as a fragment which reflects a wider process of social and cultural change, and which questions the explicit authority of the intellectual, without challenging this authority at any fundamental level.

Henriette Walter, *Le Français dans Tous les Sens*, Paris: Laffont, 1988, pp. 13–14.

1   *PRÉAMBULE*

2

3

4   Le français observé par les linguistes

5

6   Le français suscite, de la part des Français, les jugements les plus contradic-
7   toires : tantôt on le donne en exemple pour ce qu'il a été, tantôt on lui met
8   le bonnet d'âne pour ce qu'il est. Avec beaucoup de passion, on l'encense, on
9   le corrige, on le plaint, on le réprimande. On oublie de le regarder vivre.
10   Derrière ces attitudes excessives, comment redécouvrir le français tel qu'on le
11   parle, tel qu'on l'écrit, tel qu'on l'aime ?

12

13   Pour vraiment observer le français dans sa réalité, examinons-le avec l'œil du
14   linguiste. Ou plutôt servons-nous, comme lui, de nos oreilles. Car le linguiste
15   écoute plus qu'il ne s'exprime. Ne lui reproche-t-on pas de s'intéresser davan-
16   tage à la façon dont les gens parlent qu'à ce qu'ils disent ? A ses inter-
17   locuteurs, que cette attitude gêne parfois, ce professionnel du langage apparaît
18   la plupart du temps comme un personnage déconcertant et même un peu
19   inquiétant : il ne laisse rien échapper de ce que vous dites, il a l'air d'en savoir
20   plus long que vous sur votre propre langue et, pourtant, il paraît toujours ravi
21   de ce qu'il entend. Lorsque vous vous rendez compte que son premier souci
22   n'est pas de voir respecter les formes lexicales ou grammaticales, son attitude
23   en quelque sorte amorale de simple observateur vous déconcerte.

24

25   Sans nous laisser impressionner par la sévérité à peine exagérée de ces juge-
26   ments, c'est bien le point de vue du linguiste que nous adopterons dans cet
27   ouvrage : celui de « l'amateur » de langues (comme on dit qu'on est amateur
28   de musique ou de peinture). Le linguiste s'intéresse à toutes les langues sous
29   tous leurs aspects, et lorsque son examen porte sur une langue particulière, il
30   cherche essentiellement à préciser en quoi cette langue est différente de toutes
31   les autres langues, comment elle fonctionne et comment elle évolue.

32

33   Le but de cet ouvrage est donc surtout de montrer par quels traits historiques,
34   géographiques et structuraux se caractérise le français. Mais tant d'idées
35   reçues circulent sur notre langue qu'on ne pourra pas y voir clair si,
36   auparavant, on ne fait pas un sort à quelques-unes d'entre elles, qui ont la vie
37   dure. Citons pêle-mêle : « le français, c'est du gaulois », « le français, c'est du
38   latin », « le patois, c'est du français déformé », ou « le français le plus pur
39   se parle en Touraine ». Dans tout cela, il y a à prendre et à laisser.

For the original format, see page 100.

Intertextuality and the uses of irony

Satirising the World Cup

Karin Tusting

Introduction

On 12 July 1998, the captain of the French football team Didier Deschamps held the World Cup above his head for the crowd at the *Stade de France* in Paris. France, as hosts and winners of this global sporting event, had achieved a success that had never really been expected. At the beginning of the tournament, the French manager Aimé Jacquet had been so widely vilified by the media that he refused to speak to any of the mainstream newspapers or sporting press. Cafés and hotels were declaring themselves 'football-free zones' for all those looking to escape the frenzy descending on Paris, Toulouse, Marseilles and the rest. But by the time France was entering the final stages of the competition, the streets were so packed with celebrating supporters that the team coach had great difficulty negotiating its way back to the players' hotel. And no one will forget the scenes of mass celebration when a million people packed the Champs Elysées after the Cup was won, giving rise to comparisons with the Liberation and definitively changing France's relationship with football. France, generally seen as one of the second-string European football countries, had won the World Cup in style: 3–0 against Brazil. Or rather, as the crowds were singing, '*Et un, et deux, et trois – zéro!*'.

Sport in France has traditionally been closely linked with national identity. The country has always been in the forefront of hosting global sporting events. The list includes the 1900 and 1924 Olympic Games in Paris and the 1924 Winter Games in Chamonix, the 1938 World Cup, the 1968 Winter Games in Grenoble, the 1984 European Soccer Championships and the 1992 Winter Olympics in Albertville. Throughout the century, the French State has heavily subsidised sport and sporting events, an initiative which can be understood in the context of European interwar nationalism and of the Popular Front ideology of sport and leisure for all (Dauncey and Hare 1998). In recent years, this has culminated in success in the 1996 Atlanta Olympics, where a haul of medals was hailed as a national victory, and in the country's hosting the World Cup in 1998, which gave France the opportunity to play centre stage in one of the few truly global events of our time. Both de Gaulle and Mitterrand in their presidencies saw sport as one of the key arenas in which French national pride and status – *grandeur* – could be demonstrated to the world (Dine 1998).

Given the significance of the event as a whole for national pride, the success of the French team was particularly important. One of the unexpected effects of this success was a media focus on the multiracial composition of the team. It was made up largely of players originating from France's former colonies and *départements et territoires d'outre mer*, including Senegal, Guadeloupe and North Africa, and players from the regions of France seen as being the 'least' French, such as Brittany and the Basque country. The unexpected heroes of the hour were the scoring midfielder, Zinedine Zidane, the son of Algerian immigrants, and the Black defender Lilian Thuram. Against a background of growing racial tension in France, where the National Front had been gaining ever higher approval ratings, and where running battles in Marseilles between police and local youths had become regular occurrences (a city where, in the early stages of the World Cup, many cafés were televised draped in Tunisian and Algerian flags), suddenly the *Arc de Triomphe* was displaying '*Zidane Président*' signs. The crowds celebrating in the Champs Elysées were multiracial and all came together under the banner of the *tricolour*. The media began to claim that football had 'solved', at one stroke, the racial problems that politicians had been grappling with for decades. This reaction extended to even the most sober of the British press. The *Financial Times* annual country survey of France, published in October 1998, led with the positive effects of the win that 'palpably boosted the self confidence of an entire country', and 'dealt a blow to extreme right racists' (Owen 1998).

Given the general ambience of unreflective elation, the article examined here, from the satirical newspaper *Le Canard Enchaîné*, came as a refreshing change. Taking its lead from the editorials and articles which it cites, the ironic tone of the article underlines the oversimplifications and generalisations springing from the fertile ground of celebration, and provides a welcome counterbalance to the blind optimism generated by even the quality press. Close study of this article demonstrates the intertextual nature of satirical discourse, the way in which satire reproduces the features of dominant discursive formations in order to undermine them, and underlines the multivoicedness of modern culture.

The media reaction: using intertextuality to ironic effect

The article is made up of three paragraphs. The first consists of a general description of the media reaction to the World Cup, specifically the focus on the multiracial nature of the French team. The second paragraph describes the celebrations, while the third brings us down to earth again by reminding us of the realities of the situation. The first paragraph can be split into three sections. The first five

Victoire du tactico-ethnique

UN ballon de foot a réussi ce que la politique avait raté. La tête de Zidane a fait mieux que nos grosses têtes. Quelques bouts de cuir cousus ensemble ont infligé à Le Pen la gifle la plus cinglante qu'il ait jamais reçue. Onze virtuoses du crampon et voilà le modèle français d'intégration célébré dans le monde entier. C'est fou, c'est irrationnel mais c'est ainsi. En Allemagne, le vice-président de la fédération de foot en vient à se demander *comment attirer les enfants étrangers dans l'équipe nationale*. Le journal « Süddeutsche Zeitung » remarque que l'équipe de Klingsmann aurait fait meilleure figure si elle avait intégré quelques immigrés turcs. « *La victoire de l'équipe de France est aussi celle de la diversité raciale* », applaudit le « Washington Post ». Mais le plus étonnant se passe en France. On lit des choses folles dans « Le Figaro » (13/7), des éditos à la gloire de « *la France multiraciale* » sous la signature d'Alain Peyrefitte, converti sur la route de Saint-Denis par « *le Forézien Jacquet, le Kabyle Zidane, le Breton Guivarc'h, le Guadeloupéen Thuram, le Pyrénéen Barthez, le Canaque Karambeu, le Basque Lizarazu, l'Africain Desailly, l'Arménien Djorkaeff* ». Non, ce n'est pas une rafle, monsieur l'académicien, c'est l'équipe nationale... Tragique malentendu : « *La France n'a pas à avoir peur. Qui pourrait la dissoudre, quoi qu'en disent les hommes politiques qui font de l'angoisse leur pactole élec-* toral ? », sermonne Georges Suffert dans le même « Figaro » (14/7), en s'extasiant : « *Au fil des jours et des années, ils deviennent progressivement français.* »

« Ils » étaient en effet dans la rue ces jours derniers... Heureux, bondissants, avec le sentiment

ZIDANE, CELUI QUI FAIT TAIRE LE PEN

d'être enfin admis au club, ces quartiers sensibles, banlieues difficiles et zones à éduquer en priorité ont fait la fête... Sans vandalisme ! Des jeunes très civiques, avec plein de repères... Aucune zizanie grâce à Zizou ! Pas de flics, ou alors ils faisaient la ola comme tout le monde... Les petites beurettes avaient la permission de minuit pour clamer leur fierté d'être françaises et brandir le drapeau tricolore, sans complexes, les doigts en V. Elles n'ont pas fait 68, elles auront fait 98 ! Bateleur ringard. Le Pen le battu de la Coupe a cru bon de qualifier ce Mondial de « *détail de l'Histoire* ». En attendant de rejoindre les poubelles de l'Histoire, le petit Mégret croit malin de saluer en Zidane « *l'enfant de l'Algérie française* ».

Mais Zidane est né à Marseille, et « Le Parisien » (13/7) rappelle que son père Smaïl travaillait « *à quelques centaines de mètres du Stade de France, à la Plaine-Saint-Denis* » quand il a trouvé « *son premier emploi de manutentionnaire en arrivant d'Algérie* ». Ce jour-là le guichet était ouvert, et un fonctionnaire lui a donné ses papiers. Bien joué !

Frédéric Pagès

Source: Pagès, F. 'Victoire du tactico-ethnique', *Le Canard Enchaîné*, 15 July 1998, p. 1.

sentences, while not being direct quotations, are clearly mimicking the general tone of the media reaction. The article moves on to refer to reactions from the international press and community, and ends with several quotations from the French press. This gives this first paragraph something of the flavour of a news review. But it is a news review written in a heavily ironic tone. The cynicism about this optimistic reaction is evident from the very first words, '*Un ballon de foot a réussi ce que la politique avait raté*', a statement which, while not quoting directly from named papers, is clearly intertextual in that it mimics the hyperbole of the press celebrations. The writer relies on readers' background knowledge, assuming them to be aware of the general tone of rejoicing.

It is through mimicking the celebratory reaction that this text underlines its excessive nature. The first four sentences are all structured in the same way, with a simple SVComp word order in which the subject, something relatively insignificant related to the game of football, achieves great things:

Un ballon de foot	*a réussi ce que la politique avait raté.*
La tête de Zidane	*a fait mieux que nos grosses têtes.*
Quelques bouts de cuir cousus ensemble	*ont infligé à Le Pen la gifle la plus cinglante qu'il ait jamais reçue.*
Onze virtuoses du crampon	*et voilà le modèle français d'intégration célébré dans le monde entier.*

The repetition of the structure foregrounds the seemingly insignificant things in theme position which become less and less weighty with each sentence. By the end the French team is not even skilful; simply very good at hanging on. And the descriptions of their achievements become in counterpoint more and more significant, culminating in '*le modèle français d'intégration célébré dans le monde entier*'. '*Et voilà*' emphasises the almost magical nature of the way the two events are being linked; France wins the World Cup and instantly, seemingly without effort, these problems are solved. Already the scene is set for an article subtly but stingingly deconstructing these grandiose claims.

This first section of the paragraph ends with the sentence '*C'est fou, c'est irrationnel mais c'est ainsi*', the ternary structure bringing a sense of closure to the sequence of binary sentences. The use of the words '*fou*' and '*irrationnel*' is the first clear statement of the position this article is taking. So what exactly is meant by '*c'est ainsi*'? The article is surely not claiming that these '*Onze virtuoses du crampon*' have really constructed '*le modèle français de l'intégration*'?

No, but other articles are. This article is in a clearly defined intertextual relationship with the voices and texts to which it is responding, which are on two levels. First, there are the texts actually quoted, from two articles in *Le Figaro* and one in the *Washington Post*, which make up a large proportion of the article. But this article is not merely reacting to these statements; the text would make sense to readers who had never encountered the particular articles quoted. On a more general level, the extract can also be read as a response to the vast mass of media texts around the world which were commenting on the World Cup in this way. In Foucauldian terms, the citations are examples of *énoncés* taken from the discursive formation which regulates what can and cannot be said about France's winning the World Cup. '*C'est ainsi*' can only properly be understood with reference to this discursive formation. And it is through another discursive formation – that of the satirical journalism associated with *Le Canard Enchaîné* – that the folly and irrationality of these claims can be pointed out. This article therefore stands in a complex relation to the dominant discursive formation. It draws on its rules, without conforming to them. It begins by mimicking the form of statements that make up the dominant discourse, in order to point out their incoherence. It cites and refers to statements from the discourse and is dependent on it for its very existence. Yet it breaks its rules of formation by challenging them. It is this complex relationship that enables the text to be read as satire.

In the next section of the first paragraph the article continues to reproduce statements from the dominant discourse by citing statements taken from the international press and the political community. Within the genre of commentary article, such quotations would normally be used to represent the general thrust of opinion, through giving a 'flavour' of their overall response. Since the quotations selected here are represented in the text as intrinsically foolish, the reader can infer that the international response to the events has been equally unthinking.

The first citation is from the vice president of the German football federation who has been reported to be wondering how to attract foreign children into the national team. The verb used is not *il se demande* but '*[il] en vient à se demander*'. The use of the verb *en venir* connotes surprise and implies that in some way he is 'going too far'. Indeed, it is a little facile – not to say self-contradictory – to suggest that adding a few foreigners to the German team would enable them to start winning the World Cup again. This is reinforced by the reference to the article in the *Süddeutsche Zeitung*, quoted as having remarked that the team '*aurait fait meilleure figure si elle avait intégré quelques immigrés turcs*'. Of course there is no intrinsic reason why Turkish immigrants would make any better or worse footballers than native Germans. This is reinforced by the use of wordplay in the phrase, which is a summary rather than a direct citation. The use of the phrase '*aurait fait meilleure figure*' could be read as a subtle reference to the fact that Turkish immigrants can often be identified by the way that they look in Germany, by their '*figure*'; and the use of the word '*intégré*' recalls fears of Muslim fundamentalism associated with Muslim immigrants – *intégrisme* – and emphasises the fact that, while a German paper may be asking for immigrants to be integrated into the German team, they have not yet necessarily become 'integrated' as part of German national culture.

Finally, the quotation from the *Washington Post*, '*La victoire de l'équipe de France est aussi celle de la diversité raciale*', is left without comment, but is immediately followed by the phrase '*Mais le plus étonnant se passe en France*', which reframes all the preceding quotations as being themselves '*étonnants*'. This final section is the longest part of the first paragraph, and consists of quotations from the newspaper *Le Figaro*. These quotations are positioned as being examples of the general French media response, in the same way that those above were seen as representative of international comment.

This section is the most explicitly critical, using words such as '*étonnant*', '*des choses folles*' and '*Tragique malentendu*' to describe and frame the quotations selected. The use of the inclusive '*on*' in '*On lit des choses folles*' suggests that readers of these articles are likely to have shared the writer's experience of them as being '*folles*'. The ironic tone is continued through the use of hyperbole – for example, in the description of one of the writers as writing '*en s'extasiant*', a phrase which connotes a certain loss of control. This is reinforced by the use of imagery derived from religion. References to ecstasy and glory – '*des éditos à la gloire de « la France multiraciale »*' – are also references to feelings and concepts associated with religious experience. In addition, Alain Peyrefitte, writer of the editorial quoted, is described as having been '*converti sur la route de Saint-Denis*', a direct reference to the New Testament conversion of St Paul on the road to Damascus – an event which was coupled with an immediate affliction of blindness. And the verb used to describe Georges Suffert's pronouncements on the issue is '*sermonne*'. The religious associations are clear: this man is speaking from on high, from a judgemental position, very possibly speaking from one which is in some way detached from the 'real world'.

The long list of names taken from the editorial ('*le Forézien Jacquet, le Kabyle Zidane, le Breton Guivarc'h, le Guadeloupéen Thuram, le Pyrénéen Barthez, le Canaque Karambeu, le Basque Lizarazu, l'Africain Desailly, l'Arménien Djorkaeff*'), while a direct citation from *Le Figaro*, when re-embedded in this ironic text appears comic in its cumulative effect. It is followed by the comment: '*Non, ce n'est pas une rafle, monsieur l'académicien, c'est l'équipe nationale*'. '*Monsieur l'académicien*' is Alain Peyrefitte, who, in addition to writing journalism, is a right-wing politician, social commentator and member of the *Académie Française*. This aside underlines the way in which an interest in football is now being shown by the most unexpected of people. Before his 'conversion', Peyrefitte would not necessarily have been expected to have known or written about the names of the members of the French national team. And the dialogic form explicitly constructs the article as an exchange between the author and the object of satire, inviting the reader to collude with the writer's ironic approach. Through the vocabulary used, the phrase also implies that such a list, referring to several different nationalities, would historically have arisen from accounts of racial oppression rather than from French national success. The word '*rafle*' is often used in accounts of the Holocaust to refer to French Jews and other ethnic minorities being rounded up for deportation; its use here is a subtle but pointed reminder of the historical realities of racism.

The final quotation from the Suffert article, '*« Au fil des jours et des années, ils deviennent progressivement français »*', is left without explicit comment in this paragraph. But in the same way as the quotation from the *Washington Post* is reframed as being '*étonnant*' by the sentence immediately following, the contradictory nature of this quotation is highlighted by the way next paragraph begins: '*« Ils » étaient en effet dans la rue ces jours derniers . . .*'. The quotation marks around the '*ils*' underline the fact that Suffert is still referring in his writing to a 'them and us' situation. In this construction of the world, he and his readers are positioned as being 'really' French, while a mysterious 'they' is gradually being allowed to come nearer to belonging without ever truly becoming part of 'us'. This sentence continues the general tone of cynicism by underlining the fact that in the usual course of events such a phrase would be used to refer to rioting or demonstrations, rather than to street celebrations. More pointed is the description of those involved as having '*le sentiment d'être enfin admis au club*', reinforcing the message by emphasising the fact that this may still in fact be only a short-lived '*sentiment*', rather than the beginnings of true acceptance.

The celebrations: juxtaposing different voices

This second paragraph consists for the most part in describing the celebrations of the immigrant population after France had succeeded in winning the final. While not containing direct quotations from the media, it is recognisably still echoing the excessively optimistic tone of the dominant discursive formation, combining this with other voices – particularly in the use of lexis associated with bureaucratic discourse and slang – to continue the ironic effect achieved through implicit intertextuality. As with the first sentences of the article, the first sentences of this paragraph all follow a similar pattern. After the initial phrase, we find three sentence sequences, each structured in the same way:

Heureux, bondissants, avec le sentiment d'être enfin admis au club, ces quartiers sensibles, banlieues difficiles et zones à éduquer en priorité ont fait la fête . . . Sans vandalisme!

Des jeunes très civiques, avec plein de repères . . . Aucune zizanie grâce à Zizou!

Pas de flics, ou alors ils faisaient la ola comme tout le monde . . . Les petites beurettes avaient la permission de minuit pour clamer leur fierté d'être françaises et brandir le

*drapeau tricolore, sans complexes, les doigts en V. Elles n'ont pas fait 68, elles auront
fait 98!*

The description of the celebrators as '*Des jeunes très civiques, avec plein de repères*'
again underlines the tone of surprise which characterised media reporting of the
trouble-free celebrations, as does the excessive use of exclamation marks. '*Très
civiques*' and '*plein de repères*' are not descriptions normally associated with the
areas designated as '*quartiers sensibles*' and '*banlieues difficiles*'. The claim that there
was '*Aucune zizanie grâce à Zizou*' raises the question: Could Zidane's achievements
really have transformed these traditionally 'difficult' youth into effectively
different people, inculcating instantaneously in them the values denoted as 'civil-
ised' by the mainstream press? Or are there more complex reasons for both the
trouble-free celebrations and the usual trouble reported from these deprived
areas?

Within this general ironic tone, lexis drawn from particular areas signals a
mixing of different 'voices'. The first sentence cited above, describing the areas
involved as '*ces quartiers sensibles, banlieues difficiles et zones à éduquer en priorité*',
draws on designations usually associated with French bureaucracy or politicians.
They are euphemistic labels attached to areas with a high immigrant population,
high unemployment, high crime rates and very low average income. The use of
these designations underlines the social situation of the '« *ils* »' being spoken about
so blithely by the press, and reminds us that the real problems in their lives are too
complex to be resolved by a simple game of football, however strongly felt the
emotions of the moment might be. They also contain connotations of 'speaking
for' in the same way as the use of the '« *ils* »', and of 'speaking from above' in the
same way as the use of '*sermonne*'. This is reinforced by the conversion of the label
Zones d'Education Prioritaire, used by the *Education Nationale* to refer to areas
which are given extra funding for teachers because of social difficulties, into '*zones
à éduquer en priorité*', which implies that these areas are in dire need of education.

But the article also draws on slang vocabulary to construct an ironic representation of the 'popular' voice. The use of '*Zizou*' is a familiar shortening of Zinedine
Zidane, and, although '*zizanie*' is more literary than argotic, the juxtaposition of
the two lends it a similar familiar effect. The use of the phrase '*ont fait la fête*' and
'*Les petites beurettes*' (an ironic neologism?) are both part of a popular register of
vocabulary. In addition, both the vocabulary and the syntax of '*Pas de flics, ou alors
ils faisaient la ola comme tout le monde . . .*' have popular associations, with the use
of '*Pas de*' to begin a sentence belonging to a register of informal French, '*flics*'
being clearly argotic and *faire la ola* both being popular language and referring to a
popular celebratory practice. While the quotations in the first paragraph situated
the rather facile reaction within the domain of the media, the use of this popular
lexis and the implicit citation of the general 'voice' in the second widens the zone
of attack to include the tone of reaction amongst the public as a whole.

In the first paragraph we noted an implicit reminder of the horrors of World War II with the use of the word '*rafle*'. This comparison of the World Cup with other significant historical events is continued in the next paragraph. Memories of war, liberation and revolution are evoked by the description of the '*petites beurettes*' as having '*les doigts en V*', recalling the crowds along the Champs Elysées at the time of the Liberation of Paris. They are given '*la permission de minuit*', as if this event has freed them from a curfew. Finally, a direct comparison is made between these celebrations and the last notable time that the streets of Paris were blocked by huge crowds: '*Elles n'ont pas fait 68, elles auront fait 98*'. The use of the future perfect in '*elles auront fait*' underlines the fact that in the future this is an event which will be looked back on and spoken about, in the same way as ageing revolutionaries look back on the days of their protests in the streets of Paris. Again, the World Cup is placed in historical perspective: was it really as historic-ally significant an event as the Liberation of Paris or the *événements* of May 1968? The text leaves it to the reader to supply the answer, but the tone of the piece suggests otherwise.

The final section of this paragraph again relies on quotations, this time from the National Front leader Le Pen and his then-deputy Mégret, key figures in the development of the racist intolerance that the press are claiming has been des-troyed. Both are described in derogatory ways, Le Pen as a '*Bateleur ringard*', and Mégret as '*le petit Mégret*' and as being destined for '*les poubelles de l'Histoire*'. This ironically repeats the appeal to history made by Le Pen in claiming that the World Cup is a mere '*«détail de l'Histoire»*', the link underlined by the capitalisation of the word '*l'Histoire*'; but whereas Le Pen's claim is positioned as being false ('*a cru bon de*'), Mégret's ultimate destination as historical detritus is written as a categorical truth. In fact, Mégret's claim is positioned as being false using *croire* in a similar way through its introduction: '*Mégret croit malin de*'. These formulations imply that they are both wrong to believe that their statements are right or clever. Le Pen's claim contrasts with the historical significance attached to the Cup by the media and general public opinion, and the juxtaposition of these ideas carries a suggestion that neither rejecting out of hand the significance of the victory, nor blowing it out of all proportion, are reasoned or rational responses. Mégret's claim is that Zidane should be seen as '*« l'enfant de l'Algérie française »*', implicitly attributing this victory to France's colonial past which is still glorified by the extreme right wing.

The realities of the situation

This claim is corrected by the third and final paragraph, which begins: '*Mais Zidane est né à Marseille*'. The use of '*Mais*' indicates that this should be read as a qualifica-tion of the preceding text. The sentence reminds the reader that Zidane was born in Marseilles, underlining that he is in fact French by birth. This comes in contrast to the racist distinctions that are being made in the reports which describe him as a foreigner ('*le Kabyle Zidane*') in much the same way as the '« *Ils* »' of the preceding paragraph emphasised the distinction that was being made between 'them' and 'us'. The quotation from *Le Parisien* recalls those with which the article began; but whereas they were overblown opinion pieces, this final one simply recounts the facts of Zidane's father's immigrant life. The fact that Smaïl Zidane worked as a goods handler at Plaine-Saint-Denis recalls the description of Alain Peyrefitte's conversion '*sur la route de Saint-Denis*', and compares the father's labour with the son's glory, also situated in Saint-Denis but almost unimaginably different.

This paragraph is recalling to the reader the real situation of immigrants in France, reminding us of the fact that Zidane is in the French team as a result of having had a 'typical' immigrant father who came initially to do the country's manual work. The relations of power which this implies are clearly evoked in the closing image: '*Ce jour-là le guichet était ouvert, et un fonctionnaire lui a donné ses papiers.*' The use of '*Ce jour-là*' implies that on another day entry might not have been granted to him, and that the star of the French national side might only have been allowed in the country in the first place on the whim of a '*fonctionnaire*'. It is this '*fonctionnaire*' to whom the final phrase, '*Bien joué !*', is directed; using the footballing term to approve the actions of this civil servant ironically suggests that the success of the team is originally down to his actions.

This paragraph is foregrounded through the change in length – it is much shorter than the other two – through its final position, which generically would indicate a conclusion, and through a sudden change of style. While the rest of the article draws on dominant discourses in order to deconstruct them, using subtle puns and phonetic juggling to ironic effect, this paragraph includes little wordplay. Instead, it consists of simple references to 'the facts', marking it as 'unvarnished reality'. These brief sentences, after the hyperbole of the preceding paragraphs, are an abrupt reminder of the realities of life for most of the immigrant population in France.

Irony, intertextuality and the multivoicedness of contemporary culture

In this satirical article, we see the dominant discursive formation of the media response to this event being skilfully and subtly deconstructed. The irony of the text depends on the reproduction of elements from the discursive formation that it is critiquing. It also depends on the reader recognising these elements and reading the text as satirical discourse. The piece could almost be read simply as a press review, or even as an article adding to the general self-approbation, were a reader to be inattentive to or unaware of the general tone of this particular newspaper. However, *Le Canard Enchaîné* is a satirical paper. Its *raison d'être* is to critique in an amusing and subtle way the grosser absurdities of French and international public life. The features noted in this article — irony and wordplay, coupled with occasional flashes of biting criticism — make up the distinctive 'voice' of the paper and would be expected by a regular reader. In part, the success of this piece depends on the reader having a mind-set that expects and is looking for evidence of this irony.

Irony depends on the reader's recognising the implicit intertextuality of the piece, and having knowledge about the discursive formations on which the satirical piece is drawing. Satire depends for its very existence on the multiple discursive formations which it mimics in order to deconstruct and critique them. An analysis of such a satirical piece is an illustration *par excellence* of the multivoicedness and plurality of contemporary culture. Occasionally, in every country, 'events' occur which appear to 'take over' the country, when a spurious unity is attributed to the reactions of press and public. The death of Diana, Princess of Wales was one such 'event' in Britain, and France's winning the World Cup set off a similar chain of national emotional outpourings. However, when making claims about any country's 'culture', it is important to remember that no absolute claims can be made about 'unity' or the 'national mood' that apply to all the heterogeneous groups making up a national community. This article shows us that, while fulsome claims about national unity were being made by the national press, together with predictions about a France united in racial harmony, these optimistic beliefs were not necessarily shared by everybody. It also demonstrates the impossibility of making any absolute claims about 'French culture'. Culture must inevitably be read in the plural; the exploration of culture through text can only give insights into the facets of this plurality within which any particular text is situated.

Frédéric Pagès, 'Victoire du tactico-ethnique', *Le Canard Enchaîné*, 15 July 1998, p. 1.

Victoire du tactico-ethnique

Un ballon de foot a réussi ce que la politique avait raté. La tête de Zidane a fait mieux que nos grosses têtes. Quelques bouts de cuir cousus ensemble ont infligé à Le Pen la gifle la plus cinglante qu'il ait jamais reçue. Onze virtuoses du crampon et voilà le modèle français d'intégration célébré dans le monde entier. C'est fou, c'est irrationnel mais c'est ainsi. En Allemagne, le vice-président de la fédération de foot en vient à se demander « *comment attirer les enfants étrangers dans l'équipe nationale* ». Le journal « Süddeutsche Zeitung » remarque que l'équipe de Klingsmann aurait fait meilleure figure si elle avait intégré quelques immigrés turcs. « *La victoire de l'équipe de France est aussi celle de la diversité raciale* », applaudit le « Washington Post ». Mais le plus étonnant se passe en France. On lit des choses folles dans « Le Figaro » (13/7), des éditos à la gloire de « *la France multiraciale* » sous la signature d'Alain Peyrefitte, converti sur la route de Saint-Denis par « *le Forézien Jacquet, le Kabyle Zidane, le Breton Guivarc'h, le Guadeloupéen Thuram, le Pyrénéen Barthez, le Canaque Karambeu, le Basque Lizarazu, l'Africain Desailly, l'Arménien Djorkaeff* ». Non, ce n'est pas une rafle, monsieur l'académicien, c'est l'équipe nationale . . . Tragique malentendu : « *La France n'a pas à avoir peur. Qui pourrait la dissoudre, quoi qu'en disent les hommes politiques qui font de l'angoisse leur pactole électoral?* », sermonne Georges Suffert dans le même « Figaro » (14/7), en s'extasiant : « *Au fil des jours et des années, ils deviennent progressivement français.* »

« Ils » étaient en effet dans la rue ces jours derniers . . . Heureux, bondissants, avec le sentiment d'être enfin admis au club, ces quartiers sensibles, banlieues difficiles et zones à éduquer en priorité ont fait la fête . . . Sans vandalisme ! Des jeunes très civiques, avec plein de repères . . . Aucune zizanie grâce à Zizou ! Pas de flics, ou alors ils faisaient la ola comme tout le monde . . . Les petites beurettes avaient la permission de minuit pour clamer leur fierté d'être françaises et brandir le drapeau tricolore, sans complexes, les doigts en V. Elles n'ont pas fait 68, elles auront fait 98 ! Bateleur ringard, Le Pen le battu de la Coupe a cru bon de qualifier ce Mondial de « *détail de l'Histoire* ». En attendant de rejoindre les poubelles de l'Histoire, le petit Mégret croit malin de saluer en Zidane « *l'enfant de l'Algérie française* ».

Mais Zidane est né à Marseille, et « Le Parisien » (13/7) rappelle que son père Smaïl travaillait « *à quelques centaines de mètres du Stade de France, à la Plaine-Saint-Denis* » quand il a trouvé « *son premier emploi de manutentionnaire en arrivant d'Algérie* ». Ce jour-là le guichet était ouvert, et un fonctionnaire lui a donné ses papiers. Bien joué !

Frédéric Pagès

For the original format, see page 108.

Fantasy and reality
The alienation of urban youth

Karin Tusting

Introduction

Le problème des banlieues – the problem of the suburbs – has become a recurrent topic for discussion in modern France. The suburbs which were built around Paris and other large towns in the postwar years of reconstruction have become in more recent times the focus of attention of politicians, administrators and educators. Built to house the large workforce of immigrants and blue-collar labour of the 1950s and 1960s, these areas have become France's equivalent of Britain's 'inner cities' or 'sink estates'; reference to *les banlieues* in the press is often a convenient shorthand used to designate areas with high unemployment and crime rates and general social difficulties. Young people in particular are often represented as the source of the most serious problems, typically being identified with marginal or immigrant groups.

One response to this objectifying perspective which sees urban youth as a threat to society has been to tell their stories from their point of view, often in their own words. The combination of real and fictional worlds in subject matter, and the use of 'non-standard' discourse in narrative forms – a tradition established by Emile Zola in the late nineteenth century – has found more recent expression through novels such as Christiane Rochefort's (1961) *Les Petits Enfants du Siècle*, which tells the story of a young girl growing up in one of the Paris *cités*. This work bears several parallels with the story from which the present extract is taken. Written in the first person, it describes the loneliness of a young girl's life, a loneliness which is assuaged neither by the continual contact she has with her family, nor by social interaction with a 'gang' of other young people. For her, freedom comes to be associated with riding a scooter, which is used to escape from the constraints of everyday life. In a similar way, in the extract discussed here, freedom is linked to riding a moped. More recently, the film *La Haine* (1994) gained a worldwide reputation through its portrait of a day in the life of three youths from different ethnic backgrounds in one of the Parisian *banlieues*. The film, set in a bleak and threatening built environment, showed the young men managing to briefly escape from their *cité*, only for this ephemeral freedom to be destroyed in a tragic *dénouement*.

In the extract under analysis here, taken from a book of short stories by Le Clézio (1982), we are given an insight into the experiences of a young girl, Martine, as she rides a moped through an oppressive urban environment. The extract, although not written in the first person, deals with her subjective experience in a highly empathetic way. Shifting between the perspective of the young girl and that of an omniscient narrator, the text contrasts Martine's own experiences of freedom with the oppression of the environment surrounding her. Like *La Haine*, the story will end in brutal and senseless tragedy, a tragedy which is implicitly foreshadowed in the present extract.

Structure of the text

This short extract is a description of Martine's experiences as she and her friend Titi ride on mopeds along quiet urban streets at or around midday. There is also a second, fantasy setting, in which Martine imagines what it would be like to be riding with Titi's brother on a motorbike. Within the context of the short story as a whole, this extract is a rare moment of freedom, happiness and escapism. The text is centred on the character of Martine, describing her experiences and thoughts from her own perspective. The other characters in the text, Titi and Titi's brother, are only presented with reference to their relationship to Martine and her thoughts about them; thus we are given an insight into her feelings and thoughts that is not afforded to the other characters. This insight is offered from a number of points of view: through descriptions of Martine's emotions by an omniscient narrator, of her inner feelings in 'free indirect thought' (Short 1996) and of her actions as seen by an external observer. The main function of the text is to tell Martine's story, and the success of the piece depends on the construction of Martine as a character with whom the reader can identify. This identification is achieved through the use of different voices in the text, which position the reader within rather than outside Martine's subjective experience.

The extract can be split into five main sections, each of which deals with one primary topic. It begins with a description of Martine's experience as she rides the moped. The second part of the first paragraph evokes her feelings about Titi's brother, which leads on to the third topic, an imaginative episode in which Martine imagines herself sharing a motorbike ride with him. The fourth topic, at the beginning of the second paragraph, describes the external environment in which the moped ride is taking place. The final topic relates to the noises in the street and to Martine's experiences of them. The progression between topics is clearly marked in the text. Each topic is introduced by the reference to its main character(s): '*Maintenant qu'elle roule, <u>Martine</u> . . .*', '*<u>Titi</u> a eu de la chance, c'est son <u>frère</u> qui . . .*', '*<u>Martine</u> ne pense pas vraiment à <u>lui</u>, mais . . .*', '*<u>Les deux</u>*

Maintenant qu'elle roule, Martine ne ressent plus la peur à l'intérieur de son corps. Peut-être que les vibrations du vélomoteur, l'odeur et la chaleur des gaz ont empli tout le creux qu'il y avait en elle. Martine aime bien rouler en vélomoteur, surtout quand il y a beaucoup de soleil et que l'air n'est pas froid, comme aujourd'hui. Elle aime se faufiler entre les autos, la tête tournée un peu de côté pour ne pas respirer le vent, et aller vite ! Titi a eu de la chance, c'est son frère qui lui a donné son vélomoteur, enfin, pas exactement donné ; il attend que Titi ait un peu d'argent pour le payer. Le frère de Titi, ce n'est pas comme la plupart des garçons. C'est un type bien, qui sait ce qu'il veut, qui ne passe pas son temps à raconter des salades comme les autres, juste pour se faire valoir. Martine ne pense pas vraiment à lui, mais juste quelques secondes c'est comme si elle était avec lui, sur sa grosse moto Guzzi, en train de foncer à toute vitesse dans la rue vide. Elle sent le poids du vent sur son visage, quand elle est accrochée à deux mains au corps du garçon, et le vertige des virages où la terre bascule, comme en avion.

Les deux jeunes filles roulent le long du trottoir, vers l'ouest. Le soleil est au zénith, il brûle, et l'air frais n'arrive pas à dissiper l'espèce de sommeil qui pèse sur le goudron de la rue et sur le ciment des trottoirs. Les magasins sont fermés, les rideaux de fer sont baissés, et cela accentue encore l'impression de torpeur. Malgré le bruit des vélomoteurs, Martine entend par instants, au passage, le glouglou des postes de télévision qui parlent tout seuls au premier étage des immeubles. Il y a une voix d'homme, et de la musique qui résonne bizarrement dans le sommeil de la rue, comme dans une grotte.

Source: Le Clézio, J.M. (1982) *La Ronde et Autres Faits Divers*, Paris: Gallimard, pp. 15–16. ©Editions Gallimard.

jeunes filles roulent . . .', '*Malgré le bruit des vélomoteurs, Martine entend . . .*'. The first break is also foregrounded with the phrase '*et aller vite!*' which precedes it, marked structurally through *cadence mineure* and graphologically with an exclamation mark. The third change of topic is reinforced by the paragraph break.

Shifts in voice: sentence structure, tone and register

These topic changes are also characterised by a shift in voice. The first two sentences describe Martine's feelings as they are in the 'now' of the text, from the point of view of an omniscient narrator: '*Maintenant qu'elle roule, Martine ne ressent plus la peur à l'intérieur de son corps. . . . le creux qu'il y avait en elle. Martine aime bien rouler en vélomoteur. . . . Elle aime se faufiler entre les autos . . .*'. The initial deictic reference '*Maintenant qu'elle roule*' and the other uses of '*Martine*' and '*elle*' indicate that this section is written from the point of view of an external narrator with access to Martine's feelings and thoughts, rather than from her own perspective. This narrative voice shows stylistic characteristics typical of written French sentence structure. The *loi de longueur* is conformed to: the final complements of the sentences, '*à l'intérieur de son corps*' and '*tout le creux qu'il y avait en elle*', are the longest. Sentences are complex, using embedded clauses: '*Maintenant qu'elle roule*', '*tout le creux qu'il y avait en elle*'. The phrase '*les vibrations du vélomoteur, l'odeur et la chaleur des gaz*' shows a classic ternary structure typical of traditional 'literary' French style. The use of adverbials to begin both sentences – '*Maintenant qu'elle roule*' and, particularly, '*Peut-être que*' – conform to the norms of written French. Vocabulary from a high register is used: '*ressentir*', '*à l'intérieur de son corps*', '*emplir le creux*'.

In the second part of the first section, which describes what Martine enjoys about riding a motorcycle, there is a move away from the objective description of her emotions towards a more subjective perspective. While still using the third person, the style of the sentences suggests a 'voice' that belongs more to Martine herself than to a literary narrator. The deictic time reference to 'today', '*comme aujourd'hui*', relates to Martine's own temporal positioning. Sentence rhythm begins to take on the characteristics of a more informal, spoken register. Subordinate clauses come after the main clause and are coordinated with '*et*', chains of complements are linked through the use of commas, and the *loi de longueur* is broken in both sentences. This gives the impression that the final complements, '*comme aujourd'hui*' and '*et aller vite!*', are afterthoughts, added to the phrase in linear fashion as it is being constructed.

In the second section, relating to Martine's feelings about Titi's brother, this shift towards Martine's 'voice' continues, as we are given direct access to her internal thought processes. The section is introduced by the phrase '*Titi a eu de la chance*', which, coming directly after the section relating Martine's feelings, is positioned as being her own opinion rather than the narrator's. Her thought patterns are reflected in the sentence structure. The long first sentence, with clauses linked by coordination and the use of commas and semicolons, recalls the rhythms of spoken French. The correction of '*donné . . . enfin, pas exactement donné*', with the casual use of '*enfin*', suggests spoken or 'thought' language, constructing the illusion that these words are being formulated in 'real time' with all the self-correction and rethinking that this entails. The use of '*c'est*', occurring in all three sentences ('*c'est son frère qui lui a donné son vélomoteur*', '*Le frère de Titi, ce n'est pas comme la plupart des garçons*', '*C'est un type bien*'), is strongly characteristic of an informal register. The vocabulary used is slangy: '*un type bien*', '*raconter des salades*'. As in the first paragraph, the *loi de longueur* is broken with the use of the proportionately short complement '*juste pour se faire valoir*'.

While these sentences can be read as if they were a transcription of spoken French, there is no indication that Martine is actually speaking them. Since they are placed immediately after the description of her feelings in the fourth sentence, we assume that we are still dealing with her thoughts. These sentences therefore read as being 'free indirect thought' (Short 1996: 314–316). This is reinforced by the progression of ideas. Instead of constructing an argument around rational links to suggest a logically inevitable movement from one idea to the next, Martine's mind jumps between topics in a way which suggests free association. While there are logical links between individual elements, there is no overall thread: her thoughts move from Titi, to Titi's brother, to the fantasy of riding his motorbike. The unfocused train of thought suggests a daydream. Just as the moped '*se [faufile] entre les autos*', Martine's thought patterns thread their way haphazardly through her mind.

The third main section, Martine's fantasy ride with Titi's brother, begins with a direct reference to the speed and superficiality of these daydreams: '*Martine ne pense pas vraiment à lui, mais juste quelques secondes c'est comme si elle était avec lui . . .*'. This signals that we are moving away from a mode which recounts her thoughts directly, and into a mode in which comments on this thought process are possible. The point of view is no longer that of Martine herself. However, the 'voice' is still not in the register associated with the detached narrator of the opening sentences. We find several clauses linked through relations of coordination or listing, rather than using embedded structures. The use of vocabulary items from an informal register continues in '*sur sa grosse moto Guzzi*' and '*en train de foncer à toute vitesse*'. And the simulation of thought processes finds expression in the *cadence mineure* of the final simile '*comme en avion*'. So, the reader is positioned as sharing the point of view of an external narrator who has privileged access to Martine's thoughts and feelings.

The fourth section, which describes the external environment in which the ride takes place, begins with a move to 'long-shot' view, in which Martine is described as if by an external observer: '*Les deux jeunes filles roulent le long du trottoir*'. This sentence and the one after it are the parts of the extract most 'detached' from Martine's subjectivity, describing her completely 'from the outside'. Although these two sentences refer to external elements, such as the burning sun, which contribute to her experience, the reporting is not explicitly mediated through her perspective. While the sentence structure is not complex, the first sentence being syntactically simple and the second consisting of three clauses linked with commas and *et*, they do not for all that suggest informal speech. This is largely due to the use of high-register vocabulary: '*Le soleil est au zénith*', '*dissiper*', '*l'espèce de sommeil*', and to the complexity and length of the clause: '*l'air frais n'arrive pas à dissiper l'espèce de sommeil qui pèse sur le goudron de la rue et sur le ciment des trottoirs.*'

The final two sentences, which constitute the fifth section, fall between third-person narration of Martine's experiences and her own point of view. Here, a description of the noises in the street is mediated through what she hears. But the 'voice' used is not hers. While the onomatopoeic '*glouglou*' belongs to an informal register and the phrase '*par instants, au passage*' suggests Martine's perspective, the sentence-initial adverbial phrase, the embedded clause '*qui parlent tout seuls au premier étage des immeubles*' and the use of the more formal '*postes de télévision*' mark the sentence as coming from the narrator. The same is true of the final sentence which, while it continues to describe Martine's perceptions, uses high-register vocabulary and complex sentence structure.

Location in time: the deictic value of temporal reference

These shifts in voice are associated with changing spatio-temporal perspective. Most of these references are centred on Martine, moving from her position in the 'real', as it is constructed in the text, to a more generalised description of her feelings, to a fantasy world which draws on her current reality for its experiences, to a description of Martine by an outside observer.

The objective, neutral point of view of the omniscient narrator, identified at the start of the extract and in the final paragraph, is strongly associated with the events which are actually happening in the reality which the text describes. In the first two sentences, the present tense situates the current situation through the use of the negative *ne . . . plus*, which gives an insight into the recent past. The opening sentence, '*Maintenant qu'elle roule, Martine ne ressent plus la peur à l'intérieur de son corps*', presupposes that at a previous time Martine *was* afraid, and therefore locates this description just after the start of the ride. Equally, the use of the *passé composé* in '*ont empli tout le creux qu'il y avait en elle*' refers back to this immediate past. The use of these tenses links this voice clearly to the here-and-now, through tying the present and the recent past closely together. And the time adverbial '*Maintenant qu'elle roule*', foregrounded as it is by its position at the beginning of the extract, frames such descriptions as being in this 'now'.

The shift away from the voice associated with the external narrator, identified in the third sentence, is matched by a slippage in the temporal anchoring in the 'now' of the text. The third sentence links a general statement about Martine's character with reference to what is actually happening to her. It begins with the statement: '*Martine aime bien rouler en vélomoteur, surtout quand il y a beaucoup de soleil et que l'air n'est pas froid*'. However, the use of the deictic temporal reference '*comme aujourd'hui*' reframes the statement by suggesting that these conditions prevail today. Thus, we are afforded insight both into Martine's actual experiences and into her character, linking reference to the here-and-now to a more generalised claim.

On moving 'into Martine's head', in the section covering her interior mono-logue and her fantasy about riding with Titi's brother, we are almost completely divorced from her actual experiences. There is another statement relating to Martine's opinions, constructed using the present tense, this time about Titi's brother: '*Le frère de Titi, ce n'est pas comme la plupart des garçons*'. However, this statement is not anchored in Martine's present at all. Even when we identify the fifth sentence, '*Titi a eu de la chance . . .*', as interior monologue, the uses of the *passé composé*, the present and the subjunctive are not directly related to Martine and Titi's current experience. The use of the present tense in '*il attend que Titi ait un peu d'argent pour le payer*' is a reference to the present moment, but this is not situated in the here-and-now of the text. Rather, it is a more generalised present with a different aspect: he is in the process of waiting for Titi to have some money.

We return to direct reference to what is actually happening – or at least to what is not happening – with '*Martine ne pense pas vraiment à lui, mais . . .*'. '*[M]ais . . . comme si*' moves us into Martine's imaginary world, linked to textual reality only by the time adverbial in '*juste quelques secondes c'est comme si elle était avec lui*', which signals the few seconds of real time that this thought takes up. Since we know, from '<u>*comme si elle était avec lui*</u>', that this section recounts a fantasy world rather than the real one, a clear distinction is drawn between the 'real' world, as it has been constructed in the text, and Martine's fantasy. However, the experiences of riding the motorbike mirror Martine's current experience, and the present tense is used to describe both. This world is a parallel world in which she is '*en train de foncer dans la rue vide. Elle sent le poids du vent sur son visage, quand elle est accrochée à deux mains au corps du garçon, et le vertige des virages où la terre bascule, comme en avion.*' Present tenses are used to describe a scene which is not actually happening. This serves two purposes. It makes the imaginary scene seem more immediate and more real. But it also relates the imaginary experience to the real experience of riding the moped, in which she is actually feeling the wind on her face and the giddiness of the turns, suggesting that Martine is drawing on her current experience to develop her fantasy.

After this move into the imaginary, we are repositioned in the here-and-now with the objective description in the final paragraph. As has been pointed out above, the time adverbials here allow the text to describe both the general state of affairs – the sounds going on in the street – and Martine's more fleeting experience of them '*par instants, au passage*'. But both these things are situated in the realm of 'reality', rather than fantasy or thought. This move back into the here-and-now is associated with the marked shift from subjective experience to objective observation. While the whole of the first paragraph either came from Martine's perspective or related her interior monologue, in this paragraph for the first time the narration comes from an external, detached point of view. The present tenses in this section all refer to what is actually happening: '*Les deux jeunes filles roulent* . . .', '*le soleil est au zénith, il brûle* . . .', '*l'air frais n'arrive pas à* . . .', '*l'espèce de sommeil qui pèse sur le goudron de la rue* . . .', '*Martine entend par instants* . . .', '*[les] postes de télévision qui parlent tout seuls* . . .', '*Il y a une voix d'homme, et de la musique qui résonne bizarrement* . . .'.

Contrasting associations: word meaning and sound patterning

The worlds constructed through the different voices have conflicting associations. The 'real' experience of riding a moped and the 'fantasy' of riding a motorbike, both related to Martine's subjective point of view, are associated with freedom, speed and lightness. More threatening themes of stagnation and oppression are associated with the objective description in the second paragraph. Three clear descriptions of the riding experience can be identified in the first paragraph, the first two relating to the reality of the moped, the third to the fantasy of the motorbike:

1   *Peut-être que les vibrations du vélomoteur, l'odeur et la chaleur des gaz ont empli tout le creux qu'il y avait en elle.*
2   *Elle aime se faufiler entre les autos, la tête tournée de côté pour ne pas respirer le vent, et aller vite!*
3   *. . . sur sa grosse moto Guzzi, en train de foncer à toute vitesse dans la rue vide. Elle sent le poids du vent sur son visage, quand elle est accrochée à deux mains au corps du garçon, et le vertige des virages où la terre bascule, comme en avion.*

These three descriptions are striking in their appeal to the senses, to the physical experience of riding a motorbike or moped. In sentence 1, the description of '*les vibrations du vélomoteur, l'odeur et la chaleur des gaz*' sets the pattern, describing the experience by appealing to physical sensations and the sense of smell. Reference to the body continues in sentence 2, with the description of Martine liking to ride '*la tête tournée de côté pour ne pas respirer le vent, et aller vite!*'. The foregrounding of the adverb *vite*, through the exclamation mark and its final position in the sentence as a short complement breaking the *loi de longueur*, suggests that Martine has a particular attraction to the feeling of speed associated with this experience. These characteristics are mirrored in sentence 3. The theme of speed is continued with *'en train de foncer à toute vitesse dans la rue vide'*. Physical references persist: the experience of having a strong wind in your face is described again in *'Elle sent le poids du vent sur son visage'*, and there are more references to parts of the body, Martine being *'accrochée à deux mains au corps du garçon'*. In addition, the giddy feelings of turning at speed are evoked through the second complement of the verb *sentir*: *'et le vertige des virages où la terre bascule'*, foregrounded (as has been already pointed out) by the deviant sentence structure, and also by the phonetic patterns to which it contributes. This is a metaphorical use of language, transferring the motion from the motorbike to the earth – it is the *'terre'* that *'bascule'*, rather than Martine herself. The metaphor both reinforces the physicality of the experience and creates an identity between this natural landscape and Martine's fantasy experience, which contrasts with the strong distinction that is made between her subjective experiences and the urban environment through which she is actually riding.

The three descriptions are linked by strong phonetic patterns. In the first, the repetitions of /v/ and particularly /œr/ onomatopoeically evoke the purring of an engine; this is recalled in the strong /v/-initial patterns of the third description: *'vitesse'*, *'vide'*, *'vent'*, *'visage'*, *'vertige'*, *'virages'*, and in the /gr/ /s/ and /z/ of *'sa grosse moto Guzzi'*. These /v/-initial patterns are also linked by the strong /vi/-initial pattern of four of the six words, recalled with the /i/ of *'vertige'*, with the three final words linked through /v/ /i/ and /ʒ/; in fact *'visage'* and *'virages'* have only one phonetic difference. Both the /v/ and /ʒ/ phonemes as fricatives evoke the buzzing of an engine. The second description, while still strong in fricatives, particularly /v/ and /f/: *'faufiler'*, *'vent'*, *'vite'*, is also characterised by rhythmic patterns of stop consonants in /t/, /p/ and /d/, which add a 'jumpy' rhythm reflecting the semantic associations of *faufiler*: *'se faufiler entre les autos, la tête tournée de côté pour ne pas respirer le vent'*. Martine is drawing on the 'real' experience of riding a moped through the streets with her friend in imagining the 'fantasy' experience of riding a powerful motorbike through a natural setting. The many stylistic links between the two descriptions reinforce this connection between the 'real' situation of riding a moped through the streets and the fantasy of riding a motorbike in a more empty and natural setting (*'rue vide'*, *'virages où la terre bascule'*).

Both the 'real' and the fantasy riding experiences, written from Martine's perspective, are contrasted with the oppression associated with the urban environment, described as outlined above in a more objective voice. Both these paragraphs finish with a simile – *'comme en avion'* and *'comme dans une grotte'*. These similes are foregrounded rhythmically, through breaking the *loi de longueur*, through their paragraph-final position, and through the direct contrast between them. Each sums up the themes of the paragraph in which they are located. The comparison with an aeroplane brings together ideas of speed, noise, freedom and movement, while the cave simile evokes darkness, stillness and oppression.

Where riding was characterised by the freedom of the wind, the street they are riding along is oppressed by the weight of the sun: '*Le soleil est au zénith, il brûle, et l'air frais n'arrive pas à dissiper l'espèce de sommeil qui pèse sur le goudron de la rue et sur le ciment des trottoirs*'. Stillness and oppression are indicated by '*sommeil*' and '*pèse*'. The words '*goudron*' and '*ciment*' evoke hard, dull, dead man-made substances in grey and black colours, in contrast with the natural living '*terre*' at the end of the first paragraph. The noise of the mopeds is contrasted with '*le sommeil de la rue*', with the echoing sounds of the televisions coming from the flats around only serving to underline the overall silence, particularly as these noises are character-ised as being '*tout seuls*'. There is a sense of menace in this description, underlined by the implicit threat of the verbs '*brûle*' and '*pèse*'. This recalls the first sentence: '*Maintenant qu'elle roule, Martine ne ressent plus la peur à l'intérieur de son corps.*' These associations are reinforced by the metaphorical reference to fear as '*le creux qu'il y avait en elle*' in the first paragraph, which is recalled with the '*grotte*' simile that has similar associations of hollowness and emptiness.

In addition to being a strong indicator of the change in voice, the sentence structure also contributes to the atmosphere of oppression. The second sentence of the final paragraph is based on a ternary structure which respects the *loi de longueur;* but it does so in a rather exaggerated way. The final element is prolonged and complex, including a relative clause: '*qui pèse sur le goudron de la rue et sur le ciment des trottoirs*'. This completion of a ternary structure by a binary structure has the effect of foregrounding the two final complements, '*sur le goudron de la rue et sur le ciment des trottoirs*', emphasising again the urban character of the environ-ment. These are both complements of the verb '*pèse*', and the foregrounding of the double complement underlines the all-encompassing nature of this oppres-sion. In the same paragraph, there is a repetition of the word '*sommeil*': '*l'espèce de sommeil qui pèse . . . dans le sommeil de la rue*', which foregrounds the theme of drowsiness that is contrasted with the speed, noise and vibrancy of the riding experience.

Constructions of fantasy and reality

There is therefore a distinction in this text between the voice used in the objective description of the 'real' events being described in the text and that used when recounting Martine's subjective experiences. The differences in register between these two voices are signalled through distinctive features of sentence structure and lexis. While Martine's experiences and her fantasy world are associated with freedom, speed and lightness, the objective voice of the narrator describes a textually 'real' world of oppressive heat and stagnation. Martine escapes this threatening reality through the ephemeral physical pleasures of riding a moped which open the door to a fantasy world of freedom and exhilaration. However, the distinction made between fantasy and reality in this text suggests that this escape can only be temporary, and that the 'real' situation will eventually gain the upper hand. This extract is characteristic of the short story from which it has been taken, in which accounts of Martine's own experiences alternate with representations of the threatening reality of the outside world. The two eventually come together in a tragic conclusion.

The text is primarily a piece of literary fiction, which manipulates different layers of the 'real'. Although, as fiction, it is constructing an imaginary world, it deals with topics and environments which are the stuff of daily debate. By providing a window into Martine's subjectivity, the text resists the dominant tendency to objectify the youth of the suburbs. At the same time, however, the distinction between the real and fantasy worlds underlines the fact that her subjective experiences of freedom are temporary. The objective reality of the urban environment ultimately offers this young girl no prospect of escape or personal fulfilment. Paradoxically, through this representation, the text colludes with the widely held perception that life in the *banlieues* is without hope.

Jean-Marie Le Clézio, *La Ronde et Autres Faits Divers*, Paris: Gallimard, 1982, pp. 15–16.

1 Maintenant qu'elle roule, Martine ne ressent plus la peur à l'intérieur de son
2 corps. Peut-être que les vibrations du vélomoteur, l'odeur et la chaleur des gaz
3 ont empli tout le creux qu'il y avait en elle. Martine aime bien rouler en vélomo-
4 teur, surtout quand il y a beaucoup de soleil et que l'air n'est pas froid, comme
5 aujourd'hui. Elle aime se faufiler entre les autos, la tête tournée de côté pour ne
6 pas respirer le vent, et aller vite ! Titi a eu de la chance, c'est son frère qui lui a
7 donné son vélomoteur, enfin, pas exactement donné ; il attend que Titi ait un peu
8 d'argent pour le payer. Le frère de Titi, ce n'est pas comme la plupart des
9 garçons. C'est un type bien, qui sait ce qu'il veut, qui ne passe pas son temps à
10 raconter des salades comme les autres, juste pour se faire valoir. Martine ne pense
11 pas vraiment à lui, mais juste quelques secondes c'est comme si elle était avec lui,
12 sur sa grosse moto Guzzi, en train de foncer à toute vitesse dans la rue vide. Elle
13 sent le poids du vent sur son visage, quand elle est accrochée à deux mains au
14 corps du garçon, et le vertige des virages où la terre bascule, comme en avion.
15
16 Les deux jeunes filles roulent le long du trottoir, vers l'ouest. Le soleil est au
17 zénith, il brûle, et l'air frais n'arrive pas à dissiper l'espèce de sommeil qui pèse
18 sur le goudron de la rue et sur le ciment des trottoirs. Les magasins sont fermés,
19 les rideaux de fer sont baissés, et cela accentue encore l'impression de torpeur.
20 Malgré le bruit des vélomoteurs, Martine entend par instants, au passage, le
21 glouglou des postes de télévision qui parlent tout seuls au premier étage des
22 immeubles. Il y a une voix d'homme, et de la musique qui résonne bizarrement
23 dans le sommeil de la rue, comme dans une grotte.

For the original format, see page 120.

Adverts as discourse

David Steel

Advertising is an increasingly pervasive – and persuasive – factor in contemporary Western European life; indeed, in the life of all capitalist economies. Communist economies have used it chiefly in the form of political poster propaganda. In the West it has developed, through the century, from simple sales aid into mass-communication medium, artform and main financial prop of the press, radio and television. Adverts, whether as elements in consumerist culture or as elements of discourse, display uniquely complicated features when compared to those exhibited by text alone.

The discourse displayed in an advert may be uniquely linguistic, whether oral (a radio plug) or textual (a newspaper small ad), but will more often also contain one or more iconographical components – images whose meaning is more or less subtly interlinked with that of the text. It is not rare for text itself – decorative lettering, shaped typography – to be used to iconographic ends as design. Many, if not most, adverts are then icono-textual constructs which are often further complicated by music (radio jingles) or by music and drama (TV ads). In the latter instance, visuality and aurality are simultaneously involved in our perception. With many adverts we are not far from, have indeed gone well beyond, Wagner's notion of total art, though, while involving artwork, adverts are far less gratuitous than works of art *per se*. Where some adverts are concerned (for example, the impregnated page of a magazine perfume ad), the sense of smell or the sense of touch (a sample of material stuck to an ad), may be also invoked. Clever adverts may even bring into play synaesthetic (cross-sensory) perceptions. The sense of taste alone seems (notwithstanding the BT ad which claimed that the telephone 'licks stamps') not to have been appropriated by Adland.

Adverts are equally polyvalent in their mode of appearance. Whereas a literary text is usually restricted to the page of a book or magazine, the support media for adverts are multifarious and can include, apart from instances mentioned above, hot-air balloons, T-shirt fronts, hoardings, jeans pockets, the Eiffel Tower, loo paper . . . name it and an ad has probably appeared on it.

In addition, their relation to the concept of authorship is unusual. While a clever advertising slogan may have been devised in a flash of inspiration by a single individual, that person will not be named or known outside a small group of professionals. More often it will be the result of dialogue or of group work, and its integration into the ad as a whole will also involve the designers of the artwork. It follows that an advert usually has no single author and even as the product of a team its agency source will generally not be known outside the industry. Unlike many French TV ads, few other adverts ascribe themselves to agencies of origin.

Adverts often also stand in a special relationship to the viewer or reader. Unlike a novel, a poem or a letter read in private, poster adverts displayed in the street, bus shelters or public transport constitute a form of public language, simultaneously read by the crowd, and their historical origins are to be found in early legal or public-order proclamations nailed up in the street. Hoarding displays thus have affinities with road or directional signs whose authoritarian overtones advertisers are no doubt not dissatisfied to think infiltrate into their creations. *Serrez à droite, Circulez lentement* . . . , *Buvez Contrexéville, Achetez Renault* . . . – imperative forms of the verb are common to traffic signs and to adverts.

A particular feature of advertising discourse, far removed from a crudely imperative appeal, is its subtlety, even deviousness, of linguistic strategy – required in order to deflect reader resistance to the hard sell and allow its persuasive message to succeed. Much meaning in an advert may well be indirect, implied or coded, written, or rather not written, between the lines. The positing by Freud of the notion of a subconscious, whereby we are susceptible, without being aware of it, to certain message patterns, led eventually to filmic experiments in subliminal advertising, since banned. There remain, however, multiple opportunities for clever copywriters to have a subtext, a sort of ghost discourse that haunts and doubles for the printed text, clandestinely infiltrating itself behind the overtly stated discourse of the advert.

There is also a particular way in which advert texts are comparable to poetic texts. Both, for different reasons, are attracted into the use of language in compressed form. Poetic compression makes for heightened, headier meaning, which absorbs a sense of lyrical urgency and emotional power. The advertising text, to be effective on its own terms, aims for a message of similar intensity but is driven to it for propagandistic and economic reasons as well. Advertising space is extremely expensive. The more one can express in the least space, the more cost-effective is the advert. One example of the end result of such demanding linguistic economics is the slogan – a combination of meaningfulness and brevity. Advertisers' fondness for puns or similar wordplays, where a double meaning is elicited through the use of a single term, is understandable within this context. Many (if not all) of the rhetorical devices of poetry and persuasive prose – assonance, alliteration, rhyme, repetition, inversion, etc. – will also be exploited by the advert.

The advert, then, is an anonymous, multi media, icono-textual artefact, subject to unusual viewer/reader reception, which works towards a specific response – the purchase of whatever consumer good it is advertising. To this end, usually with a blend of informational and persuasive material, a mix of the real and the ideal, it will deploy a variety of seductive strategies, a rhetoric of text and image, directed towards converting the viewer into a purchaser. It is real-world action discourse, but with a seductive intent which in no way debars it from playful use of pun, poetry or dream as part of its charm campaign. It is in short both instructional, purposeful and ludic, a peculiarly hybrid, shape-shifter form of discourse.

*

The nature of an advert, its size, tone, layout and style will be determined by the medium in which it appears – its *support*. The first advert under scrutiny here appeared in *Madame Figaro* a weekly, glossy, middle-market colour magazine associated with the conservative, middlebrow daily newspaper *Le Figaro*, which no longer perpetuates the subversive impertinence of its namesake born in the eighteenth-century plays of Pierre de Beaumarchais. *Madame Figaro*, as its title implies, is a magazine aimed at a female readership, which never excludes a minority of flick-through male glancers. A stereotypical reader of *Madame Figaro* will be a reasonably well-off, conservative-ish, urban woman aged between 25 and 45.

The advert for women's shoes made by *Arche* appeared in late March 1988 and is thus time-targeted to women who, in spring, think of renewing their summer footwear. A consumer product that is subject to the shifts of fashion, as are most products – especially clothing, ones – will necessarily have to be seen within the context of *la mode du jour*. In retrospection, colour and style can lose their appeal . . . or, eventually, regain it. Adverts, like poems or other cultural artefacts, may be viewed both within and without their contemporary sociocultural environment.

This advert consists of an uncluttered mixture of textual and pictorial components on a white ground which generously separates and highlights the various elements. This is not an ad that is visually busy, and its cool elegance is designed to reflect the chic French simplicity of the product. Spacing, it is important to remember, while it may seem semantically neutral, is nonetheless a dynamic in the conveyance of meaning, in the same way that what is not said in a novel – *les silences du récit* – can be as load-bearing for our understanding of the novel as what is said.

Reading vertically, the arrangement of text and picture is more or less alternate and distinct, with the exception of the yellow '*arche*' label, where the stylish lettering seems to be framed in a gilded picture of its own, one of a number of devices by which this element in the advert is foregrounded. Although these are by far the largest letters in the ad (well over 50 point), it is the headline and, simultaneously, the main picture that attract our attention. As we read the top title we also easily see the main picture, though we cannot – note the optical

Dans la jungle des villes,
la loi du plus souple est toujours la meilleure.

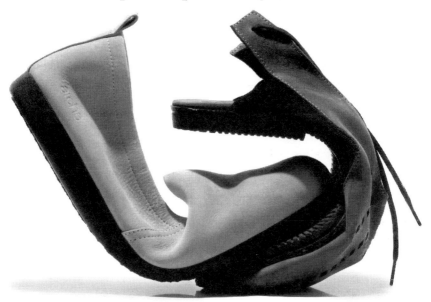

DANS L'ENFER DU BITUME, DE L'ASPHALTE ET DU MACADAM, IL Y A DES JOURS OÙ IL FAIT

BON AVOIR LES PIEDS SUR TERRE. JE MARCHE EN COULEURS, TU MARCHES TRÈS MODE,

ELLE MARCHE SOUPLESSE, NOUS MARCHONS ARCHE. ARCHE, TOUT LE CONFORT MODERNE.

•

LISTE DES POINTS DE VENTE SUR DEMANDE. SHOWROOM ARCHE:

13, RUE DES INNOCENTS, 75001 PARIS - TEL. (1) 45.08.19.45.

PARIS / NEW-YORK / DUSSELDORF / BRUXELLES / LONDRES / TOKYO

Source: L'Arche: an *Arche* shoes advert, *Madame Figaro*, 29 March 1988. Reproduced with kind permission of Arche, Madame Figaro and SC&A, Paris.

difference – read the title, even less the middle section of text, if we focus on the main picture itself.

The main picture is unusual and something of a puzzle: a pair, but not a pair, of conjoined pink and green shoes bizarrely and impossibly (without support) bent in some form of engagement. It falls into the category of enigma pictures, a technique beloved of advertisers since the early 1970s, and borrowed from those used by Dadaist or Surrealist artists, first to arrest the attention of the viewer by the visual mystery, and second, to solicit viewer participation by tempting them to resolve it. Two shoes dancing, embracing, fighting, making love? The title may hold the clue to the picture puzzle, one way in which text and image here work inseparably – as the shoes seem to be doing – together.

In a sentence of fourteen words where feminine articles – (fitting for a women's shoe ad) predominate, and which includes the superlatives so common in advertising language, '*Dans la jungle des villes, la loi du plus souple est toujours la meilleure*' establishes two analogies, one by an oxymoron metaphor – that cities are akin to jungles – and one by statement – that in them flexibility is equivalent to the highest behaviour value. The image of modern urban life as a jungle originated, with the largely unregulated and rapid expansion of London and Paris, in the popular novel of the mid-nineteenth century such as Eugène Sue's *Les Mystères de Paris* (1842–1843), and has since become a cliché (cf. the films *The Asphalt Jungle* (1950) and *The Blackboard Jungle* (1955)). Clichés are forms of conceptual or linguistic repetition and adverts can afford to resort to them as recognition devices. The city is a stressful, dangerous (and, in summer, hot) environment, where there is competition for space and life resources and where predators can lurk. The advert is drawing on the *imaginaire* of animal life, where flexibility or adaptability is the key to survival. Both language and picture are here indisputably evoking another mid-nineteenth-century text, more seminal than Sue's, – namely, Charles Darwin's *Origin of Species* (1859) with its notions of 'natural selection', 'the struggle for life' and the 'survival of the fittest', that the species which survive are those that prove most adaptable to shifting environmental conditions. The Darwinian echo in this advert, imperceptible to the uncultured reader, is however overlaid, for the French viewer, with another cultural reference, at once more distant and more accessible. Amongst the earliest textual representations of animal life that French children still today encounter at primary school are the *Fables* of La Fontaine (1688, Livre I, 10), one of the best known of which, '*Le Loup et l'Agneau*', has as first line '*La raison du plus fort est toujours la meilleure*', on which the second line of the advert title is clearly calqued. There is, of course, a direct link between shoes and animals; quality shoes are still made from the animal skin we know as leather.

Embracing, dancing, making love, perhaps – and polyvalent decipherings are plausible – but the picture may primarily be read as fighting shoe-animals caught in the struggle for survival, an act which allows the flexibility of the product, (particularly in the case of the green shoe), to be visibly demonstrated. Pink and green (*Le Rose et le Vert* was a less successful novel by Stendhal), the only colours – with yellow, white and black – used in this advert, are perhaps evocative of jungle scenery – jungle green and the bright pink of plumage, petal or fruit. Is the pink shoe a fish, a tongue, a phallus, in the process of being clamped in the teeth that are the serrated sole of the crocodile-like creature with raised green eyes or ears? Crocodile skin, one remembers, is or was a raw material for upmarket footwear. Whatever the case may be, in conformity with the message it is the suppler of the two shoes which appears to be getting the better of the bout.

Or are we viewing a sculpture for which the text beneath it serves as plinth or platform, just as the tarmac surface serves as platform for the shoed woman shopper wearily walking the warm street? For our eye moves now to the smaller-print text (the black macadam-layered pavement?) immediately below the main picture, helped to do so by the direction of the laces of the green shoe (though crocodiles don't have manes), just as the heel tag of the pink shoe serves as deliberate pointer between picture and top text.

The heat and danger of the jungle are now cross-referenced to those of hell – '*l'enfer du bitume*' – not so much *The Asphalt Jungle* as the tarmac hell, '*bitume*', '*asphalte*' and '*macadam*' being all, like '*jungle*' (Hindi *jangl*), exotic terms of Latin, Greek and Scottish origin respectively, but of virtually identical meaning (repetition again) all of which evoke, as to some degree does *jungle*, blackness. T.S. Eliot's *Waste Land* lines (1963, I, 62–63), inspired by those of Dante's *Inferno* (III, 55–57), spring to mind: 'A crowd flowed over London Bridge, so many, / I had not thought death had undone so many'. But the hell and discomfort of hot city streetwalking is alleviated by a joke *double entendre* (and, naturally, by the wearing of *Arche* shoes) since *avoir les pieds sur terre* means both to be a down-to-earth sort of person and literally to have one's feet on the ground. Walking for which, as the song nearly says, these shoes are made, becomes the insistent theme of the next sentence, as the verb *marcher* is simply but tellingly conjugated in the present tense, so evoking the physical act of doing it. Not all persons of the verb are present, however – for reasons of space and economy perhaps, but arguably more for reasons of clever psychological strategy. The male third persons *il/ils* are omitted, since the product is for women, *vous* is neglected probably as too formal compared with the companionable '*tu*', and *elles* (plural), given the previous '*elle*' (singular), is dropped as superfluous and so that the list can end on the collective in-group companionship of '*nous*'. Purchase *Arche* shoes and – a common advertising appeal to social vanity and peer-group pressure – elevate yourself to the select group of one of us. The conjugation of the verb legitimises its repetition. Furthermore, and most ingeniously, each repeated use of the verb *marcher* allows the repeated use of the crucial phoneme *arche* consolidated in the final '*nous marchons Arche*' and recapitulated, with the first word of the sentence reprising the last word of the previous one, in '*Arche, tout le confort moderne*'. In five words, both up-to-date chic and traditional comfort are claimed as the qualities of the brand.

The dislocated syntax in evidence in the middle sentence here is of special interest. Whereas '*Je marche en couleurs*' is semantically but not grammatically odd, and also lyrically beautiful (reminiscent of Byron's 'She walks in beauty, like the night'), '*tu marches très mode*' is grammatically quite unconventional since the noun '*mode*' is here used singly as an adverb for *à la mode*, just as, even more blatantly, in '*elle marche souplesse*', the noun '*souplesse*' is used adverbially, a markedly transgressive use of language in terms of grammatical norms, but increasingly common in popular space-pressured registers such as news headlines and advertisements. Transgression, as in human behaviour, can be, and in adverts *is*, a strategy for drawing attention to oneself, which adverts not only need to do but have as their *raison d'être*. Here, grammatical dissent slants the language to the colourful level of the picture above, whose pictorial distortion had already announced the linguistic twists that were to follow. 'Incorrect' or deviant syntax or, more often, spelling (cf. 'Beanz meanz Heinz') are part of the fun/surprise tactics of the composition of advertisements.

The typographical variety of the print used is noticeable both in size and style, capitals and small letters and, with exceptions, print size is seen generally to diminish as we move down the page. Compared to the persuasive and even poetically unconventional language used so far, the even smaller print below the bullet point is soberly informational in its listing of the *Arche* Parisian showroom address and phone number. Note, however, the snobbish anglicism of '*showroom*' as well as the classy central Paris address, a classiness equally apparent in the global list of chic, cosmopolitan cities which constitutes the bottom line (the placing of the city names here is determined by the number of letters in the name – shortest to longest working in from both margins). Above this latter we have a repeated image of the pink and green shoe, but this time in realistic pose, as we would wish to see them conventionally on the showroom shelf. For variety's and balance's sake, they are shown pointing in opposite directions, which is how a pair of shoes is fitted into a shoe box. That we do not have a pair here tallies with shop display practice, where, for security reasons, only single shoes are presented. In this miniaturised partial-repeat picture the advert demonstrates that, for the potential customer, the recognition factor is important, all the more so as the larger picture of the green shoe hardly displays a recognisable product.

The layout of the advert on the page is centralised. Both picture and text are equally balanced on either side of an invisible line dividing the page centrally from top to bottom and which would transfix the word '*jungle*' and twice (immediately above the bullet point) the word '*arche*'; these two words being arguably the most important in the advert – the one naming the product, the other stating the governing idea of the metaphorical device. The elegant and comfortable equilibrium of this centralised *mise en page* is broken twice; partly, in the first instance, by the contorted act of the shoes (though these are centralised), wholly by the yellow-grounded brand name of '*arche*' at the bottom right, which is pointed to by the laces of both green shoes and which almost seems attached, as if it were a brand-name tag or label, to the laces of the small green shoe. It might also seem reminiscent of a cardboard shoebox. The bottom right corner of a magazine advert, particularly of a righthand-page one, is a psychologically sensitized area. Written languages of western European origin are visually scanned top to bottom and left to right, which renders the bottom righthand corner the last point focused on by the eye before the page is turned. In adverts, especially magazine ones, the brand name of the advertised product is habitually situated in this optically loaded righthand corner (righthand-page ads cost more than lefthand ones). The *Arche* name, already reproduced elsewhere in the ad nine times, is thus significantly foregrounded by, not only its visually critical position, but its separate lettering style (note the arch-shaped 'h'), largest lettering size, being the only example of tilted text and being printed over the only instance of yellow-gold used – gold, with its connotations of scarcity and wealth, being expressive of high value (cf. gold card, Gold Blend, golden handshake, etc.).

This ultimate emphasis on the term '*Arche*' reminds us that '*arche*' is the common noun meaning 'arch', hinted at in the convex/concave shapes of the bigger shoes and evocative of numerous elegant architectural structures in Paris from bridges to monuments, the most recent of which is *l'Arche de la Défense* known as *La Grande Arche* (some earlier famous triumphal examples have *arche* abbreviated to *arc* as in *Arc de Triomphe*). English readers may associate the word 'arch' with the instep of the foot, an image not used in French, which speaks of *la voûte plantaire*. More pointedly perhaps, the optimum-value implications of the word '*arche*' are in evidence in *L'Arche de l'Alliance* (the Ark of the Covenant) and, equally biblical, but more apposite to this advertisement, *L'Arche de Noé* (Noah's Ark), with its connotations of animals, safety and protection of species and, more generally, since Noah learned how to adapt to a harshly changing environment, of survival in a hard world. The rainbow arch, interpreted biblically as the divine promise of no further Flood, is, in French, *l'arc-en-ciel*.

Behind its apparent simple elegance, the linguistic and pictorial strategies of this advert are complex and subtle, as well as being tightly interlinked. Though not a high-involvement product (*un produit impliquant*), *Arche* shoes, 'sensible', cool but chic, are not cheap. They are being marketed here to *Madame Figaro* women readers who, caught up in the game of high-street capitalist consumerism, are flatteringly urged to see themselves as the elegant and flexible-minded winners in the war of the pavement world, where the purchase of *Arche* shoes brings the promise of survival. Nor is the wearing of pretty footwear a drawback in other combats where all is fair, an inference hardly present in this ad (in which women's legs – and indeed the word *chaussure* itself – are noticeably absent), except perhaps indirectly through an erotic reading of the main picture. Let us not forget, either,

that in the very act of advertising its product here the firm Arche is itself engaged
in the jungle combat of capitalism, this very advert a weapon in its fight against
rival manufacturers of women's shoes. '*La loi du plus souple est toujours la meilleure*'
– La Fontaine's moral and Darwinian theory apply equally as well to the hard
human world of commerce as to the animal kingdom.

*

We turn now to an advert for a banking product placed on behalf of Paris-based
banks and using the beauty and charms of Paris to persuade a largely Parisian-
based potential clientele. The title of the magazine in which this advert appeared,
L'Etudiant, is clear evidence of the precise market the advert is targeting: students,
whether they be in the upper levels of secondary school or already at university
and, possibly, more widely, young people in general between the ages of 16 and
22. The start of the academic year is an appropriate time at which to target
students. Nowhere in the advert, it will be noticed, is the word *étudiant* to be seen,
the less restrictive '*les jeunes*' being used instead (but once only).

Like most magazine adverts, it traditionally combines, in a mixture of black and
white and colour, textual and pictorial elements which supportively lock into each
other's meaning. The product advertised is a *Union de Banques à Paris* bank account
for young people, *Le Compte Basique*, whose phonetic near-equivalence to the
French-pronounced name of the well-known jazz musician Count Basie, popular
in France, is perhaps a coincidence. Product names, as is perhaps most obvious
with the names of models of cars, are an important element of marketing strategy.
As a neologism, the adjective '*basique*' may well have appeal for the young. In use
since the Renaissance as a chemical, geological and technical term, it is only in
recent decades that it has acquired the meaning, from English, of 'elementary' or
'fundamental'. Neither the late nineteenth-century *Littré*, nor the 1966 *Robert*, nor
surprisingly the most recent and complete *Trésor de la Langue Française* (CNRS
1971–1994) dictionaries include this new meaning of *basique*. Only the 1970
Supplément of the *Robert*, quoting a 1953 occurrence in Jacques Perret's novel
Bâtons dans les Roues, includes it as such and as a neologism. With the managers of
the account promoted being the '*Banques à Paris*', it might also be noted that
'*basique*' has a curious aural affinity both with the word '*banque*' (through its first
and last consonants) and with the word '*Paris*' (through its two vowels), being a
sort of slightly deformed phonetic fusion of the two words.

Under the title which, in soberly informational fashion, is the product name,
we read a text, in four lines of variable length, which evokes childhood and
adolescent habits of acquiring, managing or saving money by, respectively, piggy
bank, savings book or Saturday-night pouting pleas to mother or father for pocket
money. This first section of text includes no complete sentences with direct verbs,
but is one long construction using repeated syntactical inversion that allows the

LE COMPTE BASIQUE

**Oubliées les tirelires,
dépassés les livrets d'Epargne,
terminées les moues quémandeuses des adolescents
du samedi soir !**

Un véritable compte bancaire.
Un chéquier bien à soi.
Une carte de retrait d'espèces.
...... des services identiques à ceux proposés aux adultes.

**Avec l'Union de Banques à Paris :
accédez au monde bancaire
gagnez votre autonomie financière
en un mot, devenez responsable de votre argent.**

Aujourd'hui, les jeunes les plus exigeants ont
déjà ouvert leur propre COMPTE BASIQUE.

Vous aussi, rejoignez la banque des battants !

Union de Banques à Paris

22 place de la Madeleine Tél. (1) 42.68.33.33

Source: *Le Compte Basique*: an advert for *Le Compte Basique* of *L'Union de Banques à Paris*, *L'Etudiant*, October 1990. Reproduced with kind permission of *L'Etudiant* and *L'Union de Banques à Paris*, which, since 1998, has discontinued 'Le Compte Basique', designed for the 1980s, updating and restyling it for 16- to 25-year olds as 'Jeunes'.

verb *être* to be omitted. In an emphatic verbal phrase structure which, unlike French, English cannot replicate by use of an initial past participle ('*Oubliées les tirelires*' would have to be rendered either by 'Goodbye piggy banks' or an imperative 'Forget piggy banks'), the use of three '-*er*' verbs allows for further emphatic reiteration through the internal rhyme of the past-participle endings, internal rhyme being present also in '*tirelire*'. Added emphasis is signalled by the use of the exclamation mark. The use of these past participles of three different verbs – but which each have related meanings of 'forgotten', 'outdated' or 'finished' – as the first words of the first three lines deliberately accentuates a sense of outmodedness as though, paradoxically, the habits of youth are devalued as old. There is a resonance of this complex understanding of the new as old (i.e. childhood as old-fashioned) in the image that underscores this section, which shows one of the most beautiful and the oldest of Paris bridges, still however known by the name of *Le Pont-Neuf*. Shortly after this advert appeared, it was raised to cult status amongst the young with Leos Carax's costly cinematographic avant-garde failure *Les Amants du Pont-Neuf* (1991).

Whereas this initial section of text is of purely persuasive character, playing on the desire of the child or adolescent to achieve adulthood, the haste to be grown-up, the four lines of text immediately below the image of the bridge, with the exception, perhaps, of the loaded adjective '*véritable*', are largely informational, outlining the facilities included in the product advertised – a bank account, a personalised cheque book, a cash card – identical services to those offered to adults. Each of the three items has a line devoted to itself, with the fourth line summarising that these are the same facilities as those available to grown-ups, a line which plays on the same feelings as those exploited in the earlier section of text, the desire of the young to acquire the trappings of maturity.

Again, as with the previous text, nouns predominate and no direct verb is used. The only verbal form is yet another past participle, '*proposés*', but here delayed until the end of the section. Where the first three lines of the earlier text each began with a repeated -*er* verb past participle, the first three lines of this second section each begin with a repeated indefinite article, a part of speech avoided in the earlier passage, which was strongly characterised by the definite article. In this second section we see four noun phrases each terminating in a full stop (the third of which, after '*espèces*', and preceding the suspension dots, is superfluous if not erroneous), which allows the use of the following emphatic capital letter of the indefinite article.

There are, then, lexical and syntactical distinctions, as well as differences in function and tone, to be made between the text below the picture of the bridge and the text above it. The latter makes dismissive reference to money matters of childhood; the former points forcefully to the financial advantages that adulthood can bring. It is to underline these distinctions that the main pictorial element in the advert comes into play. The separating factor between these two ages is marked and symbolised by the image of the bridge, which, on the page, cuts off the past from the present and the future that is promised by the product advertised. The carriageway supported by *le Pont-Neuf* draws a line under childhood. Linking riverbank to riverbank, the bridge spans the divide between the past of the juvenile and the dawning world of adulthood. The sun filtering through the arches offers the promise of the new in appropriately coin-shaped discs of light.

A third section of text, again in four lines and, like the first section, in bold type, now marshals a triple battery of forceful forward-looking imperatives that negate the retrospection of the past participles of section one and urge the viewer to present or future action by acquiring the product. The central rhyming couplet – '*bancaire*'/'*financière*' – adds resonance to the exhortative message. Freedom is the prize to be won, in the shape of financial independence, which flatteringly assumes the purchaser's sense of responsibility, although one does not purchase a bank account in quite the same sense as one buys a pair of shoes. Access to the banking world is offered by the *Union de Banques à Paris*, the advertiser, named here for the first time. The more formal *vous* form of address is chosen, perhaps to cast the net wide for all young people, perhaps because we are in the sober world of banking and more particularly of French banking, less informal, less user-friendly than its British counterpart.

A final line of persuasive text, in bold, brings a last fourth imperative into play, in the same way as a fourth past participle had been added earlier, '*rejoignez la banque des battants*' with alliteration and assonance equally displayed in the last three words. '*Battants*' (go-getters/whiz-kids) is the only term in the advert whose register – slang – leans towards the colloquial everyday language of the young. Its positioning as last word (before an exclamation mark that repeats the one used after the first section of text) conveys upon it an especially emphatic function. The '*Vous aussi*' refers back to the two previous lines, in roman lettering, claiming, questionably, that the most demanding – note the superlative – young people have already opened their '*COMPTE BASIQUE*', the capital letters of which here reprise those of the same words in the title, the only examples of capitals used in the advert. The psychological strategy at work is commonplace: conform with the practice of the elite in order to become a member of it, the elite naturally being defined as the product purchasers. The fashionable up-to-dateness of the practice is underscored by the '*Aujourd'hui*' (whose sense of the present gives the lie to the past participles used at the outset) and the '*déjà*' used respectively at the head of the two lines.

The logo, a miniaturised and stylised version of the main image, using two-tone silhouette shapes framed in a small square, precedes the underlined name of the advertiser, in bold and slightly larger lettering, before the address and telephone number. The logo design is emblematic of two notions – that of Paris and that of union – the bridge being the structure which unites separate banks, crosses a divide and allows passage to and fro. In both logo and main picture, the bridge and its reflection appear to form a chain whose rounded links are shaped by the arches. Links between banks and cooperation between different areas of Paris is thus symbolised. The logo offers a stylised view of the *Pont-Neuf*, differently orientated from the one in the main picture, and seen outlined against the shapes of *Notre-Dame* and the dome of the *Panthéon*, a deliberate mock-up which symbolically evokes the imposing heart of the ancient city. The main photographic image, on the other hand, hazily romantic in its autumnal shading, is a more realistic photographic reproduction of the *Pont-Neuf*, perhaps the loveliest of Paris bridges, on which Laurence Sterne commented, in his *Sentimental Journey Through France and Italy* (1768), that it was 'the noblest, the finest, the grandest, the lightest, the longest, the broadest that ever conjoined land and land together upon the face of the terraqeous globe'. Or, more particularly, it is a photograph of that half of the bridge which links the extreme end of the *Ile de la Cité* to the *Rive Droite* and was originally so built to allow the commercial extension of the constricted *Cité* to the northern side of the Seine, ever since associated with finance and commerce, the *Rive Gauche*, on the other hand, still being traditionally associated with student life and the arts. Fittingly, the advert under review aims to introduce students to the financial world, bridging the different associations of the two *rives*. The solidity, tranquillity and tradition connoted by the picture are suitable qualities for a bank to advertise itself by.

Banks desire to project an image of economic soundness and solidity. '*Se porter comme le Pont-Neuf*' is a French expression meaning 'to be in robust health'. The balanced calm of the whole advert is therefore particularly appropriate for the promotion of a banking product – one speaks of bank balance and financial equilibrium – and is deliberately generated by the page layout and design. Just as scarcely a ripple breaks the surface of the placid Seine, atypically empty of boats or barges, so the entirety of the unjustified text and of the two images is regularly centred – the bridge alone interrupting the flow of language – arranged round an invisible median line from top to bottom of the page, which follows the run of the river. This centralised verticality of the text is itself counterbalanced by the graded horizontals of variable length that are the lines, these in turn paralleled by the bridge itself, the parapet of which, scored by its corbels and spiked by its lamp-posts, reads almost like a long line of esoteric script, running (the only element in the advert to do so) from margin to margin. The steady alternation of normal and bold type adds to the sense of regularity. Nothing is tilted, nothing out of kilter. No quirks or visual jokes here. It is through its air of deliberate quiet confidence and Parisian charm that the advert, so fitted to its product, works.

A further and final telling feature of this advert is how evocative it is, visually, of a poem on a page. It displays a title; it has a text composed of short lines of variable length; the grouping of the lines resembles stanzas, four quatrains, followed by a couplet, then by single lines. Generous margins give it added typographical self-possession. We note the use of end-line rhyme ('*banc<u>aire</u>*'/ '*banc<u>aire</u>*'/'*financ<u>ière</u>*'), of end-line para-rhyme ('*soir*'/'*soi*'), of internal rhyme ('*tirelires*', homophonic past participle and imperative endings, <u>-ée</u> and <u>-ez</u>), of assonance and alliteration. The density of the language, the varying syntactic structures and the deliberate linguistic strategies peculiar to each section are pointedly and carefully worked. The logo is not unlike a traditional woodcut illustration to a poem, whereas the main image, 'poetic' in its expression of nature, historic architecture and autumnal mood, is expressive of a more modern approach to the illustration of poetry. Of course this icono-textual construct is a hard commercial artefact, far removed from the inspiration and aims of poetry. It nonetheless borrows a range of devices from poetic rhetoric and copies from the typographical conventions of poetic page layout. With its *Pont-Neuf* advert, the *Union de Banques à Paris* is seeking to exploit a *créneau* that is a moment in the flow of biological time: a first bank account may, after all, be seen as a rite of passage between adolescence and adulthood. In one of the most famous and haunting of modern poems, well-known to French students, it was with an uglier, more modern Paris bridge, the *Pont Mirabeau*, that Apollinaire sought to capture a different moment in the flux of human experience:

> *Sous le Pont Mirabeau coule la Seine*
> *Et nos amours faut-il qu'il m'en souvienne . . .*

Young love lost is one thing; the opening of a first bank account, quite another. In the advert with which we are concerned it is not lost love ebbing downstream, but, rather, as it were, commercially seductive text that is flowing under the gracefully solid *Pont-Neuf*. Adverts – generally sexist, ageist and idealist, and which habitually dream up scenarios of permanent prettification – can scarcely afford to include ungainly bridges. Poems can.

*

The two adverts we have analysed are different one from the other in several ways. *Arche* shoes advertise a consumer product made by the manufacturing sector, one which is particularly susceptible to the vagaries of shifting female fashion and which is relatively expensive in terms of its competitor products. The *Union de Banques à Paris*, part of the service sector, *le secteur tertiaire*, advertises a financial service which may involve no initial direct cost to the customer. Advertising a service such as a bank account, which is not in itself a concrete entity is, in a way, less straightforward than publicising a pair of shoes: you can't exactly produce a pink and green photograph of the product. Each advert targets a different specific niche of the market: the ad for *Arche* shoes being gender- and possibly social class-orientated; the one for the *Compte Basique* being age- and occupation-orientated.

The adverts differ, too, in the adventurousness of the techniques they employ, verbal pirouettes, syntactical twists, image deformation and humour in the case of *Arche* shoes; staider, though in some ways equally subtle approaches with the *Compte Basique*. Strangely, it is the advert selling shoes to conservative, middle-class women that displays the jazzier techniques of language and imagery (perhaps it takes a radical to shift a conservative), whereas students – and students and the young are usually enthusiastic vectors of linguistic slippage and lexical novelty – are tackled, in the bank advert, in more traditional registers of discourse. Or are the advertisers riding on profounder psychological insights into the insecurity (financial and other) of the young who, unconsciously perhaps, crave steadiness, while moneyed conservative women shoppers, deep down, are susceptible to more mischievous advertising ploys? Is it that women, after all, need to be seen as young, and students as mature, and that the respective advertisers here are deviously playing on those needs?

At the same time, the adverts display many common features. Both eschew presentation of the human figure, thereby avoiding ageism, racism and sexism, though the bank advert falls into the commonplace of prettification. Each has a refined sense of economy and layout style. Both have embedded in their text or imagery, though one more firmly than the other, intracultural referents, which interrogate and simultaneously reassure the reader about their cultural identity as French men or women. Both call up classic poetic imprints, schoolday inscriptions, indented early on the French mind: one from the *grand siècle*, the snatch of La Fontaine's famous fable, the other from twentieth-century modernism, Apollinaire's song of love lost, *Sous le Pont Mirabeau*, itself a subcategory of that lyrical mythologising that has accrued around the idea of, to quote a more popular song, *sous les ponts de Paris*. This form of cultural complicity, seen also in the evocation of Paris as perhaps the most visually satisfying city in the world (*Compte Basique*), and of France as the home of *haute couture* and female elegance (*Arche*), echoes and cunningly reinforces advertisers' furtherance of what might be called consumerist complicity: the pressure for all to join together as purchasers of their product; subscribe to our firm as you subscribe to your Frenchness (*société*, interestingly, can mean both French firm and French society).

While both adverts are typical of advertising discourse and show the extreme care and craft which has been channelled into the composition of text and artwork, exploiting an impressive, some might say worrying, array of icono-textual rhetorical devices, the *Arche* shoes advert in particular demonstrates how adverts have become important instruments at the cutting edge of linguistic change and expansion. Borrowing the language of different tranches of society to target specific markets, but displaying that language before the public at large – using slang, flouting accepted lexical registers, defying, in the name of brevity, fun or surprise, conventional 'rules' of spelling or syntax – the advert has become, alongside the pop song and the tabloid headline (but perhaps more so than them) an important factor not only in the popular appreciation of language but in linguistic evolution itself. Adverts both reflect the linguistic status quo and budge it, just as they both reflect social mores and in turn no doubt influence them. There are those who object to experiments on live words in public laboratories; there are those who delight in them. Advertisers may scarcely care, swayed by the adage that all publicity is good publicity.

There remains the question of reader response. Adverts are actantial discourse. They adopt a variety of textual and pictorial postures, evident or covert, to persuade the reader/observer to act in a way that will have financial consequences for them. They solicit their money. Of the hundreds of adverts of one sort or another which, more or less haphazardly, cross our gaze each day, most will form part of the passing visual paraphernalia, natural or other, which scarcely retains the eye. Others may distract us with momentary entertainment, elements of the 'three-minute culture' for which the age is known. Of those few which may detain us or be sought out for special scopic scrutiny, reader attitudes will vary according to age, education or mood. The sophisticated consumer, however, and consumers are increasingly sophisticated, will read an advert with at least a modicum of suspicion. Adverts are not fiction, nor, though they may contains facts, are they quite fact, but stand perhaps as a subcategory of the 'faction' that has become so important an element in contemporary visual and textual culture. Certainly suspension of disbelief is less beneficial for the observer of an advert than for the reader of a novel. The *Bureau de Vérification de la Publicité* may prosecute an advertiser for issuing *une pub mensongère*, just as the Advertising Standards Authority is there to enforce levels of social acceptability, but the borderline between untruth and the seduction of certain superlatives wrapped in glitzy advertising rhetoric is hazy.

Madame Figaro readers, while being amused and possibly mildly flattered at the jauntily rejuvenating pictorial and linguistic fun of the *Arche* shoe advert, may distrust its unverifiable claim, which it takes care not quite to state, but certainly to convey, that *Arche* shoes are the most flexible on the market. They may still, however, be seduced into buying them. Young readers of *L'Etudiant* may be swayed by the psychological pressures and discreet poetry of the *Compte Basique* advert, but will be alert to the fact that there are other competitors for their custom in the field. Reader scepticism and rival advert rhetoric are factors that composers of advertising discourse must constantly take into account. Rival texts and reader resistance are two of the factors (shifting linguistic and artistic fashions, and evolving technology in mass reproduction, are others) which ensure that advertising language, understood in its fullest icono-textual sense, is under constant self-scrutiny to hone its effectiveness as language of persuasion, another reason for its need to operate, within enervating constrictions of space and finance (and of time, for radio/TV/cinema ads), at the experimental edge of contemporary discourse.

***L'Arche*: an advert for *Arche* shoes, *Madame Figaro*,
29 March 1988.**

1	**Dans la jungle des villes,**
2	**la loi du plus souple est toujours la meilleure.**
3	
4	
5	
6	**[image]**
7	
8	
9	
10	DANS L'ENFER DU BITUME, DE L'ASPHALTE ET DU MACADAM, IL Y A
11	DES JOURS OÙ IL FAIT BON AVOIR LES PIEDS SUR TERRE. JE MARCHE
12	EN COULEURS, TU MARCHES TRÈS MODE, ELLE MARCHE SOUPLESSE,
13	NOUS MARCHONS ARCHE. ARCHE, TOUT LE CONFORT MODERNE.
14	
15	•
16	
17	LISTE DES POINTS DE VENTE SUR DEMANDE, SHOWROOM ARCHE:
18	13, RUE DES INNOCENTS, 79001 PARIS – TEL. (1) 45.08.19.45.
19	
20	
21	**[image]**
22	**arche**
23	
24	PARIS / NEW YORK / DUSSELDORF / BRUXELLES / LONDRES / TOKYO

For the original format, see page 133.

Le Compte Basique: an advert for *Le Compte Basique* of *L'Union de Banques à Paris*, **L'Etudiant**, October 1990.

LE COMPTE BASIQUE

**Oubliées les tirelires,
dépassés les livrets d'Epargne,
terminées les moues quémandeuses des adolescents
du samedi soir !**

Un véritable compte bancaire.
Un chéquier bien à soi.
Une carte de retrait d'espèces.
...... des services identiques à ceux proposés aux adultes.

**Avec l'Union de Banques à Paris :
accédez au monde bancaire
gagnez votre autonomie financière
en un mot, devenez responsable de votre argent.**

Aujourd'hui, les jeunes les plus exigeants ont
déjà ouvert leur propre COMPTE BASIQUE.

Vous aussi, rejoignez la banque des battants !

Union de Banques à Paris
22 place de la Madeleine Tél. (1) 42.68.33.33

For the original format, see page 139.

Enterprise and empire on the eve of the millennium

The case of Antoine Riboud

Benoît Heilbrunn

Introduction

The social and economic context

As in the UK, the 1980s saw an explosion in the growth of French enterprise. The election of François Mitterrand to the presidency in July 1981 was followed by a large-scale programme of nationalisation accompanied by massive state borrowing. This led in its turn to the economic crisis of 1983, which ushered in a regime of austerity marked by a tight control of the money supply. In order to foster growth, the government launched a campaign to stimulate the spread of enterprise. Advertisements all over the country and the promotional literature of business schools captured the mood of young people enthused by the appeal of dynamism and initiative, which, as in Thatcher's Britain, took precedence over the ethical scruples that might have been expected to accompany the first Socialist government in France for over twenty years. Small and medium enterprises grew in number and prospered and there was a huge rise in the number of applications to the regionally funded business schools which sprang up throughout the country. This culture of enterprise founded on the individual, made possible by the more ready access to venture capital (*capital risque*), was at variance with the republican tradition of state support to major corporations which had been a feature of French national life since World War II.

Following the change of government in 1986, leading self-made businessmen such as Bernard Tapie and Alain Gomez emerged as icons who, straddling the worlds of business and politics, were held up as models for the public to emulate. The growth of the East Asian countries and the expansion of the world economy, the surge of belief in the idea of European Union following the ratification of the Single European Act in 1986 and the build up to its implementation in 1992 under the presidency of the charismatic Jacques Delors, created an atmosphere of optimism in which French business flourished. While the relatively small size of the French financial marketplace made it difficult for French companies to raise sufficient private capital to expand overseas, and in an environment where large, partly nationally owned companies formed mutually supportive groups (*noyaux durs*), the individuals who were prepared to go it alone and to take risks were thought to be pointing the way to a brave new world.

Ten years on, it was a different story. The inevitable downturn in the world economy, the high interest rates imposed on French firms by the need to maintain parity with the Deutsche Mark and reduce the national deficit, the lack of disposable income and the onset of recession, had forced larger firms to restructure and sent thousands of PMEs (*Petites et Moyennes Entreprises*) to the wall, particularly in the black year of 1993, when pressure on the French franc practically forced it out of the European Monetary System. Things did not improve as the Mitterrand presidency drew to its close in 1994. There was rioting in the streets throughout the country in November 1995 as public-sector employees protested against the reduction in their personal benefits, accompanied by widespread public reaction against an overprotected civil service and individuals who were seen to have been augmenting their personal fortunes through corrupt practices. A number of the leading businessmen who had been held up as public heroes in the late 1980s found themselves under investigation. The euphoria of the previous decade had given way to a hard-headed realism where survival and sustainable growth were the watchwords. In the last few years of the millennium, independently funded overseas expansion based on merger and takeover was the main safeguard for the national economy. Such a strategy would be hard to maintain in a global context threatened by the collapse of the 'tiger' economies of the Far East and overshadowed by the threat of recession. Figures apparently untainted by corruption, yet who were playing a leading role in a national economic revival, were ripe for resurrection to the status of figureheads, raising in turn the vital issue of their succession.

A dual profile

Such are the context and the themes which underpin the profile of Antoine Riboud, Chairman and creator of the BSN group, written by François Renard and published in *Le Monde* on 4 May 1996. As grammatical subject of the subheading to the article (though not of the headline itself), the focus is on the personality of one of France's most long-standing and successful business leaders: '*Anticonformiste de nature, exigeant, . . . , l'homme qui a fait BSN . . .* '; yet the topic of the first paragraph of the text and its principal focus throughout all but the last few paragraphs is the growth of the company. Two discourse types coexist: the portrait of the individual, and historical narrative which traces the development of the firm. The piece was, moreover, written at a turning point in the group's history. Antoine Riboud had just handed over its direction to his son, Franck. The company was therefore facing the challenge of demonstrating its durability despite the

La passion selon Antoine

Anticonformiste de nature, exigeant, Antoine Riboud, l'homme qui a fait BSN, a mis trente ans pour transformer une entreprise familiale lyonnaise en empire. Il passe le témoin à son fils

IL a fallu cent trente ans au groupe suisse Nestlé pour devenir le numéro un mondial de l'alimentation avec près de 230 milliards de francs de chiffre d'affaires, avant l'américain Philip Morris (200 milliards de francs) et l'anglo-américain Unilever (135 milliards de francs). Il n'en aura fallu que trente à Antoine Riboud pour faire d'une fabrique familiale de bouteilles de la région lyonnaise le numéro un mondial pour les produits laitiers frais et les biscuits, le numéro deux pour les eaux minérales, le numéro un européen pour les sauces et condiments, le numéro deux pour les pâtes alimentaires et la bière, le numéro trois pour les plats cuisinés, avec un effectif de soixante-quatorze mille personnes, dont vingt-six mille seulement en France, un chiffre d'affaires d'environ 80 milliards de francs, 36 milliards de francs de fonds propres et 55 milliards de francs de capitalisation boursière.

Paradoxalement, c'est d'un échec, celui de l'OPA lancée fin 1968 sur un verrier concurrent, Saint-Gobain, qu'est issu cet empire, le premier groupe agro-alimentaire français. Tout, en fait, avait commencé en 1943, lorsque, à l'âge de vingt-cinq ans, Antoine Riboud, fils d'un banquier de Lyon, peu enthousiasmé pour les études (il était sorti dernier de l'Ecole supérieure de commerce de Paris), entra, « par protection », dans une firme lyonnaise, Souchon-Neuvesel, présidée par son grand-oncle, M. Souchon. Antoine se pique au jeu. Secrétaire général de la firme en 1952, il accède à sa présidence en 1961 et y amorce son grand jeu de Meccano en réunissant sous la raison sociale Souchon-Neuvesel une douzaine de verreries. En 1966, un premier grand coup : la fusion avec l'un des deux fabricants français de verre plat (deux tiers du verre à vitre et un tiers des glaces en France), Boussois, dont les deux actionnaires principaux, le belge Solvay et la Générale de Belgique, se chamaillaient.

C'est un sacré pari, car Boussois représente les deux tiers des actifs apportés dans l'opération, mais Antoine devient PDG de Boussois-Souchon-Neuvesel, désormais BSN, qui représente, au surplus, 80 % du chiffre d'affaires français du grand rival Saint-Gobain. L'idée vient à Antoine Riboud d'un rapprochement avec ce rival, d'autant que Boussois avait, dès 1962 – le premier en France –, acheté à l'anglais Pilkington le brevet du *float-glass*, à savoir la coulée du verre sur un bain d'étain en fusion parfaitement lisse, ce qui ramenait le prix de la glace à celui du verre à vitre. Les deux groupes collaborent déjà et pourraient envisager une rationalisation de la production ainsi qu'une diminution des frais et coûts. Mais les dirigeants de Saint-Gobain, vieille dame tricentenaire qui remonte à Colbert, ne l'entendent pas de cette oreille, surtout le PDG, Arnaud de Vogüé. En décembre 1968, encouragé, affirme-t-il, par Georges Pompidou, Antoine Riboud lance, avec le concours de la Banque Lazard, une offre publique d'achat, la première en France, sur 30 %, puis sur 100 % des actions Saint-Gobain.

Une bataille épique se livra durant un mois, pendant laquelle les dirigeants de Saint-Gobain firent monter les cours de leurs titres au-dessus du prix de l'OPA (230 francs) en les faisant racheter en Bourse par centaines de milliers, pour plus de 1 milliard de francs de l'époque – 8 à 10 milliards de francs actuels – empruntés pour une bonne part à l'étranger... L'OPA naturelle échoua, avec une belle plus-value pour BSN, Lazard et leurs alliés, qui revendirent... à Saint-Gobain, le dernier jour de l'OPA, les titres achetés par leurs soins. Pour la création d'un groupe verrier européen, c'était fichu. Mais, à cette occasion, la France découvrit Antoine Riboud, PDG d'un groupe jusqu'alors peu porté sur la communication, pour lequel un tel échec accéléra la prise de conscience d'un phénomène, celui, perceptible dès 1969, du boom des emballages perdus, qui allait faire ôter au verre le monopole de l'emballage. D'où l'idée de passer du contenant au contenu. Depuis 1915, Souchon Neuvesel, soucieux de contrôler ses débouchés, détenait 20 % du capital pour l'eau d'Evian, dont Antoine était même devenu PDG en 1965. Un an seulement après l'OPA manquée, c'est le début du virement de bord sur l'alimentaire avec l'absorption d'Evian, de la bière Kronenbourg et de l'Européenne de brasseries Champignolles, payée en actions BSN, comme l'avait été Boussois cinq ans auparavant. Le tout à la grande satisfaction du gouvernement français, qui luttait contre l'offensive des anglo-saxons sur les entreprises françaises isolées et trop petites (10 000 entreprises dont moins de 100 employaient plus de 500 salariés). Le numéro un de la profession, convoité par les britanniques, avait été constitué en 1967 par la réunion de deux affaires laitières, Gervais (fromages frais), de Jacques Corbière, et Danone (yaourts), de Daniel Carasso, fondé

> « La dimension sociale ne peut être dissociée de la gestion de l'entreprise »

en 1929, plus le rachat des pâtes Panzani Millat.

Au début de 1973, BSN rachète à Gervais-Danone 40 % de son chiffre d'affaires, toujours en payant en actions. Du coup, l'alimentation représente 52 % des actifs de BSN, qui, en 1980, pousse un nouveau pion en acquérant à la Générale occidentale de Jimmy Goldsmith l'ancienne Générale alimentaire, à savoir les moutardes et condiments Amora, Grey-Poupon, Maille et Parisot, La Pie qui chante (confiseries), Vandamme (pâtisserie industrielle), toujours payée en titres. En 1982, c'est l'achat au groupe britannique Brooks Bank de Liebig et Viandox (potages en boîte et extraits de viande). En 1986, nouvelle étape après la prise de contrôle de la Générale biscuit, créée en 1920 par Claude-Noël Martin, qui fédéra une trentaine de firmes dont Heudebert, L'Alsacienne des frères Thèves et LU-Brun. 7 milliards de francs de chiffre d'affaires au total. Claude-Noël Martin, très ambitieux, prône des *« rapprochements européens, notamment avec l'anglais United Biscuit »*. Ces projets inquiètent Antoine Riboud, qui passa à l'action avec le concours des actionnaires de la Générale et M. Brossolette, patron de MM. Worms et compagnie, et annexa la création de Claude-Noël Martin, qui préféra s'en aller.

Six ans auparavant, le PDG de BSN avait officialisé le changement de cap vers l'alimentaire en déclarant : *« A mes yeux, Gervais-Danone est le Coca-Cola français »* et en annonçant une décision capitale : l'abandon du verre plat. Cette activité était devenue un boulet financier, rendue coûteuse par le premier choc pétrolier de 1973, grosse consommatrice d'investissements lourds d'une valeur ajoutée relativement réduite sur les marchés stagnants et qui avait infligé à BSN, en 1975, le premier déficit de son histoire. Il fallait vendre, mais auparavant remettre le verre sur pied au prix de 2,5 milliards de francs d'investissement entre 1974 et 1979, de la fermeture de vingt-deux fours en Europe et d'une perte de 700 millions de francs en cinq ans, comblée par l'alimentaire. En mars 1980, c'est la cession à l'anglais Pilkington des filiales allemandes. En avril 1980, celle, au japonais Asashi, des filiales néerlandaises et surtout belges Glaverbel, et enfin, en décembre 1981, la vente à l'américain Pittsburgh Paints Glass de la filiale Boussois. Plus de verre plat donc, mais pas question de céder le verre creux, les bouteilles de Souchon-Neuvesel, dont le groupe BSN absorbe la moitié de la production pour loger ses eaux minérales et ses bières.

Après la France, l'Europe, notamment l'Italie et l'Allemagne. *« Il nous reste cinq ans pour européaniser nos marques »*, affirme Antoine en 1987. Une première tentative est faite en 1985, mais c'est l'échec : BSN se fait souffler *in extremis* les pâtes Buitoni par Carlo De Benedetti, patron d'Olivetti, qui fait jouer auprès des autorités la carte nationaliste. Antoine avait compris à ses dépens que, dans l'inextricable jungle des affaires italiennes, il ne pouvait percer sans un parrain puissant, influent et bien introduit. Il le trouve avec le groupe Agnelli, véritable empire de la Péninsule dont le joyau est Fiat. En 1986, le premier fruit de l'alliance est l'entrée dans les eaux minérales (San Gemini), qui sera bouclée à 100 % en 1991. Suivie en 1987 par l'acquisition d'Agnesi, numéro deux de cette chasse gardée qu'est l'industrie des pâtes alimentaires, dominée par le géant Barilla. Après un échange de participations entre les groupes français et italien, Agnelli rachète progressivement pour le compte de BSN Galbani, numéro un des fromages, numéro deux de l'agroalimentaire transalpin, véritable coup de maître au nez et à la barbe des grandes multinationales que sont Unilever, Philip Morris et naturellement Nestlé, qui a fini par racheter Buitoni à Benedetti. Suivra l'acquisition des mains de l'italien Fossati de 45 % de Star, grosse affaire de sauces, épices et condiments. Entre-temps, BSN est devenu numéro un de la bière en Italie, Wuhrer et Peronni prenant pied en Espagne chez Mahou, puis San Miguel.

AUX Etats-Unis, le grand événement de 1989 est le rachat de cinq filiales européennes du géant de l'agroalimentaire RJR Nabisco, que le célèbre établissement new-yorkais KKR avait acquis en 1988 pour le prix record de 25 milliards de dollars (170 milliards de francs de l'époque). Après quatre semaines de négociations serrées menées par l'entremise de Michel David-Weill, *senior partner* de Lazard Frères à New York et de Félix Rohatyn, associé de la même maison, Antoine Riboud enlève le marché. Son directeur financier, Christian Lauble, après vingt-quatre heures de discussions épuisantes, signe un chèque de 2,5 milliards de dollars (17 milliards de francs) tiré sur le Crédit lyonnais. Deux des filiales acquises seront revendues pour peu, mais Antoine exulte : BSN est désormais numéro un du biscuit sucré et maintenant salé en Europe. Belin, raflé par Nabisco dans les années 60, redevient français. La célèbre marque britannique Huntley et Palmer le devient, après Worcester Sauce, de Lea and Perrins, acquise l'année précédente.

L'offensive sur l'Europe était certes indispensable, mais la consommation y augmente peu et la véritable croissance, c'est l'Asie. Dès 1993, Antoine avait fait un voyage en Chine, mais BSN, malgré une association difficile pour les yaourts avec le japonais Ajinomoto et une présence ancienne en Malaisie, partait bon dernier. En 1989, une première étape est franchie avec le rachat à Nabisco de Britannia, numéro un du biscuit en Inde, avec plus de 35 % du marché et 200 000 points de vente. En 1992, c'est l'acquisition d'Amoy, la marque alimentaire la plus connue et la plus ancienne de l'Asie du Sud-Est, numéro un de la sauce au soja à Hongkong. Puis c'est la percée en Chine avec six entreprises communes pour produire du yaourt à Guangzhou (Canton) et Shanghaï, où des biscuits sont produits dès 1992 sous la marque LU. Biscuits également en Indonésie, en Nouvelle-Zélande, et le tandem biscuit-yaourt en Thaïlande. Autre zone de croissance, l'Amérique latine, où BSN vient de devenir le numéro deux de l'agroalimentaire argentin.

La chute du mur de Berlin en 1989 ouvre à BSN, selon son PDG, *« une chance stratégique et imprévisible et pratiquement sans limites, puisque cela concerne 400 millions d'habitants qui aspirent à une alimentation de meilleure qualité »* : les yaourts en RDA, Hongrie, Bulgarie, Tchécoslovaquie, Pologne et Russie, où Danone Volga a démarré en 1995, numéro un de la confiserie et du biscuit en Tchécoslovaquie, en association avec Nestlé, avec la prise de contrôle en 1994 de Bolshevik, premier biscuitier de Russie.

Sans doute, une telle réussite n'est pas vraiment un miracle. Il existe une recette maison dont les ingrédients sont : restructuration, réorganisation, productivité, abaissement des coûts, marketing et publicité. Après chaque acquisition, la mécanique du groupe (ses détracteurs ou victimes parlent parfois de *« rouleau compresseur »*) se met en route. Les dépenses de fonctionnement sont sabrées, les produits harmonisés et les ventes relancées grâce à une publicité coûteuse. *« Si l'on veut être entendu, il faut dépenser 5 à 6 % du chiffre d'affaires »*, estimait Pierre Bonnet, redresseur de la Générale biscuit.

Danone, c'est bien connu, a le premier ou deuxième budget de publicité en France, qui dépasse largement le milliard de francs par an. Ce n'est pas par hasard que les grands collaborateurs initiaux d'Antoine Riboud, Francis Gautier et Georges Lecallier, étaient des anciens de la filiale française de l'américain Colgate, des hommes de marketing s'il en fut. La mécanique est parfois douloureuse, notamment la rationalisation de l'outil industriel : les vingt brasseries du groupe Champignolle furent ramenées à deux puis une, la Générale biscuit, conglomérat de sociétés moyennes, fut « compressée » avec fermeture du siège et de la célèbre usine LU à Nantes. Et tout cela n'a pas manqué parfois de déclencher des conflits sociaux.

EN ce domaine, pourtant, Antoine Riboud a été une personnalité tout à fait à part. Jeune bourgeois lyonnais, il avait été frappé par la dureté du travail ouvrier et, tout au long de son existence, s'est attaché à améliorer sans cesse le climat social de son groupe. Très frappé par les événements de Mai 68, il fera scandale aux assises nationales du patronat français, en octobre 1972 à Marseille, en développant le thème « Croissance et qualité de vie », estimant que *« la dimension sociale ne peut être dissociée de la gestion de l'entreprise, que son absence compromettrait »*. Plus tard, il s'opposera aux salaires au mérite prônés par le patronat français, leur mise en œuvre, selon lui, ne pouvant que *« devenir une source permanente de conflits et même ranimer une nouvelle lutte des classes »*, tout au moins jusqu'à deux fois le revenu du SMIC.

Pour les cadres, en revanche, il recommande vivement de tenir compte des *« performances individuelles »*. Cette *« dimension sociale »*, il s'efforcera d'en tenir compte en instituant très tôt un intéressement du personnel, qui a atteint les deux tiers de la distribution aux actionnaires en 1995 et a pu l'égaler dans le passé, en innovant l'organisation du travail, par exemple par la création d'une cinquième équipe dans les usines de bouteilles à feu continu et en augmentant très tôt les budgets de formation.

La mèche en bataille, des yeux pétillants, « Antoine », anticonformiste de nature, est un affectif, un passionné, colérique à l'occasion, exigeant vis-à-vis de ses collaborateurs, dont bien peu l'ont quitté néanmoins. L'exception fut, en 1985, le responsable des produits frais, parti en guerre contre les grandes surfaces qui interdisent de rayons la marque Gervais-Danone, véritable catastrophe. Il fut viré sans états d'âme. Passionné, Antoine le fut pour le sort de son entreprise. Cette obsession, il l'a transmise à son fils, Franck, entré en 1980 dans le groupe, où il a « tourné » dans tous les métiers, à la direction générale d'Evian comme à celle du développement, notamment en Asie et en Amérique latine. Dans les milieux financiers, certains ont pu se montrer sceptiques sur cette succession qui a, pourtant, un immense mérite aux yeux des cadres de Danone, à savoir l'arrivée aux commandes d'un homme sorti du sérail, rompu à ses mécanismes et familier de ses arcanes.

François Renard

Dessin : Pancho

Source: Renard, F. 'La Passion selon Antoine', *Le Monde*, 4 May 1996, p. 13. Reproduced with kind permission of *Le Monde*.

change in chief executives, a transition which had echoes of medieval politics and kingship (see Kantorowicz 1957).

As Kantorowicz explains, the king is in fact two beings: he has a mortal condition as an individual and, at the same time, a political identity, whose essence lies in extending the kingdom in time and space. It is this dual status which explains how a monarchic system of government is able to survive the physical death of kings as human beings. Both the administrative body and the physical entity of the headship of state perpetuate themselves through the principle of heredity. In the case of BSN and its monarchic chairman, it would be difficult to imagine a more marked separation between, on the one hand, the changes of name and corporate activity undergone by the group and, on the other, the image of constancy and stability represented by Riboud. Thus, paradoxically, it was the person himself who, despite instigating change, stood for the organisation and sustained the myth of its continuity.

The story of the firm is clearly one of success, covering a thirty-year period during which a regional French glass manufacturer survived mixed fortunes to become the national leader in packaging and then one of the largest food producers in the world. The central topics of the text as well as its genre are highlighted by the key words ('*portrait*', '*agro-alimentaire*', '*historique*' and '*instance*'), which allow it to be accessed on *Le Monde*'s electronic *fiche documentaire*. The main subjects of the paragraphs are referred to impersonally as objects or concepts – sometimes expressed metaphorically: '*Il a fallu cent trente ans au groupe suisse, Nestlé...*'; '*c'est d'un échec . . . qu'est issu cet empire . . .* '; '*Au début de 1973, BSN rachète à Gervais-Danone 40 per cent de son chiffre d'affaires . . .* ' etc. These objective references, suggestive of a text whose primary function is apparently to inform, are matched by the mentions of Antoine Riboud himself, whose name occurs no less than nineteen times, either in its full form or simply as the more familiar forename '*Antoine*'.

Just as the topic of the whole article is dual, so it seems that there are two main characters explored through the portrait of Antoine Riboud: '*Antoine Riboud*', named in the third person or, as suggested above, an implied presence underpinning objective events, and the more familiar '*Antoine*' whose personality – entrepreneurial, dynamic, emotional, paternalistic – takes on a more affective colouring. While the former is generally represented in the past (*passé composé* and *passé simple*), the latter is expressed in the present: as if to emphasise the opposition between the integrated and essentially unchanging nature of the human being and the evolving state of the businessman which follows the development of the firm.

Of the two, it is the human being which dominates. The man whom many consider to be the greatest French *patron* of the postwar era has above all been successful in placing human qualities at the core of the organisation and in creating a management culture which is distinct from corporations such as Procter and

Gamble, Nestlé and Unilever, whose main focus has been on profit. As the title suggests, Antoine Riboud is being presented in evangelical terms. Not only does he show the way forward but inspires devotion in his followers, even when pursuing high-risk financial operations against the odds. And this devotion extends to the consumers, whose faith in BSN's products are linked by implication as much to the chairman as to the name of the firm.

The text follows an esssentially chronological sequence, which moves from the present global position of BSN to the start of Riboud's career in 1943 via the failed takeover of Saint-Gobain in 1969 which marked the turning point in the group's development. It is both a *'portrait'* and an *'historique'*. Virtually every paragraph begins with a reference to time: *'cent trente ans'*, *'lancée fin 1968'*, *'durant un mois'*, *'Au début de 1973'*, *'Six ans auparavant'*, *'Après la France . . .'*, *'le grand évènement de 1989 . . .'*, *'Dès 1993 . . .'*, and so on. The reader is thereby positioned as a listener rather than as participant; a spectator in the dramatic success story of a French institution and, simultaneously, that of a man.

The narrative construction of the hero

A model of narrative structure

The text tells the story of a double transformation: that of a small family firm into an empire in which the scale, work and conception of the company is recast, and that of the main protagonist from anti-hero to hero. Riboud's first steps in the business world are marked by failure: he seems not to have enjoyed studying, was offered a post through family influence, his first attempt at a takeover was a disastrous failure. The text recounts the path from unpromising beginnings to the status of national hero. One is not born a hero. Heroic status is only achieved as a result of overcoming a number of obstacles. In this text, this path can be reduced to four major stages corresponding to the four stages in Greimas' (1970) model of narration:

Table 2 A general framework for a structure of narrative

Mission	Action		Sanction
Contract	Qualifying test (competence)	Decisive test (performance)	Sanction
Project proposed by the beneficiary	Acquisition of the qualities necessary to realise the project	Completion of the project	Comparison of the completed project with the contract to be fulfilled

(Adapted from Floch 1990: 61)

- *The contract*. This corresponds to the protagonist's 'mission' or programme of action, in this case the need on the part of the protagonist to establish himself in an organisation to which he has been admitted through 'grace and favour' and then to conceive and realise a strategic programme in a rapidly changing environment (the opening up of the market, the power of the main competitors in the food industry, the change in the packaging market, etc.). The significance of this 'contract' is all the greater for the fact that Antoine Riboud is only the general manager of the company. As holder of only a minute proportion of the shares of the company, he is theoretically removable at any stage by the shareholders.

- *The acquisition of competence*. As already suggested, the process is described by implication through the actions themselves. The qualifications which make the actions possible are presented as human qualities and are only mentioned towards the end of the article: '*anti-conformisme*', '*exigence*', '*nature passionnée*', etc.).

- *The performance*. This is expressed through the different actions undertaken by the hero in order to realise his strategic programme: the idea of the merger with the rival Boussois, the attempted takeover of Saint-Gobain, the reversal of strategy in order to concentrate on food products instead of packaging, the internationalisation of the group. As presented in the text, these appear as conjuring tricks: sudden, wilful actions taken by an all-knowing magician of which the most dramatic is the switch from the container to the content.

- *The sanction*. The hero is recognised for what he is in virtue of what he has accomplished. This is established in the first paragraph of the text through the use of numbers, and underlined at the close. The case is therefore made retrospectively. '*Antoine*' is known to be a hero. The article acknowledges this and addresses the question of how he got there.

The article therefore presents the reader with the four stages of Riboud's progressive acquisition of hero status, even though the human qualities which have enabled him to achieve this are not revealed explicitly until the last stages of the text. The narrative manages the chronological order of events so as to create a state of suspense, lending a spirit of nobility and national salvation to the mission of '*grand patron*' and elevating its status to that of '*Roi*' or '*Empereur*'. Its structure is formed by a series of mini-narratives, each of which recounts an event or stage in the progressive constitution of Danone's industrial empire and the canonisation of its figurehead.

Narrative tone: lexis and metaphor

As might be expected, the lexical fields are a direct reflection of the text's subject matter: money ('*francs*', '*chiffre d'affaires*', '*actifs*', '*frais*', '*coûts*', '*fonds propres*', '*capitalisation boursière*', '*cours*', '*plus value*', '*titres*'), food products ('*alimentation*', '*produits laitiers*', '*biscuits*', '*eaux minérales*', '*sauces et condiments*', '*pâtes alimentaires*', '*bières*', '*plats cuisinés*', '*fromage frais*', '*yaourts*', '*confiseries*'), glass ('*verreries*', '*verre plat*', '*verre à vitre*', '*verre creux*', '*glace*', '*float-glass*'), packaging and containers ('*emballages*', '*contenant*', '*bouteille*'), and companies – too numerous to name comprehensively and, in many cases, linked to the names of their chairmen – '*Riboud*', '*Arnaud de Vogüé*' (Saint-Gobain), '*Jacques Corbière*' (Gervais), '*Daniel Carasco*' (Danone), '*Jimmy Goldsmith*' (Générale occidentale), '*Claude-Noël Martin*' (Générale biscuit), '*M. Brossolette*' (MM. Worms), '*Carlo De Benedetti*' (Olivetti), '*Agnelli*', '*Fossati*', and so on. The battles between the firms and the countries they represent are also duels between individuals, from which one party or another inevitably emerges victorious.

Accordingly, most of the metaphors employed to describe the actions of the different agencies are derived from the fields of games, risk-taking, military campaigns and imperialism ('*empire*' [×3], '*se pique au jeu*', '*sacré pari*', '*rival*', '*bataille épique*', '*offensive des anglo-saxons*', '*pion*', '*faire jouer la carte nationaliste*', '*annexa . . .*'). Selective features are transferred metonymically to Riboud himself ('*mèche en bataille*', '*les yeux pétillants*' . . .). Apart from being a fighter and a risk-taker, a systematically ruthless, even mechanical approach to management is a feature of his style ('*meccano*', '*mécanique*' [×2]). But the noun phrase which dominates the piece is without doubt '*numéro un*', which recurs no less than nine times in the text – a clear reminder, if any were needed, that the piece is primarily concerned with winning an unremitting international competition and (by extension) maintaining France's place in the economic world.

The link with nationalism and the identification of Antoine Riboud with the national cause is central to the text. It is vested in the statement '*Mais, à cette occasion, la France découvrit Antoine Riboud*', suggesting explicitly that Riboud is being cast in the role of national saviour. As in the second and fourth paragraphs, there is a marked shift in level from the more formal '*Antoine Riboud*' to the familiarity of the forename '*Antoine*', which positions Riboud *vis-à-vis* his employees as well as the general public. The forename, presented in inverted commas in the last paragraph – an indication of how he is viewed within the firm – is, in virtually all cases, collocated with an affective term: '*La passion selon Antoine*', '*Antoine se pique au jeu*', '*Antoine avait compris . . .*', '*Antoine exulte*', '"*Antoine*", *anticonformiste de nature, est un affectif, un passionné*', '*Passionné, Antoine le fut*'.

The commitent which Riboud brings to the mission of expanding BSN's international empire is set within the sphere of global competition by the recurrent reference to the national identities of the commercial groups. Nestlé is the '*groupe suisse*', which has striven for 130 years to become the world number-one food company – against BSN's meteoric thirty year progress – while the Belgian firms Solvay and la Générale de Belgique are seen to be squabbling ('*se chamaillaient*').

The French government shows '*satisfaction*' in 1969 at BSN's expansion into the food industry, which enables the country to stem the inroads made by Britain into French business. Having ceded large portions of his holdings in the glass sector to different international groups in Britain, Japan, The Netherlands, Belgium and the United States, Riboud first '*annexa*' Générale biscuit's holdings in France, then systematically expands his base beyond national borders: '*Après la France, l'Europe, notamment l'Italie et l'Allemagne . . .*'. In winning the battle for the biscuit sector with the American giant, Nabisco, Belin, formerly '*raflé*' (implying violation and illegitimacy), '*redevient français*', while prestige brands in the UK fall under the French group's control. These European developments are described as an '*offensive*', while BSN's rapid domination of the Asian and Chinese markets are a '*percée*'. *L'Amérique latine* is presented as territory ripe for invasion while, following the fall of the Berlin Wall, the launch of Danone Volga and the takeover of Bolshevik represent the metaphorical subjugation of central and eastern Europe and the new Russia.

Narrative structure: the role played by tense and mood

In short, as the sub-headline suggests, what is being presented is the establishment of a (quintessentially French) empire which owes its existence to the Napoleonic drive and ambition of one man (« *A mes yeux, Gervais-Danone est le Coca-Cola français* »). The historical dimension of the narrative as well as the imperative force of BSN's expansion is embodied in the use of tense and mood. The anaphoric use of the modal '*Il a fallu . . .*', '*Il n'en aura fallu . . .*', while making melodramatically explicit the contrast between Nestlé and BSN, locates the argument simultaneously in past, present and future, and prepares the ground for the main narrative focus of the text. As already mentioned, there are two turning points: the failed takeover of Saint-Gobain in 1968, which marked the start of BSN's onslaught on the food industry, and the inauspicious beginning of Riboud's career in 1943. As indicated by the use of the pluperfect '*avait commencé*', 1968 is pivotal, as the momentary mixing of metaphors ('[*un*] *virement de bord*' or '*changement de cap*') implies.

Having engineered the time-shift from 1968 to 1943, Renard's combination of historic present and past historic lends a conventional immediacy to the narrative. The absence of the verb foregrounds the statement which marks Riboud's first major success: '*En 1966, un premier grand coup . . .*' immediately projected into the present by the sequence of present tenses which follows in paragraph three. Amongst these, the reader is arrested by the foregrounded conditional: '*Les deux groupes collaborent déjà et <u>pourraient</u> envisager une rationalisation de la production ainsi qu'une diminution des frais et coûts . . .*', which is both inclusive (of the reader) and points strongly towards the speculative nature of Riboud's 1968 bid. The stages of the failed takeover itself are lent greater impact though the use of the past historic, which gives the impression of an accumulation of individual and seemingly uncontrollable events. These are followed by France's 'discovery' of Riboud as a result of his decision – again foregrounded by a verbless sentence – to change direction (*'D'où l'idée de passer du contenant au contenu'*), signalling a return to the historic present. In this way, the text successively moves backwards and forwards as it traces the post-1968 growth of the group before shifting perspective in the last third to concentrate on the managerial techniques on which the success of the group is built and – finally – on the character of Riboud himself. This last section brings the different tenses together, allowing for an unusual combination of perfect, pluperfect, historic future and present.

Register and writer–reader relationships

As has been suggested, the reader is positioned essentially as a passive interlocutor. However, shifts in tone vary the flow of facts and introduce a more familiar, complicitous element into the relationship, conventionally marked by French colloquialisms: *'Antoine se pique au jeu'*, *'les dirigeants de Saint-Gobain, vieille dame tricentenaire qui remonte à Colbert, ne l'entendent pas de cette oreille'*, *'Pour la création d'un groupe verrier européen, c'était fichu'*, *'L'entrée dans les eaux minérales sera baclée en 1991'*. Riboud's son, Franck, destined to take over his father's company, is already *'rompu à ses mécanismes'*. The series of quoted statements by Riboud, typical of the genre and which recur intermittently throughout the text, define the personality of the leading protagonist and establish a direct relationship between him and the reader: « *A mes yeux, Gervais-Danone est le Coca-Cola français* », « *Il nous reste cinq ans pour européaniser nos marques* », « *une chance stratégique et imprévisible et pratiquement sans limites . . .* », etc. Similarly, short verbless sentences establish a sense of dialogue internal to the text in which the phrases have a dual voice: that of the author and that of Riboud (*'Plus de verre plat donc, mais pas question de céder le verre creux . . .'*). The combination of ellipsis, deictic phrases and adverbial qualifiers reinforce cohesion while maintaining a sense of spoken dialogue: *'C'est un sacré pari'*, *'Après la France, l'Europe . . .'*, *'L'offensive sur l'Europe était certes indispensable'*, *'D'où l'idée de passer du contenant au contenu'*, *'Sans doute, une telle réussite n'est pas vraiment un miracle'*.

Sentence structure, word order and rhythm

Switches from conventional word order further contribute to the blend of rhetoric and familiarity which is the hallmark of the genre, inviting the reader to share the author's conversational, mildly populist perspective: *'Suivra l'acquisition . . . de 45 per cent de Star . . .'*, *'des hommes de marketing s'il en fut . . .'*, *'Passioné, Antoine le fut pour son entreprise . . .'*, etc. At the same time, more classical rhetorical devices are deployed to give an enhanced view of BSN's empire-building project.

Perhaps the most striking example of this is found in the first paragraph, where the magnitude of Riboud's achievement is conveyed by the accumulation of verb complements and the repetition of '*numéro* . . .' which build up to the strong ternary structure that closes the paragraph:

> . . . *un chiffre d'affaires d'environ 80 milliards de francs, 36 milliards de fonds propres et 55 milliards de francs de capitalisation boursière.*

The same effect occurs later in the text in the seventh paragraph – '. . . *grosse affaire de sauces, épices et condiments*' – and the eleventh – '*Les dépenses de fonctionnement sont sabrées, les produits harmonisés et les ventes relancées grâce à une publicité coûteuse.*'

The regularities of rhythm which these examples illustrate are the exception rather than the rule. Elsewhere, the rhythms are resolutely irregular and fragmented, typical of a superficially disorganised style designed to give the impression of conversation – or possibly simply the product of an experienced journalist writing to a deadline. The sentence structure is characterised by frequent parentheses, in the form of asides or afterthoughts, which reconstruct a natural thought process:

> *un tel échec accéléra la prise de conscience d'un phénomène, celui, perceptible dès 1969, du boom des emballages perdus.*

> *Son directeur financier, Christian Laubie, après vingt-quatre heures de discussions épuisantes, signe un chèque de 2,5 milliards de dollars (17 milliards de francs) tiré sur le Crédit lyonnais.*

Examples such as the above, frequent in the text, follow the logical progression of ideas, communicating a profusion of facts within a clearly structured narrative frame. Many do not follow the conventions of increased length of clauses (*loi de longueur*) or of *cadence majeure*. Sentences are extended, often through the use of participial clauses which, rather than being 'fronted', fall late in the sentence, giving the impression of careless accumulation rather than deliberate construction:

> *En 1966, un premier grand coup : la fusion avec l'un des deux fabricants français de verre plat (deux tiers du verre à vitre et un tiers des glaces en France), Boussois, dont les deux actionnaires principaux, le belge Solvay et la Générale de Belgique, se chamaillaient.*

> *Il fallait vendre, mais auparavant remettre le verre sur pied aux prix de 2,5 milliards de francs d'investissement entre 1974 et 1979, de la fermeture de vingt-deux fours*

en Europe et d'une perte de 700 millions de francs en cinq ans, comblée par l'alimentaire.

Entre temps, BSN est devenu numéro un de la bière en Italie, Wuhrer et Peroni prenant pied en Espagne chez Mahou, puis San Miguel.

One sentence, unique within the text, marks the transition from narrative to generic description: '*Il existe une recette maison dont les ingrédients sont : restructuration, réorganisation, productivité, abaissement des coûts, marketing et publicité.*' While conveying admirably the ruthless approach adopted by Riboud following a takeover – incidentally and in a slightly forced way playing on the metaphor of cooking – its cumulative construction sums up the condensed, hasty tenor of the whole piece. Similarly, the occasional examples of onomatopoeia and assonance ('*prenant pied*', '*la chute du mur*, '*numéro un de la confiserie et du biscuit*', '*en instituant un intéressement*', etc.), seem more coincidental than deliberate and can hardly be said to enhance the communicative impact of the message. In general, the emphasis is not on the poetic and emotive functions but rather on the referential and the conative, with the overriding object of engaging the reader's admiration for Antoine Riboud.

Conclusion

In linking the global expansion of a national firm to the portrayal of a monarchic yet quintessentially human personality, '*La passion selon Antoine*' constructs a heroic model of national regeneration with which the readership is invited to identify. Yet in foregrounding Antoine Riboud's success and force of personality, the hero's human qualities override the social cost which international expansion implies. Riboud's concern for his workforce masks the real effects of his systematic approach to cost-cutting: '*le rouleau compresseur*'. Reconciling these conflicting pressures is the subject matter of the last part of the text. Streamlining implies closure and social conflict, for which paternalistic empathy can hardly be seen as adequate compensation. As constructed in the text, the person of Antoine Riboud rises above the paradox in a schematic and simplistic way. His supposed even-handedness in his dealings with the workforce, which includes the introduction of joint shareholding and training schemes, is matched by his aggressive attitude towards management performance.

As presented in '*La passion selon Antoine*', Antoine Riboud combines the traditional attributes of the '*Grand Patron*' – a highly visible profile, incarnation of the values of the company, a clear and direct relationship with his employees, a readiness to take responsibility – with the qualities of the modern entrepreneur needed for France to emerge victorious in the imperialistic climate of modern global business. At the same time, the dependence on the individual rather than on the State as a means of securing national expansion raises the question of succession indicated in the title and again in the closing sentence. Despite casting a shadow on the model which is being offered to the reader, this issue does not detract from the force of the portrait which remains the main focus of the text: that of the entrepreneurial figure motivated less by a desire for self-aggrandisement and personal profit than by a vision for his company and, by extension, for the future of France.

François Renard, 'La Passion selon Antoine', *Le Monde*,
4 May 1996, p. 13.

1   # HORIZONS
2   ### PORTRAIT
3
4   # La passion selon Antoine
5
6   **Anticonformiste de nature, exigeant, Antoine Riboud, l'homme qui a**
7   **fait BSN, a mis trente ans pour transformer une entreprise familiale**
8   **lyonnaise en empire. Il passe le témoin à son fils**
9
10   Il a fallu cent trente ans au groupe suisse Nestlé pour devenir le numéro un
11   mondial de l'alimentation avec près de 230 milliards de francs de chiffre d'affaires,
12   avant l'américain Philip Morris (200 milliards de francs) et l'anglo-américain
13   Unilever (135 milliards de francs). Il n'en aura fallu que trente à Antoine Riboud
14   pour faire d'une fabrique familiale de bouteilles de la région lyonnaise le numéro
15   un mondial pour les produits laitiers frais et les biscuits, le numéro deux pour les
16   eaux minérales, le numéro un européen pour les sauces et condiments, le numéro
17   deux pour les pâtes alimentaires et la bière, le numéro trois pour les plats cuisinés,
18   avec un effectif de soixante-quatorze mille personnes, dont vingt-six mille seule-
19   ment en France, un chiffre d'affaires d'environ 80 milliards de francs, 36 milliards
20   de francs de fonds propres et 55 milliards de francs de capitalisation boursière.
21
22   Paradoxalement, c'est d'un échec, celui de l'OPA lancée fin 1968 sur un verrier
23   concurrent, Saint-Gobain, qu'est issu cet empire, le premier groupe agro-
24   alimentaire français. Tout, en fait, avait commencé en 1943, lorsque, à l'âge de
25   vingt-cinq ans, Antoine Riboud, fils d'un banquier de Lyon, peu enthousiasmé
26   pour les études (il était sorti dernier de l'Ecole supérieure de commerce de Paris),
27   entra, « par protection », dans une firme lyonnaise, Souchon-Neuvesel, présidée
28   par son grand-oncle, M. Souchon. Antoine se pique au jeu. Secrétaire général de
     la firme en 1952, il accède à sa présidence en 1961 et y amorce son grand jeu
29   de Meccano en réunissant sous la raison sociale Souchon-Neuvesel une douzaine
30   de verreries. En 1966, un premier grand coup : la fusion avec l'un des deux
31   fabricants français de verre plat (deux tiers du verre à vitre et un tiers des glaces
33   en France), Boussois, dont les deux actionnaires principaux, le belge Solvay et la
34   Générale de Belgique, se chamaillaient.
35
36   C'est un sacré pari, car Boussois représente les deux tiers des actifs apportés dans

37 l'opération, mais Antoine devient PDG de Boussois-Souchon-Neuvesel, désor-
38 mais BSN, qui représente, au surplus, 80 % du chiffre d'affaires français du grand
39 rival Saint-Gobain. L'idée vient à Antoine Riboud d'un rapprochement avec ce
40 rival, d'autant que Boussois avait, dès 1962 – le premier en France –, acheté à
41 l'anglais Pilkington le brevet du *float-glass*, à savoir la coulée du verre sur un bain
42 d'étain en fusion parfaitement lisse, ce qui ramenait le prix de la glace à celui du
43 verre à vitre. Les deux groupes collaborent déjà et pourraient envisager une
44 rationalisation de la production ainsi qu'une diminution des frais et coûts. Mais les
45 dirigeants de Saint-Gobain, vieille dame tricentenaire qui remonte à Colbert, ne
46 l'entendent pas de cette oreille, surtout le PDG, Arnaud de Vogüé. En décembre
47 1968, encouragé, affirme-t-il, par Georges Pompidou, Antoine Riboud lance, avec
48 le concours de la Banque Lazard, une offre publique d'achat, la première en
49 France, sur 30 %, puis sur 100 % des actions Saint-Gobain.
50
51 Une bataille épique se livra durant un mois, pendant laquelle les dirigeants de
52 Saint-Gobain firent monter les cours de leurs titres au-dessus du prix de l'OPA
53 (230 francs) en les faisant racheter en Bourse par centaines de milliers, pour plus
54 de 1 milliard de francs de l'époque 8 à 10 milliards de francs actuels – empruntés
55 pour une bonne part à l'étranger . . . L'OPA naturelle échoua, avec une belle
56 plus-value pour BSN, Lazard et leurs alliés, qui revendirent . . . à Saint-Gobain, le
57 dernier jour de l'OPA, les titres achetés par leurs soins. Pour la création d'un
58 groupe verrier européen, c'était fichu. Mais, à cette occasion, la France découvrit
59 Antoine Riboud, PDG d'un groupe jusqu'alors peu porté sur la communication,
60 pour lequel un tel échec accéléra la prise de conscience d'un phénomène, celui,
61 perceptible dès 1969, du boom des emballages perdus, qui allait faire ôter au
62 verre le monopole de l'emballage. D'où l'idée de passer du contenant au contenu.
63 Depuis 1915, Souchon Neuvesel, soucieux de contrôler ses débouchés, détenait
64 20 % du capital pour l'eau d'Evian, dont Antoine était même devenu PDG en
65 1965. Un an seulement après l'OPA manquée, c'est le début du virement de
66 bord sur l'alimentaire avec l'absorption d'Evian, de la bière Kronenbourg et de
67 l'Européenne de brasseries Champignolles, payée en actions BSN, comme l'avait
68 été Boussois cinq ans auparavant. Le tout à la grande satisfaction du gouverne-
69 ment français, qui luttait contre l'offensive des anglo-saxons sur les entreprises
70 françaises isolées et trop petites (10 000 entreprises dont moins de 100 employai-
71 ent plus de 500 salariés). Le numéro un de la profession, convoité par les britan-
72 niques, avait été constitué en 1967 par la réunion de deux affaires laitières,
73 Gervais (fromages frais), de Jacques Corbière, et Danone (yaourts), de Daniel
74 Carasco, fondé en 1929, plus le rachat des pâtes Panzani Millat.
75
76 Au début de 1973, BSN rachète à Gervais-Danone 40 % de son chiffre d'affaires,
77 toujours en payant en actions. Du coup, l'alimentation représente 52 % des actifs
78 de BSN, qui, en 1980, pousse un nouveau pion en acquérant à la Générale

79   occidentale de Jimmy Goldsmith l'ancienne Générale alimentaire, à savoir les
80   moutardes et condiments Amora, Grey-Poupon, Maille et Parisot, La Pie qui
81   chante (confiseries), Vandamme (pâtisserie industrielle), toujours payée en titres.
82   En 1982, c'est l'achat au groupe britannique Brooks Bank de Liebig et Viandox
83   (potages en boîte et extraits de viande). En 1986, nouvelle étape après la prise de
84   contrôle de la Générale biscuit, créée en 1920 par Claude-Noël Martin, qui fédéra
85   une trentaine de firmes dont Heudebert, L'Alsacienne des frères Thèves et LU-
86   Brun. 7 milliards de francs de chiffre d'affaires au total. Claude-Noël Martin, très
87   ambitieux, prône des « *rapprochements européens, notamment avec l'anglais United*
88   *Biscuit* ». Ces projets inquiètent Antoine Riboud, qui passa à l'action avec le
89   concours des actionnaires de la Générale et M. Brossolette, patron de MM.
90   Worms et compagnie, et annexa la création de Claude-Noël Martin, qui préféra
91   s'en aller.
92
93   Six ans auparavant, le PDG de BSN avait officialisé le changement de cap vers
94   l'alimentaire en déclarant: « *A mes yeux, Gervais-Danone est le Coca-Cola français* » et
95   en annonçant une décision capitale : l'abandon du verre plat. Cette activité était
96   devenue un boulet financier, rendue coûteuse par le premier choc pétrolier de
97   1973, grosse consommatrice d'investissements lourds d'une valeur ajoutée rela-
98   tivement réduite sur les marchés stagnants et qui avait infligé à BSN, en 1975, le
99   premier déficit de son histoire. Il fallait vendre, mais auparavant remettre le verre
100   sur pied au prix de 2,5 milliards de francs d'investissement entre 1974 et 1979, de
101   la fermeture de vingt-deux fours en Europe et d'une perte de 700 millions de
102   francs en cinq ans, comblée par l'alimentaire. En mars 1980, c'est la cession à
103   l'anglais Pilkington des filiales allemandes. En avril 1980, celle, au japonais Asahi,
104   des filiales néerlandaises et surtout belges Glaverbel, et enfin, en décembre 1981,
105   la vente à l'américain Pittsburgh Paints Glass de la filiale Boussois. Plus de verre
106   plat donc, mais pas question de céder le verre creux, les bouteilles de Souchon-
107   Neuvesel, dont le groupe BSN absorbe la moitié de la production pour loger ses
108   eaux minérales et ses bières.
109
110   Après la France, l'Europe, notamment l'Italie et l'Allemagne. « *Il nous reste cinq ans*
111   *pour européaniser nos marques* », affirme Antoine en 1987. Une première tentative
112   est faite en 1985, mais c'est l'échec : BSN se fait souffler *in extremis* les pâtes
113   Buitoni par Carlo De Benedetti, patron d'Olivetti, qui fait jouer auprès des
114   autorités la carte nationaliste. Antoine avait compris à ses dépens que, dans
115   l'inextricable jungle des affaires italiennes, il ne pouvait percer sans un parrain
116   puissant, influent et bien introduit. Il le trouve avec le groupe Agnelli, véritable
117   empire de la Péninsule dont le joyau est Fiat. En 1986, le premier fruit de
118   l'alliance est l'entrée dans les eaux minérales (San Gemini), qui sera bouclée à 100
119   % en 1991. Suivie en 1987 par l'acquisition d'Agnesi, numéro deux de cette
120   chasse gardée qu'est l'industrie des pâtes alimentaires, dominée par le géant

121 Barilla. Après un échange de participations entre les groupes français et italien,
122 Agnelli rachète progressivement pour le compte de BSN Galbani, numéro un des
123 fromages, numéro deux de l'agroalimentaire transalpin, véritable coup de maître
124 au nez et à la barbe des grandes multinationales que sont Unilever, Philip Morris
125 et naturellement Nestlé, qui a fini par racheter Buitoni à Benedetti. Suivra l'acqui-
126 sition des mains de l'italien Fossati de 45 % de Star, grosse affaire de sauces, épices
127 et condiments. Entre-temps, BSN est devenu numéro un de la bière en Italie,
128 Wuhrer et Peroni prenant pied en Espagne chez Mahou, puis San Miguel.
129
130 Aux Etats-Unis, le grand événement de 1989 est le rachat de cinq filiales euro-
131 péennes du géant de l'agroalimentaire RJR Nabisco, que le célèbre établissement
132 new-yorkais KKR avait acquis en 1988 pour le prix record de 25 milliards de
133 dollars (170 milliards de francs de l'époque). Après quatre semaines de négocia-
134 tions serrées menées par l'entremise de Michel David-Weill, *senior partner* de
135 Lazard Frères à New York et de Félix Rohatyn, associé de la même maison,
136 Antoine Riboud enlève le marché. Son directeur financier, Christian Laubie, après
137 vingt-quatre heures de discussions épuisantes, signe un chèque de 2,5 milliards de
138 dollars (17 milliards de francs) tiré sur le Crédit lyonnais. Deux des filiales
139 acquises seront revendues pour peu, mais Antoine exulte : BSN est désormais
140 numéro un du biscuit sucré et maintenant salé en Europe. Belin, rafleé par
141 Nabisco dans les années 60, redevient français. La célèbre marque britannique
142 Huntley et Palmer le devient, après Worcester Sauce, de Lea and Perrins, acquise
143 l'année précédente.
144
145 L'offensive sur l'Europe était certes indispensable, mais la consommation y aug-
146 mente peu et la véritable croissance, c'est l'Asie. Dès 1993, Antoine avait fait un
147 voyage en Chine, mais BSN, malgré une association difficile pour les yaourts avec
148 le japonais Ajinomoto et une présence ancienne en Malaisie, partait bon dernier.
149 En 1989, une première étape est franchie avec le rachat à Nabisco de Brittania,
150 numéro un du biscuit en Inde, avec plus de 35 % du marché et 200 000 points de
151 vente. En 1992, c'est l'acquisition d'Amoy, la marque alimentaire la plus connue
152 et la plus ancienne de l'Asie du Sud-Est, numéro un de la sauce au soja à Hong-
153 kong. Puis c'est la percée en Chine avec six entreprises communes pour produire
154 du yaourt à Guangzhou (Canton) et Shanghaï, où des biscuits sont produits dès
155 1992 sous la marque LU. Biscuits également en Indonésie, en Nouvelle-Zélande,
156 et le tandem biscuit-yaourt en Thaïlande. Autre zone de croissance, l'Amérique
157 latine, où BSN vient de devenir le numéro deux de l'agroalimentaire argentin.
158
159 La chute du mur de Berlin en 1989 ouvre à BSN, selon son PDG, « *une chance
160 stratégique et imprévisible et pratiquement sans limites, puisque cela concerne 400 millions
161 d'habitants qui aspirent à une alimentation de meilleure qualité* » : les yaourts en RDA,
162 Hongrie, Bulgarie, Tchécoslovaquie, Pologne et Russie, où Danone Volga a

163 démarré en 1995, numéro un de la confiserie et du biscuit en Tchécoslovaquie, en
164 association avec Nestlé, avec la prise de contrôle en 1994 de Bolshevik, premier
165 biscuitier de Russie.
166
167 Sans doute, une telle réussite n'est pas vraiment un miracle. Il existe une recette
168 maison dont les ingrédients sont : restructuration, réorganisation, productivité,
169 abaissement des coûts, marketing et publicité. Après chaque acquisition, la
170 mécanique du groupe (ses détracteurs ou victimes parlent parfois de « *rouleau*
171 *compresseur* ») se met en route. Les dépenses de fonctionnement sont sabrées, les
172 produits harmonisés et les ventes relancées grâce à une publicité coûteuse. « *Si*
173 *l'on veut être entendu, il faut dépenser 5 à 6 % du chiffre d'affaires* », estimait Pierre
174 Bonnet, redresseur de la Générale biscuit.
175
176 Danone, c'est bien connu, a le premier ou deuxième budget de publicité en
177 France, qui dépasse largement le milliard de francs par an. Ce n'est pas par hasard
178 que les grands collaborateurs initiaux d'Antoine Riboud, Francis Gautier et
179 Georges Lecallier, étaient des anciens de la filiale française de l'américain Colgate,
180 des hommes de marketing s'il en fut. La mécanique est parfois douloureuse,
181 notamment la rationalisation de l'outil industriel : les vingt brasseries du groupe
182 Champignolle furent ramenées à deux puis une, la Générale biscuit, conglomérat
183 de sociétés moyennes, fut « compressée » avec fermeture du siège et de la célèbre
184 usine LU à Nantes. Et tout cela n'a pas manqué parfois de déclencher des conflits
185 sociaux.
186
187 En ce domaine, pourtant, Antoine Riboud a été une personnalité tout à fait à part.
188 Jeune bourgeois lyonnais, il avait été frappé par la dureté du travail ouvrier et,
189 tout au long de son existence, s'est attaché à améliorer sans cesse le climat social
190 de son groupe. Très frappé par les événements de Mai 68, il fera scandale aux
191 assises nationales du patronat français, en octobre 1972 à Marseille, en dévelop-
192 pent le thème « Croissance et qualité de vie », estimant que « *la dimension sociale ne*
193 *peut être dissociée de la gestion de l'entreprise, que son absence compromettrait* ». Plus tard,
194 il s'opposera aux salaires au mérite prônés par le patronat français, leur mise en
195 oeuvre, selon lui, ne pouvant que « *devenir une source permanente de conflits et même*
196 *ranimer une nouvelle lutte des classes* », tout au moins jusqu'à deux fois le revenu du
197 SMIC.
198

Pour les cadres, en revanche, il recommande vivement de tenir compte des
200 « *performances individuelles* ». Cette « *dimension sociale* », il s'efforcera d'en tenir
201 compte en instituant très tôt un intéressement du personnel, qui a atteint les deux
202 tiers de la distribution aux actionnaires en 1995 et a pu l'égaler dans le passé, en
203 innovant l'organisation du travail, par exemple par la création d'une cinquième

204 équipe dans les usines de bouteilles à feu continu et en augmentant très tôt les
205 budgets de formation.
206
207 La mèche en bataille, des yeux pétillants, « Antoine », anticonformiste de nature,
208 est un affectif, un passionné, colérique à l'occasion, exigeant vis-à-vis de ses
209 collaborateurs, dont bien peu l'ont quitté néanmoins. L'exception fut, en 1985, le
210 responsable des produits frais, parti en guerre contre les grandes surfaces qui
211 interdisent des rayons la marque Gervais-Danone, véritable catastrophe. Il fut viré
212 sans états d'âme. Passionné, Antoine le fut pour le sort de son entreprise. Cette
213 obsession, il l'a transmise à son fils, Franck, entré en 1980 dans le groupe, où il a
214 « tourné » dans tous les métiers, à la direction générale d'Evian comme à celle du
215 développement, notamment en Asie et en Amérique latine. Dans les milieux
216 financiers, certains ont pu se montrer sceptiques sur cette succession qui a,
217 pourtant, un immense mérite au yeux des cadres de Danone, à savoir l'arrivée aux
218 commandes d'un homme sorti du sérail, rompu à ses mécanismes et familier de
219 ses arcanes.
220
221   *François Renard*

For the original format, see page 150.

Rewriting the French Revolution

Robert Crawshaw

Introduction

Interdiscursivity and the narration of historical events

Few events in history have been more written about than the French Revolution of 1789. The interpretation of its causes and the attitude towards its legacy within French society have always been a mirror of prevailing political beliefs and a representation of French citizens' changing views of the Nation and the State. These views and explanations find expression in academic books and monographs, comment in the written press, the texts of radio or television broadcasts and other discourses of all kinds. All compete for space and readership in order for their particular perspectives to be more widely shared within French society. A central argument of this book has been that the struggle for dominance between discourses has to do not simply with the subject matter but in the manner in which ideas are formulated in language – that is, in the structure and progression of the texts through which the discourses find expression. The written texts relating to the French Revolution bear out the truth of this hypothesis, as is demonstrated by three texts from a similar genre whose discursive formations could be said to be 'in conflict' with each other.

Conflicting views of the French Revolution and the interests of modern politics

In 1989, Bétourné and Hartig published *Penser l'Histoire de la Révolution*. Its title was derived directly from François Furet's *Penser la Révolution Française* (1978), which had been seen as a direct challenge to the analysis of the Revolution then regarded as orthodox by leading French historians. Bétourné and Haig's publication was timed to coincide with the 1989 bicentenary celebrations in France. This event provided the government of the day with an opportunity to re-evaluate France's relationship with its past and to claim that the politics of the centre which it represented was a worthy standard-bearer for post-revolutionary republicanism. Much therefore hinged on what the aims and outcomes of the Revolution were judged to have been. The attitudes of French people towards 'their' Revolution could be linked directly to their current political affiliation. At a time when the Soviet Empire was about to collapse, and following a period of rapid economic growth in France and the world, it seemed as though French social democracy might be able to lay to rest the instability and confrontation which had been the hallmark of French politics for the previous two hundred years – provided that a reduced dependence on the State was not seen by the French people as a betrayal of their republican heritage. The centre-left presidency of François Mitterrand and the centre-right majority in parliament led by Jacques Chirac both needed to appeal to a concept of French nationhood which was in tune with the country's radical past and, at the same time, able to accommodate the more pragmatic direction of the government's economic policy.

It is hardly surprising, therefore, that, in the buildup to the celebrations of 1989, the interpretations of the causes and consequences of the French Revolution should have been seen to mirror the beliefs and ideologies of late twentieth-century political parties in France and that each should have sought to appropriate the heritage of the Revolution to validate their positions. The three texts I have chosen for analysis represent three different political strands within contemporary French society. In the buildup to 1989, they can be seen to represent three conflicting discourses, reflecting the standpoints which the government had to reconcile in constructing its own interpretation of the heritage of modern France.

Three narrations

The first text represents the point of view of extreme reaction expressed by the right-wing monarchist and member of the *Académie Française*, Pierre Gaxotte (1895–1982). His massive best-seller *La Révolution Française*, first published in 1928, ran to over 100 editions and at least four revised versions, of which the latest was published in 1988. These figures alone point to its status as a symbol of nationalist sentiment. For Gaxotte, the Revolution was responsible for overthrowing a just and prosperous system under which France had flourished for centuries, definitively undermining the authority and moral security of the Catholic Church (Bétourné and Hartig 1989: 156). It was the weakness of the monarch which had led to a progressive and fatal transfer of power to constituent assemblies and ultimately to the descent into anarchy. The *Ancien Régime* was the hallmark of France's glorious past, an often misrepresented utopia in relation to which France's twentieth-century republicanism was a tawdry compromise.

The second text is an extract from the orthodox socialist/communist analysis which was most memorably articulated in Albert Soboul's book, *La Révolution Française* (1982). For Soboul, the holder of the Chair in the history of the French

Revolution from the mid-1960s until his death, the Revolution was a necessary stage in the evolution towards capitalism and – ultimately – communism. It was caused by the progressive rise of the bourgeoisie and made possible its establishment as the dominant class in the nineteenth century. According to Soboul, the ruthless violence of the terror was an inevitable part of an historical process which could be explained in terms of economic forces.

The third consists of a short section of François Furet's controversial 1978 publication, *Penser la Révolution Française*. Taking issue with Soboul's analysis, Furet suggested that no definitive interpretation of the Revolution was possible. It was inherent to the nature of historical explanation that new analyses of the Revolution should emerge as an ongoing expression of social and political change. There were important events which had still not been satisfactorily explained or understood; the individuals who had perpetrated the mass executions of 1793–1794 could not simply be absolved by history, but bore a share of the responsibility for the actions undertaken in the name of the State. The Revolution had left a legacy in France which was only now being resolved in the union between monarchic (presidential) and democratic principles. Not surprisingly, as contemporary press reports make clear, Furet's stance was seen to be directly undermining the orthodox communist analysis of the Revolution and was approved by President Mitterrand, who wished to make the 1989 celebrations a cause for conciliation and national unification.

Pierre Gaxotte (1928/1970): *L'Ancien Régime*

Structure and content

The extract selected for analysis is the opening of the book, the beginning of Chapter 1, entitled '*L'Ancien Régime*'. Its subject matter is the foundation of the French nation. Immediate pride of place is given to the longevity of pre-revolutionary France and to its gradual and progressive evolution. This is seen as cumulative and reassuring. Reference to the relative size of the population and the quality of life point towards the geographical advantages offered by the area which would become recognised as French national territory. The *Ancien Régime* is presented as a building, an image which appeals to a sense of domesticity and territoriality. The metaphor is extended to the next foregrounded paragraph of three lines, which introduces the Church as the active agent in the construction of the nation. Once again, the long, painstaking character of the project is emphasised. The 400 years of Roman domination are disparagingly referred to as dour and oppressive ('*dur et froid*'), implying that the authentic ethnic origins of the French lay in the culture of Gallic tribes. In contrast, the Catholic Church is simplistically represented as the embodiment of life-enhancing qualities, the guardian of justice and culture and a force for order and peace.

1.
L'Ancien Régime

La France de l'Ancien Régime était un très grand et très vieil édifice qu'avaient bâti cinquante générations, embrassant plus de quinze cents années. Elles y avaient laissé chacune sa marque, ajoutant toujours au passé sans presque jamais rien en abattre, ni retrancher. Aussi, le plan en était-il confus, les styles disparates, les morceaux irréguliers. Quelques parties abandonnées menaçaient ruine ; d'autres étaient incommodes ; d'autres, trop luxueuses. Mais, somme toute, l'ensemble était cossu, la façade avait grand air, on y vivait mieux et plus nombreux qu'ailleurs.

Les fondations les plus anciennes et les plus profondes étaient l'œuvre de l'Eglise. Pendant douze siècles, elle y avait travaillé seule, ou presque seule.

Au temps de Rome, dans un monde dur et froid, elle avait apporté la consolation des misères, le courage de vivre, l'abnégation, la charité, la patience, l'espoir d'une vie meilleure et juste. Quand l'Empire se fut écroulé sous les coups des Barbares, elle avait été le refuge des lois et des lettres, des arts et de la politique. Elle avait caché, dans ses monastères, tout ce qui pouvait être sauvé de la culture humaine et de la science. En pleine anarchie, elle avait formé une société vivante et ordonnée dont la police et l'esprit rappelaient à eux seuls les temps calmes et les faisaient regretter. Bien mieux, la voici qui va au-devant des envahisseurs, les gagne, les apaise, les convertit, canalise leur flot, limite leurs dévastations. Devant l'évêque, représentant d'un au-delà mystérieux, le Germain a peur et recule. Il épargne les gens, les maisons, les terres. L'homme de Dieu devient le chef des cités, le défenseur des foyers et des métiers, le seul protecteur des humbles en ce monde.

Plus tard, quand le moment des pillages et des brûleries sera passé, quand il faudra reconstruire, administrer, négocier, les assemblées et les conseils s'ouvriront tout grands devant les clercs seuls capables de rédiger un traité, de conduire une ambassade, de haranguer un prince.

Dans les malheurs renaissants, dans cette nuit du IXe siècle remplie de bruits d'armes, tandis que de nouvelles invasions hongroises, sarrasines et normandes, entament ou recouvrent le pays, tandis que le peuple épars flotte sans direction, l'Eglise, une fois encore, tient bon. Elle renoue les traditions interrompues, combat les désordres féodaux, réglemente les guerres privées, impose des trêves et des paix. Les grands moines Odon, Odilon, Bernard élèvent, au-dessus des donjons et des villes, le pouvoir moral de l'Eglise, l'idée de l'Eglise universelle, le rêve de l'unité chrétienne. Prédicateurs, pacificateurs, conseillers de tout le monde, arbitres de toutes les querelles, ils interviennent partout et dans tout, véritables puissances internationales auxquelles les puissances terrestres ne résistent qu'en tremblant.

Autour des grands sanctuaires et des saintes abbayes se nouent relations et voyages. Le long des pistes de terre où cheminent les longues processions de pèlerins, naissent les chansons épiques. Les forêts attaquées par les moines défricheurs reculent. A l'ombre des monastères, les villages se repeuplent. Des villages en ruine se relèvent. Les vitraux des églises et les sculptures des cathédrales sont le livre d'images où le peuple s'instruit. Le pape est le dictateur de l'Europe. Il ordonne les croisades et défait les rois. Dotations, richesses, honneurs, on met tout aux pieds des clercs et l'excès même de cette reconnaissance mesure la grandeur de leurs bienfaits.

Mais déjà un autre ouvrier s'était mis à l'œuvre : le seigneur.

Source: Gaxotte, P. (1970) *La Révolution Française*, Paris: Fayard, pp. 11–13. Reproduced with kind permission of Librairie Arthème Fayard.

The remaining paragraphs of the extract are devoted more or less exclusively to the central position held by the Church throughout the different phases of the early Middle Ages. As an institution, it is seen as a humanising, civilising influence, a bastion against the destructiveness of barbaric invaders, identifiable by implication with the Germany of 1870 and 1914 (*'le Germain'*). The text traces the subsequent development of the Church's role as administrative adviser through that of pacifier, moral arbiter and protector to its medieval apotheosis as militant, totalitarian power. It is only with the last, heavily foregrounded paragraph of one sentence that the link with the next phase of the extended text is made. This marks the transition from the tyranny of warlords to the secular structure of land-ownership and loyalty on which the feudal system was to be based.

Genre and text type: the positioning of writer and reader, deixis and reference

The chronological progression of the text, the deliberate links between the paragraphs, its location in time and the magisterial style of the author clearly identify the text as belonging to the genre of 'history as narrative'. The reader is positioned as a receiver of value-judgements who is expecting as much to be entertained and reassured as to be informed. Yet neither reader nor author are ever referred to or acknowledged. The implied presence of the one and the absolute authority of the other are taken entirely for granted. The author offers no asides or comments on his own statements. His identity as in interlocutor is embedded in his style. In the first paragraph, the recurrence of the verb *être* followed by nominal and adjectival complements (*'très grand et très vieil édifice'*, *'confus'*, *'disparates'*, *'irréguliers'*, *'incommodes'*, *'luxueuses'*, *'cossu'*, and so on) presents readers with an *état de fait*. They are positioned as passive receivers of assertions which the text invites them to accept as true.

But the statements in the text cannot be verified as true or false. They are too general and loaded with connotation to have the status of fact. Beliefs are presented as certainties, to be shared or rejected according to where you stand ideologically. Simplification and emotional appeal take precedence over objective analysis. In the extreme, history as chronology demands minimal effort from the reader. The sequence of the text follows the sequence of events. But despite following a broad chronological progression, this text does not in fact refer to events at all, but to tableaux and processes. The support provided by the Church is described in abstract, moral terms (*'consolation'*, *'courage'*, *'abnégation'*, *'charité'*, *'patience'*, *'espoir'*). Institutions and races are translated into metonymies (*'l'évêque'*, *'le Germain'*). Even the temporal domination of the papacy is described in a single, brief sentence (*'Le pape est le dictateur de l'Europe'*). Ideas are replaced by images, the relationship between writer and reader being one in which the text positions the author as the purveyor of truth and the reader as consumer – or communicant.

Within the text, the positioning of characters and institutions has already been described. The Church is portrayed as a hard-working agent for good (*'œuvre'*, *'bienfaits'*, *'ouvrier'* . . .) in a world constantly threatened by violence and disorder. In the third paragraph, the verbs associated with the Church are ones of moderation during a period when invasion and chaos are in the ascendant (*'apaiser'*, *'convertir'*, *'canaliser'*, *'limiter'* . . .), which give way to nouns referring to moral leadership and protection (*'chef des cités'*, *'défenseur des foyers'*, *'protecteur des humbles'* . . .). In the fourth, the lexis is drawn from the field of rhetoric, as befits the clerical role of civil servant (*'rédiger'*, *'conduire'*, *'haranguer'* . . .), to become in the fifth a vocabulary of action and involvement in secular affairs (*'renouer'*, *'combattre'*, *'réglementer'*, *'imposer'*, *'élever'*, *'intervenir'* . . .). The sixth paragraph bears witness to a new period of stability in which, with the exception of the Pope's imperious behaviour (*'ordonner'*, *'défaire'*), the emphasis is entirely on the animation of normally inanimate features of the natural or cultural world. Forests *'reculent'*, epic *chansons de geste* *'naissent'*. The establishment of order is expressed through the repeated use of reflexive and pronominal verbs suggesting an almost biological process (*'se nouer'* *'se repeupler'*, *'se relever'*, *'s'instruire'*).

In situating the Catholic Church at the centre of the text by identifying it as the principal architect of the *Ancien Régime*, Gaxotte makes abundant use of the deictic *'elle'* (*'Les fondations les plus anciennes et les plus profondes étaient l'œuvre de l'E̲g̲l̲i̲s̲e̲. . . . e̲l̲l̲e̲ y avait travaillé seule . . . e̲l̲l̲e̲ avait apporté la consolation des misères . . . e̲l̲l̲e̲ avait été le refuge des lois et des lettres . . . e̲l̲l̲e̲ avait caché . . . tout ce qui pouvait être sauvé de la culture humaine et de la science'*). Apart from reinforcing the coherence of the third paragraph, this anaphora is a constant reminder of the Church's engagement in the nation-building project, since it shifts the focus to the various actions which the Church undertook on behalf of the community. The initial, general personification, with its combination of militant and maternal connotations, gives way, as we have seen, first to metonymy (*'L'évêque'* / *'L'homme de Dieu'*) and then in the following paragraph to a feature known as onomasia - taking a name to symbolise a quality or an action. This finds expression in the names of the monastic leaders *'Odon'*, *'Odilon'*, *'Bernard'*, in which the historical impact of a national institution is figuratively channelled through the actions of a few known individuals. Their identification with the Church is confirmed by the repetition of the word *'Eglise'*, which is expanded and made abstract by the following expression: *'le rêve de l'unité chrétienne'*, raising their status to that of apostles or prophets.

Location in time

Although the subject matter of the text follows a chronological progression, the reader's position in relation to the phenomena described is carefully manipulated by Gaxotte's use of tense. The text opens at a symbolic moment towards the end of the *Ancien Régime* at a point when – by implication – the French Revolution is about to begin. This is made clear from the first sentence of the text through the combination of the imperfect and pluperfect tenses, the first representing the general state of the regime and the second referring back to the centuries of effort which had been expended in bringing it into being: '*La France de l'Ancien Régime était un très grand et très vieil édifice qu'avaient bâti cinquante générations*'. Longevity is foregrounded as one of the main characteristics – and strengths – of the *Ancien Régime*, an implied contrast with the relative brevity of the events of the years 1787 to 1795. It is also one of the key features which lend the text coherence. This is evident from the many temporal expressions in the text ('*cinquante générations*', '*quinze cents années*', '*douze siècles*') and from the phrases which mark its gradual establishment ('*Au temps de Rome*' , '*Plus tard*' , '*dans cette nuit du IXe siècle*' , '*Mais déjà*').

The weaknesses and inequities of the regime in the second half of the eighteenth century are absorbed into adjectives ('*incommodes*', '*trop luxueuses*'). As such, they appear as minor irritants, to be subsumed in the sense of complacency and well-being which the reader is invited to share through the engagingly familiar qualifier '*somme toute*' . The reader is thus located in the mood of an historical moment which is essentially static rather than troubled by any sense of crisis and confusion. The repeated pluperfects which follow in the third paragraph ('*avait travaillé*', '*avait apporté*', '*avait été*' . . .) indicate clearly that these are long, sustained efforts of preservation and protection which took place over a previous historical period, the major development of the era being marked by the past anterior '*se fut écroulé*', which reduce the collapse of the Roman Empire in western Europe to the status of a sudden event. This reiteration of the pluperfect serves as a constant reminder to the reader that the origins of the *Ancien Régime* are being looked at from the point of view of the regime's later years; that is, from a pre-revolutionary perspective. This standpoint positions writer and reader in terms of ideological attitude as well as chronologically. According to the description of the *Ancien Régime* provided in the first paragraph, the social system offered as agreeable a way of life as was available anywhere in Europe at the time.

In the middle of the third paragraph, a striking time-shift takes place. The deictic '*la voici*' is followed by the repetition of historic present tenses: ' *qui va au-devant des envahisseurs, les gagne, les apaise, les convertit, canalise leur flot, limite leurs dévastations.*' Although highly active in the sense that, through its initiatives, the Church was able to control and direct the impact of 'barbaric' invaders, these verbs are more stative than iterative (that is, they deal with 'states of affairs' rather than with a series of successive events). Their repetition draws the reader into the time frame and, in a sequence of short sentences which have the effect of a series of intercut camera shots, lists the actions which trace the transfer of power from the invaders to the Church. Having situated the reader within the context of the early middle ages, Gaxotte is then able to move the frame forward by using the historic future and future perfect in the fourth paragraph to represent progress and consolidation (*'quand le moment des pillages et des brûleries sera passé, quand il faudra reconstruire, administrer, négocier'*), only to move back to the present when the next set of invasions, or threats to the Church's authority, takes place (*'tandis que de nouvelles invasions . . . entament ou recouvrent le pays . . . l'Eglise, une fois encore, tient bon'*). In this way, the text moves through a series of modulations which correspond to the shifts in power from the external social environment to the Catholic Church and back again. It is only in the final paragraph that there is a chronological reversal marked by the return to the pluperfect: *'Mais déjà un autre ouvrier s'était mis à l'œuvre : le seigneur'*. The foregrounded contrast highlights a process which has been taking place in parallel with the long-standing actions of the Church and represents a radical change of narrative perspective.

Rhetorical cohesion: syntactic patterning, rhythm and sentence structure

The manner in which Gaxotte's prose situates writer, reader and character depends therefore on the essentially simple structure of its progression, its assertive tone, its use of imagery, the repetition of nouns and pronouns and its foregrounded exploitation of tense. To these features should be added the highly developed sense of rhetoric which pervades the rhythm and structure of the sentences. As might be expected of a future academician who passed out first of the 1920 History graduation of the *Ecole Normale Supérieure*, the style has a classical sonority, combining regularity of rhythm with variations of syntactic pattern. These reinforce the authority of the author and add to the assertiveness of the message. The unambiguous stance taken by the text forces the reader to take a position towards the ideology which it represents. For the most part, the apparent simplicity of the style lies in the SVComp (Subject-Verb-Complement) order of the sentences. The principle of syntactic symmetry is repeatedly applied, lending a sense of measure to the prose, a feature which is perhaps best illustrated by the repetition of articles, nouns and adverbial qualifiers with coordinating conjunctions (*'un très grand et très vieil édifice'*, *'les plus anciennes et les plus profondes'*, *'de la culture humaine et de la science'*, *'des pillages et des brûleries'*, *'au-dessus des donjons et des villes'*, *'Autour des grands sanctuaires et des saintes abbayes'*, *'Les vitraux des églises et les sculptures des cathédrales'*), and finds typical expression in the combination of the two simple clauses: *'ordonne les croisades et défait les rois'*. The effect of order which results from this use of parallelism within the sentence is balanced by the variation between long and short sentences and the use of accumulation. The number of highly foregrounded features locates the text in a rhetorical tradition that draws attention to itself. Its monarchist message is embedded in the style.

Elles y avaient laissé chacune sa marque, ajoutant toujours au passé sans presque jamais rien en abattre, ni retrancher. (1) Aussi, le plan en était-il confus, les styles disparates, les morceaux irréguliers. (2) Quelques parties abandonnées menaçaient ruine ; d'autres étaient incommodes ; d'autres, trop luxueuses. (3) Mais, somme toute, l'ensemble était cossu, la façade avaient grand air, on y vivait mieux et plus nombreux qu'ailleurs. (4)

Apart from the repetition of articles, the anaphora of '*d'autres*', the triple/double use of *être* and *avoir* and the exploitation of '*en*' as a linking device between sentences 1 and 2, not a single word in the above extract recurs. Indeed, in the text as a whole, where verbal repetition occurs, it is used deliberately to foreground a particular institution or idea ('*Eglise*', '*puissances*') or, in the case of individual syllables, to further reinforce cohesion ('*partout et dans tout*'; '*défait . . . bienfaits*'). The binary structure of sentence 1 leads to the *cadence mineure* of '*ni retrancher*' which emphasises the cumulative effect of France's development as a nation. There is the cohesive balance and contrast between the conjunctions '*aussi*' and '*mais*'. But the most striking feature of the paragraph is the repetition of the three ternary rhythms in sentences 2, 3 and 4 above, between which there are nevertheless carefully modulated differences in syntactic structure. This combination of balance and variation which is built on anaphora, parallelism and rhythmic patterning is a recurrent feature of Gaxotte's style. It is found in the '*reconstruire, administrer, négocier*' and the '*rédiger . . . conduire . . . haranguer*' of paragraph four, the repetition of '*tandis que*' in paragraph five, the ternary progression of the adjectives '*hongroises, sarrasines et normandes*' and the quaternary succession of the verbs '*renoue . . . combat . . . réglemente . . . impose . . .*' and so on. These self-conscious devices are matched by the regular accumulation of nouns and verbs signalling an intensity of activity by the Church ('*la consolation des misères, le courage de vivre, l'abnégation, la charité, la patience, l'espoir d'une vie meilleure et juste*'; '*va au-devant des envahisseurs, les gagne, les apaise, les convertit, canalise leur flot, limite leurs dévastations*'; '*Prédicateurs, pacificateurs, conseillers de tout le monde, arbitres de toutes les querelles*').

Summary: the unity of style, content and genre

Overall, the style of *L'Ancien Régime* – its pictorial character, serious tone and absence of self-doubt – carries the evangelical conviction of a sermon. The text's appeal to the traditional values of the home, to territorial protection and the moral rectitude of the Catholic Church are at one with the tenor and structure of its composition. The obvious care and deliberation which have gone into every aspect of its creation, its sonority and the grandeur of its rhythms – which nevertheless do not preclude the occasional familiar qualification to maintain the collusion of the reader – earmark the text as a discursive archetype: the popular history book. For the more sceptical commentator, the attitude embedded in its rhetorical refinement excites irony – if not derision (Betourné and Hartig 1989: 155–156). It reinforces a certain readership's belief in the values of the past and in the enduring, fundamentally simple character of nationhood. Its emotional appeal, which finds an echo in the rhetoric of Charles de Gaulle, sustains an essentially centralising, hierarchically structured concept of political and ecclesiastical power. Against such a view of French history observed from the perspective of the pre-revolutionary period, the upheaval which was to follow could only appear evil and degrading.

Albert Soboul (1982): *La Révolution Française*

Background: Albert Soboul and the theory of 'La Révolution bourgeoise'

It is instructive and intriguing to compare the discursive structure of Pierre Gaxotte's text with that of a book having the same title which could arguably be seen as its Marxist counterpart. Albert Soboul's *La Révolution Française*, pub-lished in 1982 following Soboul's death the same year, was a revised and updated version of his world-famous *Précis d'Histoire de la Révolution Française* of 1962, itself a development of his 1948 publication *La Révolution Française (1789–1799)*. It was popularised in summary form in the *Que sais-je?* title *La Révolution Française*, which appeared in 1965. Holder of the *Chaire d'Histoire de la Révolution française* at the Sorbonne from 1967 to 1982 and Director of the *Centre d'Études de la Révolution Française*, Albert Soboul inherited the mantle of Georges Lefeb-vre as the principal proponent of the theory of the '*révolution bourgeoise*'. In essence, this doctrinaire Marxist argument holds that the Revolution was caused by the enlightened middle classes' drive for power. It was they who enacted the constitutional basis for equality which empowered the representatives of the peasantry and the urban poor. The excesses of the centralised revolutionary government in 1793–1794 were, according to this analysis, a necessary stage in the evolution towards 'liberalism'; that is, a free-market economy controlled by the bourgeoise (Soboul 1982: 530–533). Economically speaking, the outcome of the Revolution was the establishment of a capitalist state which prepared the foundation on which communist ideology would be built (Bétourné and Hartig 1989: 74–75).

The 'liberal' state which Soboul saw as leading the French Revolution created the context for a totally different concept of national identity from that espoused by Pierre Gaxotte. Citizenship of the French Republic implied a sworn commit-ment to the principle of total equality on which the new state was founded and of which it saw itself as the sole defender (Soboul 1982: 540):

Dès 1789, le mot nation s'était chargé d'une valeur nouvelle, précisée dans les élans passionnés du coeur, dans des mouvements collectifs spontanés qu'animaient des sentiments de foi et d'espérance. La nation, c'était le corps entier, la masse des citoyens fondus en un seul bloc; il n'y avait plus d'ordre, plus de classe; tout ce qui était français composait la nation.

It was therefore not a nation founded on order, tradition and religious belief but the embodiment of a social philosophy to which all citizens were obliged to subscribe and which found form in the acts on weights and measures, military conscription, French language, education and the general right to male suffrage (Soboul 1982: 540–556). The Terror of 1793–1794 was the result of the struggle between the defenders of the new social ideal and the members of the bourgeoisie, from which the bourgeoisie eventually emerged victorious.

Structure, progression, tone and genre

What is striking about the comparison between the two texts are their structural similarities. Both take the closing period of the *Ancien Régime* as their starting point and engage in an initial description of its defining characteristics. Both deal with a *rapport de force* between two agents: the established order and the forces of change. In one, however, change is seen primarily as a source of disorder and chaos, with credit being given to slow but constructive progress. In the other, it is the established order which is presented as oppressive and deficient, change being seen as necessary and inevitable. This is in part due to the fact that the main focus of the texts is on different points in the *Ancien Régime*'s development: Gaxotte's on its origins and Soboul's on the period preceding its dissolution. Nevertheless, each ascribes similar spiritual qualities to the agent which appears to him to have historical right on its side: the Church in the case of Gaxotte; for Soboul, the rational belief in universal human rights developed by the *philosophes*. Both agents have the power to restore a sense of dignity and purpose to a society under physical and moral threat; both are seen to take the initiative in a confrontational situation which forces the opposing elements on to the defensive ('*Devant l'évêque, . . . le Germain a peur et recule*' – Gaxotte; '*Face à cet idéal nouveau, l'Ancien Régime en était réduit à la défensive*' – Soboul); and both are portrayed as having an influence described as '*universelle*'.

Like the text by Pierre Gaxotte, Albert Soboul's extract opens with a short scene-setting statement about France and the *Ancien Régime*, which marks it as deriving from the beginning of a chapter, if not of a book. The main difference between the two texts is their positioning in time. In Soboul's case, it is much more precise. He leads the reader to suppose that the text will go on to explain the immediate reasons for the outbreak of the Revolution. For Gaxotte, the objective was more to give a portrait of the regime's historical origins and to defend the principles on which it was founded. Soboul's portrayal of the *Ancien Régime* is indeed more theoretically grounded. It depends on the interaction of

En 1789, la France vivait dans le cadre de ce que l'on a appelé depuis l'*Ancien Régime*.

La société demeurait d'essence aristocratique ; elle avait pour fondements le privilège de la naissance et la richesse foncière. Mais cette structure traditionnelle se trouvait minée par l'évolution de l'économie qui accroissait l'importance de la richesse mobilière et la puissance de la bourgeoisie. En même temps, les progrès de la connaissance positive et l'élan conquérant de la philosophie des Lumières sapaient les fondements idéologiques de l'ordre établi. Si la France demeurait encore, à la fin du XVIIIe siècle, essentiellement rurale et artisanale, l'économie traditionnelle se transformait par l'essor du grand commerce et l'apparition [*encore très réduite et très récente*]* de la grande industrie. Les progrès du capitalisme, la revendication de la liberté économique suscitaient sans doute une vive résistance de la part des catégories sociales attachées à l'ordre économique traditionnel : ils n'en apparaissaient pas moins nécessaires aux yeux de la bourgeoisie, dont les philosophes et les économistes avaient élaboré une doctrine conforme à ses intérêts sociaux et politiques. La noblesse pouvait bien conserver le premier rang dans la hiérarchie officielle ; elle n'en était pas moins en déclin [*relatif*] dans sa puissance économique et dans son rôle social.

Sur les classes populaires, paysannes surtout, pesait tout le poids de l'Ancien Régime et de ce qui demeurait de la féodalité. Ces classes étaient encore incapables de concevoir quels étaient leurs droits et combien elles étaient puissantes ; la bourgeoisie leur apparaissait naturellement, avec sa forte armature économique et son rayonnement intellectuel, comme le seul guide. La bourgeoisie française du XVIIIe siècle avait élaboré une philosophie qui correspondait à son passé, à son rôle, à ses intérêts : mais avec une telle largeur de vues et en prenant si solidement appui sur la raison, que cette philosophie qui critiquait l'Ancien Régime et contribuait à le ruiner, revêtant une valeur universelle, s'adressait à tous les Français et à tous les hommes.

* Les passages en italique entre crochets sont ceux qui ont été modifiés par rapport à l'édition du *Précis* de 1972. Pour plus de précisions, se reporter, dans ce volume, à l'avant-propos de Claude Mazauric.

La philosophie des Lumières substituait à la conception traditionnelle de la vie et de la société, un idéal de bonheur social fondé sur la croyance au progrès indéfini de l'esprit humain et de la connaissance scientifique. L'homme retrouvait sa dignité. La liberté entière dans tous les domaines, économique aussi bien que politique, devait stimuler son activité : les philosophes lui donnaient pour but la connaissance de la nature pour la mieux dominer, et l'augmentation de la richesse générale. Ainsi les sociétés humaines pourraient pleinement s'épanouir.

Face à cet idéal nouveau, l'Ancien Régime en était réduit à la défensive. La monarchie demeurait toujours de droit divin ; le roi de France était tenu pour le représentant de Dieu sur terre ; il jouissait de ce fait d'un pouvoir absolu. Mais il manquait une volonté à ce régime absolutiste. Louis XVI avait finalement abdiqué son pouvoir absolu entre les mains de l'aristocratie. Ce qu'on a appelé *la révolution aristocratique* (mais qui est plutôt une *réaction nobiliaire* ou mieux une *réaction aristocratique* ne reculant pas devant la violence et la révolte) a précédé dès 1787 la révolution bourgeoise de 1789. Malgré un personnel administratif souvent remarquable, les tentatives de réformes structurales de Machault, de Maupeou, de Turgot échouèrent devant la résistance opiniâtre des Parlements et des États provinciaux, bastions de l'aristocratie. Si bien que l'organisation administrative ne s'améliora guère et que l'Ancien Régime demeura comme inachevé.

Source: Soboul, A. (1982) *La Révolution Française*, Paris: Editions Sociales, pp. 51–53.

economic forces over a span of only sixty to seventy years, as opposed to Gaxotte's '*quinze cents siècles*'.

Soboul's tone is professorial rather than evangelical. Instead of the grandiose and static '*édifice*', the more neutral term '*cadre*' is used, lending the text a more ideational, less interpersonal perspective. At the same time, the act of qualification and definition, '*ce que l'on a appelé depuis . . .*', lends the discourse a predominantly explanatory function. It acknowledges the presence of the reader as interlocutor. This aspect of the text is re-echoed in the parentheses of the phrases in brackets: '[*encore très réduite et très récente*]' and '[*relatif*]' in paragraph two and the much more extended clause of paragraph four: '*mais qui est plutôt une <u>réaction nobiliaire</u> ou mieux une <u>réaction aristocratique</u> ne reculant pas devant la violence et la révolte*' – again preceded by the qualifying '*Ce qu'on a appelé*'. These features, which are notably absent from the text by Gaxotte, belong more to the genre of an academic seminar than that of a sermon or public oration – no less assertive but more deferential to its readership.

The combination of statements which leave little scope for disagreement with the effort to qualify and explain is demonstrated in the extended second paragraph. The text depicts a state of tension between the established order and the economic forces which were undermining it. Soboul uses the imperfect tense in two different ways, which together encapsulate the essence of the confrontation. '*Demeurait*' and '*avait*' are static and passive, '*sapaient*' and '*suscitaient*' more active and evocative of movement. As in Gaxotte's text, the reflexive verbs '*se trouvait*', '*se transformait*' suggest an historical process over which the subject has little control, a point which is reinforced in each case by the use of the preposition '*par*' followed by a Noun + Complement linked by '*de*' ('*se trouvait minée par l'évolution de l'économie*'; '*se transformait par l'essor du grand commerce*'). However, in Soboul's text, the process is directly activated by the development of commercial forces, whereas, for Gaxotte, the use of the reflexive verbs denotes a more natural, evolutionary progression which reinforces the conservative perspective of the text.

Already in the second paragraph, which sets the tone of the piece, the process of argumentation and reasoning is more clearly marked than in Gaxotte's text. The structure is less chronological and more dependent on a series of concessive clauses followed by a main clause which asserts that the economic agency of the *bourgeoisie* was the prevailing force for change: '*La société <u>demeurait</u> d'essence aristocratique . . . <u>Mais</u> cette structure se trouvait minée par l'évolution de l'économie . . .*'; '*<u>Si</u> la France demeurait encore, . . . essentiellement rurale et artisanale, l'économie traditionnelle <u>se transformait</u> par l'essor du grand commerce . . .*'; '*Les progrès du capitalisme . . . suscitaient <u>sans doute</u> une vive résistance . . .; ils n'en apparaissaient <u>pas moins</u> nécessaires aux yeux de la bourgeoisie . . .*'; '*La noblesse <u>pouvait bien</u> conserver le premier rang dans la hiérarchie officielle; elle n'en était <u>pas moins</u> en déclin . . .*'. This form of argument through counterpoint ('x' is true . . . but 'y' is also true . . . therefore 'z' . . .) is typical of academic discourse. In this instance, it structures the paragraph and represents the rhetorical dynamic around which the whole thesis of the book is to be built. It seeks not merely to assert but to *demonstrate* through dialectic. This tone is reinforced at the end of paragraphs four and five, each of which closes with causal conjunctions ('*Ainsi les sociétés humaines pourraient pleinement s'épanouir*' . . . '*Si bien que l'organisation administrative ne s'améliora guère . . .*').

The fact that Soboul's text is structured around ideas or perspectives rather than time is indicated by the opening and closing of each paragraph. Having introduced the text with a paragraph consisting of a single sentence, the second paragraph considers the relationship between the Ancien Régime and the rise of the bourgeoisie. The third goes on to consider the attitude of the so-called '*classes populaires*' to the promise of enlightenment; the fourth, the ideal which the new philosophy represented; and finally the fifth, the reaction of the established powers to the new political challenge. In contrast to Gaxotte's text, Soboul's perspective is essentially static. It defines a social context rather than telling a story.

Syntax and 'point of view'

However, as has been mentioned, Soboul's text shares a number of features with that of Gaxotte which demonstrate that the basic tenets of his analysis, although fundamentally different, are just as deeply entrenched. The certainty of his assertions comes through, as with the first text, in the repeated use of *être*: '*elle n'en était pas moins en déclin . . .*', '*Ces classes étaient encore incapables de concevoir quels étaient leurs droits et combien elles étaient puissantes.*', '*L'Ancien Régime en était réduit à la défensive.*'. Similarly, the word order of the sentences suggests that the prime function of the text is to inform and demonstrate rather than to be reflective and self-analytical. This assertive quality is softened in the fourth paragraph by a shift in position, which is expressed through a subtle change of mood. The rise of the bourgeoisie is presented simultaneously from the point of view of the author and that of the '*classes populaires*'. Soboul initially presents their perceptions as if they were realities in the form of short statements based on standard SVO/SVComp patterns, which move from the imperfect of the indicative to the conditional mood: '*L'homme retrouvait sa dignité. La liberté entière [. . .] devait stimuler son activité . . . Ainsi les sociétés humaines pourraient pleinement s'épanouir.*' In the following (fifth) paragraph, the author again speaks exclusively with his own voice: '*La monarchie demeurait toujours de droit divin ; le roi de France était tenu pour le représentant de Dieu sur terre . . .*'.

The modals '*devait*' and '*pourraient*' reflect the active potential which the Enlightenment held for human kind in general. A strong sense of intention is present, in which the principal agents are the *philosophes*, who are effectively mapping out a programme for society to follow. In a sense, the shift from imperfect to modal and conditional in Soboul's text is equivalent to that from historic present to future in Gaxotte's. In both texts, the reader is invited to share the perspective of the author by being forced to adopt a different chronological position. The difference between them is one of mood. Whereas in Gaxotte's, the future designates initiatives which supposedly actually took place, in Soboul's, the intention is to create a context of aspiration which the reader is invited to share. The manner in which the reader is implicated in the text is more subtle. Later, Soboul uses the perfect tense ('*a appelé', 'a précédé'*) as if to address the reader in an aside. In the following sentences, however, he employs the past historic ('*échouèrent', 'ne s'améliora guère', 'demeura'*). These individual events take place within a self-contained block of time during which the effects of the so-called '*réaction aristocratique*' made themselves felt. At no point does he allow himself the more populist indulgence of the historic present that is so heavily foregrounded in the text by his predecessor.

Shared rhetorical features

Elsewhere there are resemblances between the two texts which situate them both in a rhetorical tradition that seeks to represent opposing ideological affiliations. Soboul, like Gaxotte, creates sentences which combine parallel structures and balanced rhythms: '*l'importance de la richesse mobilière et la puissance de la bourgeoisie*', '*l'essor du grand commerce et l'apparition . . . de la grande industrie*', '*dans sa puissance économique et dans son rôle social*', '*quels étaient leurs droits et combien elles étaient puissantes . . .*', '*au progrès indéfini de l'esprit humain et de la connaissance scientifique*'. Similarly, his recourse to ternary rhythms is powerfully foregrounded on at least two occasions: '*qui correspondait à son passé, à son rôle, à ses intérêts . . .*' and '*les tentatives de réformes structurales de Machault, de Maupeou, de Turgot . . .*'. In both cases, the effect is to reinforce a contrast. The first emphasises the self-interest of the bourgeoisie in initiating reform. This allows Soboul to make the universal impact of the Enlightenment all the more marked – because it is surprising. In the second case, the sequence of three chief ministers who made successive attempts at reform is an indication of how difficult it was to undermine the power of the aristocracy. Despite their best efforts, they were unable to bring about change.

Thus, the two texts share a common rhetorical tradition and use many similar features to support analyses which are almost diametrically opposed to each other. Yet the first is undoubtedly more ostentatiously grandiose and relies more heavily on rhetorical flourishes than the second. It is more dependent on metaphor and metonymy and on pictorial statements delivered in short, vivid sentences, which are contrasted with the heavily foregrounded, deliberately overstated accumulations of nouns and verbs. The second text is more sober, relying as it does on argument and persuasion and on a greater sense of dialogue with the reader. Structured around ideas and social categories rather than historical chronology, it is more discursive but just as unrelenting and coherent in the consistency of its thesis. As contextualisations of historical arguments, both are archetypes of their genre. Their similarities and differences provide an insight into the different relationship which each is seeking to establish with its respective readership. Equally, they illustrate well the discursive tensions which exist between two competing interpretations of French history.

François Furet (1978): *Penser la Révolution Française*

Content and intertextuality

The third text, written by François Furet and published in 1978, is clearly an intertext of the other two in the sense that its subject is not the *Ancien Régime* and the Revolution themselves but the nature of the historical analysis which has been applied to them. As this extract shows, *Penser la Révolution Française* is a history book about history and the historical process. Since it deals with basic philosophical principles, it seems that the extract is situated early in the book and is mounting an argument which the main body of the text will go on to prove. While the first two texts we have considered are essentially affirmatory, the dominant tone of Furet's style is one of challenge or interrogation. Furet starts by setting up an historical view of the French Revolution which is based on two propositions: first, that events in retrospect are always seen as inevitable, and second, that the Revolution represents a watershed or break in time between an '*avant*' and an '*après*' which are completely separate from each other. Both in Furet's view are false and he goes on to show why. By making the rise of capitalism both the cause and the consequence of the Revolution, it distorts our understanding of the *Ancien Régime*. By arguing backwards (or deductively), says Furet, we falsify our view of the past.

Genre and the positioning of writer and reader – irony and pastiche

Furet, like Soboul, defines the reader as informed listener. However, his text has, by implication, a dual audience: the actual reader and the representatives of the theory which Furet is attacking. This representative is of course not named. Rather, he is subsumed in a concept – '*le postulat de la nécessité de « ce qui a eu lieu »*' – which opens the extract. This immediately situates the text in the genre of a debate, allowing the author to remain superficially detached. At the same time, his use of irony makes his position unmistakable to the reader. Like Soboul, Furet argues by antithesis; only, instead of doing it sentence by sentence, he establishes a point of view in a whole paragraph and then uses the whole of the following paragraph to demolish the argument he has just put forward. Soboul's more modulated approach moves within the same paragraph from counter-statement to

Le postulat de la nécessité de « ce qui a eu lieu » est une illusion rétrospective classique de la conscience historique : le passé est un champ de possibles à l'intérieur duquel « ce qui est arrivé » apparaît après coup comme le seul avenir de ce passé. Mais dans le cas de l'histoire de la Révolution, ce postulat en recouvre un deuxième, dont il est inséparable : celui de la coupure chronologique absolue que représente 89, ou les années 89-93, dans l'histoire de France. Avant, c'est le règne de l'absolutisme et de la noblesse (comme si ces deux figures de l'Ancien Régime marchaient la main dans la main). Après, la liberté et la bourgeoisie. Tapies enfin dans le bruit et la fureur de cette Révolution, les promesses d'une annonciation socialiste. Comme l'avaient dit ses acteurs, la rupture révolutionnaire érige ainsi l'histoire de France en recommencement, et l'événement lui-même en une sorte de point focal où vient s'abolir le passé, se constituer le présent et se dessiner l'avenir. Non seulement ce qui a eu lieu est fatal, mais le futur aussi y est inscrit.

Or, le « concept » dominant l'historiographie révolutionnaire. aujourd'hui, celui de « révolution bourgeoise », me paraît précisément, dans l'acception où il est utilisé. moins un concept qu'un masque sous lequel se cachent ces deux présupposés. celui de la nécessité de l'événement et celui de la rupture du temps : « concept », ou masque, providentiel, qui réconcilie tous les niveaux de la réalité historique, et tous les aspects de la Révolution française. En effet. les événements de 1789-1794 sont censés accoucher à la fois du capitalisme. au niveau économique; de la prépondérance bourgeoise. dans l'ordre social et politique; et des valeurs idéologiques qui sont supposées lui être liées. D'un autre côté. ils renvoient au rôle fondamental de la bourgeoisie comme classe dans le déroulement de la Révolution. Ainsi, l'idée confuse de « révolution bourgeoise » désigne inséparablement un contenu et un acteur historiques, qui s'épanouissent ensemble dans l'explosion nécessaire de ces courtes années de la fin du xviiie siècle. A une « œuvre » considérée comme inévitable, elle donne un agent parfaitement adapté. En systématisant l'idée d'une coupure radicale entre l'avant et l'après. l'interprétation « sociale » de la Révolution française couronne une métaphysique de l'essence et de la fatalité.

Dans cette mesure. elle est beaucoup plus qu'une interprétation de la Révolution; annexant à son sujet tout le problème des origines. c'est-à-dire toute la société française d'avant 89, elle est aussi une vision rétrospective de l' « Ancien Régime », défini *a contrario* par le nouveau.

Source: Furet, F. (1978) *Penser la Révolution Française*, Paris: Gallimard, pp. 35–36. ©Editions Gallimard.

statement, yet it always tends in the same positive direction. Furet's approach is more destructive. His main object is to discredit an established theory. He deliberately takes the voice of the opposing point of view, putting words in its mouth and making it appear foolishly simplistic through the use of the present tense '*c'est . . .*', the over-formal contrast between '*avant*' and '*après*', and through the use of parentheses, which allows him to pass ironic comment '(*comme si ces deux figures de l'Ancien Régime marchaient la main dans la main*)'. This irony is further expressed through the use of a metaphor, '*Tapies*', which has '*les promesses d'une annonciation socialiste*' cowering in the sound and fury of the revolutionary confusion. Furet uses a mixture of abstract terms, casual quotations, metaphor and ellipsis ('*Après, la liberté et la bourgeoisie*') as a source of wry humour to engage the reader's sympathy. In taking the voice of his opponents, he gently mocks their style with words such as '*annonciation*' and '*érige*' followed by a very explicit ternary structure – '*s'abolir le passé, se constituer le présent et se dessiner l'avenir*' – emphasised by the binary pattern in the next sentence ('*Non seulement . . ., mais . . .*'), all of which, through pastiche, belittles their point of view.

There can be no doubt as to where the author stands as regards current theory, or as to the position which he is inviting the reader to take up. Despite the abstraction of the debate, his approach is direct and personal, as the opening to the second paragraph makes clear. The '*postulat*' of the first paragraph has become the '«*concept*»' of the second . . . but only between quotation marks, suggesting a false premise. He does not hesitate to use the indirect object pronoun '*me*' to personalise his standpoint and, in so doing, to make a direct appeal to the reader in a manner which is in marked contrast to both the other two texts. The heavy recourse to deictics – '*ces deux présupposés, celui de la nécessité de l'événement et celui de la rupture du temps . . .*', – refer the reader to the first paragraph and the 'false' arguments he had attacked there. They, too, enhance the interpersonal dimension of the discourse – as well as its coherence – by acting as a conscious reminder of the point already made. The technique is even more pronounced in the second part of the sentence, where Furet again repeats the words '*concept*' and '*masque*', immediately followed by the – heavily ironic – '*providentiel*'. '*En effet*' only compounds the situation, followed as it is by the – again ironic – '*censés accoucher*' and the ternary structure which is a further throw-back to the earlier pastiche. The tone continues to the end of the paragraph, where the same effect of cohesion through repetition is achieved, this time through translating the adverbs '*avant*' and '*après*' into nouns, and ending with the cynical '*métaphysique de l'essence et de la fatalité*'. This leitmotif refers once again to the twin concepts Furet is attacking and which bind the whole text together: the view of the Revolution as a watershed, and the notion of historical necessity.

Argumentation, cohesion, imagery and satire

Furet's style is dense, abstract and highly verbal in the sense that he is seeking to undermine the meaning of the words used by his fellow historian. Following the exposition of the first paragraph, the second is built around the adverbial markers: '*Or*', '*En effet*' , '*D'un autre côté*'' and '*Ainsi*'. These expressions are a repeated reminder of the passage's insistent, ironic tone, since the causality of the established point of view is precisely what he is criticising. By quoting out of context or by putting ironic references between quotation marks, Furet is able to build his own metaphors, which enhance the sense of satire. The 'concept' itself is personified: so the '*idée confuse de « révolution bourgeoise » . . . donne un agent parfaitement adapté . . .* ' to bring about an '*« oeuvre » considérée comme inévitable*'. The events of 1789–1794 '*sont censés accoucher*' – give birth to – three phenomena which, according to Furet, cannot be straightforwardly linked.

Furet is not simply attacking the *idea* of the *révolution bourgeoise*. In using irony to expose what he sees as the flaws in the argument, he deliberately undermines the discourse in which the idea is expressed. It is this play with language which points towards the discursive tension between the different texts and underlines the fact that what we are witnessing is not simply a clash of ideology but a confrontation between two contexts of culture. He deliberately uses a playful and self-referring style to expose what he sees as the rigidity and abstraction of Soboul's analysis. In so doing, he earmarks himself as an opponent of logically grounded argument who has opened up the French Revolution to new interpretations.

Conclusion

The relationship between the three texts we have considered is essentially conflictual. The texts by Gaxotte and Soboul are generically demarcated. They espouse diametrically opposed analyses of the French Revolution and situate their readers through their style. The one is simplistic, highly visual and virtually devoid of factual information, positioning addressees as readers who either share the authors' presuppositions or who – like Bétourné and Hartig (1989) – are forcing themselves to swallow a bitter and indigestible pill. The other is more discursive and respectful of its audience; the presence of its author is more explicit. The qualifications in brackets suggest a measure of self-qualification, though Soboul's belief in the rightness of his argument is never in doubt. Generically, it defines itself as an academic text whose objective is to defend a thesis, positioning the reader as ally or protagonist in an ideological debate.

Furet, on the other hand, turns deductive logic on its head by revealing its contradictions. He deliberately distances himself from a prioristic theorising, engaging the collusion of the reader through irony and metaphor. This approach allows him the discursive space to offer a more sceptical, open-ended view of history in which the implementation of the principles on which the Revolution of 1789 was based are constantly being redefined. In terms of French national identity, the Revolution has been and remains the benchmark against which social justice is measured, and the State is the guardian responsible for maintaining its tradition. The nationwide protests against Alain Juppé's attempts in 1995 to overhaul the tax and social security systems were a clear indication that even if Frank Eskenazi (1988: 11) could claim in his summary of Furet's work that '*l'idée révolutionnaire est en train de mourir dans la société française*', seven years on, it was still showing some signs of life. Nevertheless, in undermining existing orthodoxies, Furet has enabled present-day interpretations of the Revolution to support a consensual, less ideologically informed view of democracy which seeks to reconcile the principle of social equality with the global economic pressures of the new millennium. It is hardly surprising that he has been seen as a harbinger of uncertainty and a threat to the contradictory values on which the notion of French nationhood has rested for so long.

Pierre Gaxotte, *La Révolution Française*, **Paris: Fayard, 1970**
(1st ed. 1928), pp. 11–13.

1. L'Ancien Régime

La France de l'Ancien Régime était un très grand et très vieil édifice qu'avaient bâti cinquante générations, embrassant plus de quinze cents années. Elles y avaient laissé chacune sa marque, ajoutant toujours au passé sans presque jamais rien en abattre, ni retrancher. Aussi, le plan en était-il confus, les styles disparates, les morceaux irréguliers. Quelques parties abandonnées menaçaient ruine ; d'autres étaient incommodes ; d'autres, trop luxueuses. Mais, somme toute, l'ensemble était cossu, la façade avait grand air, on y vivait mieux et plus nombreux qu'ailleurs.

Les fondations les plus anciennes et les plus profondes étaient l'œuvre de l'Eglise. Pendant douze siècles, elle y avait travaillé seule, ou presque seule.

Au temps de Rome, dans un monde dur et froid, elle avait apporté la consolation des misères, le courage de vivre, l'abnégation, la charité, la patience, l'espoir d'une vie meilleure et juste. Quand l'Empire se fut écroulé sous les coups des Barbares, elle avait été le refuge des lois et des lettres, des arts et de la politique. Elle avait caché, dans ses monastères, tout de qui pouvait être sauvé de la culture humaine et de la science. En pleine anarchie, elle avait formé une société vivante et ordonnée dont la police et l'esprit rappelaient à eux seuls les temps calmes et les faisaient regretter. Bien mieux, la voici qui va au-devant des envahisseurs, les gagne, les apaise, les convertit, canalise leur flot, limite leurs dévastations. Devant l'évêque, représentant d'un au-delà mystérieux, le Germain a peur et recule. Il épargne les gens, les maisons, les terres. L'homme de Dieu devient le chef des cités, le défenseur des foyers et des métiers, le seul protecteur des humbles en ce monde. Plus tard, quand le moment des pillages et des brûleries sera passé, quand il faudra reconstruire, administrer, négocier, les assemblées et les conseils s'ouvriront tout grands devant les clercs seuls capables de rédiger un traité, de conduire une ambassade, de haranguer un prince.

Dans les malheurs renaissants, dans l'effondrement de l'Etat carolingien, dans cette nuit du IXe siècle remplie de bruit d'armes, tandis que de nouvelles invasions hongroises, sarrasines et normandes, entament ou recouvrent le pays, tandis que le peuple épars flotte sans direction, l'Eglise, une fois encore, tient bon. Elle renoue les traditions interrompues, combat les désordres féodaux, réglemente les

37 guerres privées, impose des trêves et des paix. Les grands moines Odon, Odilon,
38 Bernard élèvent, au-dessus des donjons et des villes, le pouvoir moral de l'Eglise,
39 l'idée de l'Eglise universelle, le rêve de l'unité chrétienne. Prédicateurs, pacifica-
40 teurs, conseillers de tout le monde, arbitres de toutes les querelles, ils intervien-
41 nent partout et dans tout, véritables puissances internationales auxquelles les
42 puissances terrestres ne résistent qu'en tremblant.
43
44 Autour des grands monastères et des saintes abbayes se nouent relations et voy-
45 ages. Le long des pistes de terre où cheminent les longues processions de pèlerins,
46 naissent les chansons épiques. Les forêts attaquées par les moines défricheurs
47 reculent. A l'ombre des monastères, les campagnes se repeuplent. Des villages en
48 ruine se relèvent. Les vitraux des églises et les sculptures des cathédrales sont le
49 livre d'images où le peuple s'instruit. Le pape est le dictateur de l'Europe. Il
50 ordonne les croisades et défait les rois. Dotations, richesses, honneurs, on met
51 tout aux pieds des clercs et l'excès même de cette reconnaissance mesure la
52 grandeur de leurs bienfaits.
53
54 Mais déjà un autre ouvrier s'était mis à l'oeuvre : le seigneur.

For the original format, see page 169.

Alfred Soboul, *La Révolution Française*, Paris: Editions Sociales, 1982, pp. 51–53.

Introduction

1
2
3   En 1789, La France vivait dans le cadre de ce que l'on a appelé depuis l'*Ancien*
4   *Régime*.
5
6   La société demeurait d'essence aristocratique ; elle avait pour fondements le
7   privilège de la naissance et la richesse foncière. Mais cette structure traditionnelle
8   se trouvait minée par l'évolution de l'économie qui accroissait l'importance de la
9   richesse mobilière et la puissance de la bourgeoisie. En même temps, les
10   progrès de la connaissance positive et l'élan conquérant de la philosophie des
11   Lumières sapaient les fondements idéologiques de l'ordre établi. Si la France
12   demeurait encore, à la fin du XVIIIe siècle, essentiellement rurale et artisanale,
13   l'économie traditionnelle se transformait par l'essor du grand commerce et
14   l'apparition [*encore très réduite et très récente*]* de la grande industrie. Les progrès du
15   capitalisme, la revendication de la liberté économique suscitaient sans doute une
16   vive résistance de la part des catégories sociales attachées à l'ordre économique
17   traditionnel : ils n'en apparaissaient pas moins nécessaires aux yeux de la bour-
18   geoisie, dont les philosophes et les économistes avaient élaboré une doctrine
19   conforme à ses intérêts sociaux et politiques. La noblesse pouvait bien conserver
20   le premier rang dans la hiérarchie officielle ; elle n'en était pas moins en déclin
21   [*relatif*] dans sa puissance économique et dans son rôle social.
22
23   Sur les classes populaires, paysannes surtout, pesait tout le poids de l'Ancien
24   Régime et de ce qui demeurait de la féodalité. Ces classes étaient encore incapa-
25   bles de concevoir quels étaient leurs droits et combien elles étaient puissantes ; la
26   bourgeoisie leur apparaissait naturellement, avec sa forte armature économique et
27   son rayonnement intellectuel, comme le seul guide. La bourgeoisie française du
28   XVIIIe siècle avait élaboré une philosophie qui correspondait à son passé, à son
29   rôle, à ses intérêts : mais avec une telle largeur de vues et en prenant si solidement
30   appui sur la raison, que cette philosophie qui critiquait l'Ancien Régime et con-
31   tribuait à le ruiner, revêtant une valeur universelle, s'adressait à tous les Français
32   et à tous les hommes.
33

* Les passages en italique entre crochets sont ceux qui ont été modifiés par rapport à l'édition du *Précis* de 1972. Pour plus de précisions, se reporter, dans ce volume, à l'avant-propos de Claude Mazauric.

34 La philosophie des Lumières substituait à la conception traditionnelle de la vie et
35 de la société, un idéal de bonheur social fondé sur la croyance au progrès indéfini
36 de l'esprit humain et de la connaissance scientifique. L'homme retrouvait sa
37 dignité. La liberté entière dans tous les domaines, économique aussi bien que
38 politique, devait stimuler son activité : les philosophes lui donnaient pour but la
39 connaissance de la nature pour la mieux dominer, et l'augmentation de la richesse
40 générale. Ainsi les sociétés humaines pourraient pleinement s'épanouir.
41
42 Face à cet idéal nouveau, l'Ancien Régime en était réduit à la défensive. La
43 monarchie demeurait toujours de droit divin ; le roi de France était tenu pour le
44 représentant de Dieu sur terre ; il jouissait de ce fait d'un pouvoir absolu. Mais il
45 manquait une volonté à ce régime absolutiste. Louis XVI avait finalement abdiqué
46 son pouvoir absolu entre les mains de l'aristocratie. Ce qu'on a appelé *la révolution*
47 *aristocratique* (mais qui est plutôt une *réaction nobiliaire* ou mieux une *réaction*
48 *aristocratique* ne reculant pas devant la violence et la révolte) a précédé dès 1787 la
49 révolution bourgeoise de 1789. Malgré un personnel administratif souvent
50 remarquable, les tentatives de réformes structurales de Machault, de Maupeou, de
51 Turgot échouèrent devant la résistance opiniâtre des Parlements et des Etats
52 provinciaux, bastions de l'aristocratie. Si bien que l'organisation administrative ne
53 s'améliora guère et que l'Ancien Régime demeura comme inachevé.

For the original format, see page 177.

François Furet, *Penser la Révolution Française*, Paris: Gallimard, 1978, pp. 35–36.

La Révolution française est terminée

Le postulat de la nécessité de « ce qui a eu lieu » est une illusion rétrospective classique de la conscience historique : le passé est un champ de possibles à l'intérieur duquel « ce qui est arrivé » apparaît après coup comme le seul avenir de ce passé. Mais dans le cas de l'histoire de la Révolution, ce postulat en recouvre un deuxième, dont il est inséparable : celui de la coupure chronologique absolue que représente 89, ou les années 89–93, dans l'histoire de France. Avant, c'est le règne de l'absolutisme et de la noblesse (comme si ces deux figures de l'Ancien Régime marchaient la main dans la main). Après, la liberté et la bourgeoisie. Tapies enfin dans le bruit et la fureur de cette Révolution, les promesses d'une annonciation socialiste. Comme l'avaient dit ses acteurs, la rupture révolutionnaire érige ainsi l'histoire de France en recommencement, et l'événement lui-même en une sorte de point focal où vient s'abolir le passé, se constituer le présent et se dessiner l'avenir. Non seulement ce qui a eu lieu est fatal, mais le futur aussi y est inscrit.

Or, le « concept » dominant l'historiographie révolutionnaire, aujourd'hui, celui de « révolution bourgeoise », me paraît précisément, dans l'acception où il est utilisé, moins un concept qu'un masque sous lequel se cachent ces deux présupposés, celui de la nécessité de l'événement et celui de la rupture du temps : « concept », où masque, providentiel, qui réconcilie tous les niveaux de la réalité historique, et tous les aspects de la Révolution française. En effet, les événements de 1789–1794 sont censés accoucher à la fois du capitalisme, au niveau économique; de la prépondérance bourgeoise, dans l'ordre social et politique; et des valeurs idéologiques qui sont supposées lui être liées. D'un autre côté, ils renvoient au rôle fondamental de la bourgeoisie comme classe dans le déroulement de la Révolution. Ainsi, l'idée confuse de « révolution bourgeoise » désigne inséparablement un contenu et un acteur historiques, qui s'épanouissent ensemble dans l'explosion nécessaire de ces courtes années de la fin du XVIIIᵉ siècle. A une « œuvre » considérée comme inévitable, elle donne un agent parfaitement adapté. En systématisant l'idée d'une coupure radicale entre l'avant et l'après, l'interprétation « sociale » de la Révolution française couronne une métaphysique de l'essence et de la fatalité.

Dans cette mesure, elle est beaucoup plus qu'une interprétation de la Révolution; annexant à son sujet tout le problème des origines, c'est-à-dire toute la société française d'avant 89, elle est aussi une vision rétrospective de l' « Ancien Régime », défini *a contrario* par le nouveau.

For the original format, see page 182.

Part 3

Concluding comments

Text and national identity

Robert Crawshaw and Karin Tusting

The main objective of this book has been to draw the attention of students and academic colleagues to the value of a rhetoric which both explains and contextualises. It has sought first to make the close reader of a written French text aware of the linguistic instruments or features which have been brought into play by different authors in different circumstances. This implies that choices have been made by speaker/writers from the brute matter of the linguistic system, moulding the language into a message in order to achieve a particular communicative objective. In doing so, conscious or subconscious devices have been mobilised, lending texts a particular character and producing an effect on an implied reader. In drawing attention to the features available to speaker/writers, the book has aimed to give its own readers an insight into the creative potential of the French language. This insight has inevitably been limited by the number, range and type of texts chosen and by the particular contexts from which they have been drawn. The book's implied interlocutors are students and professional linguists who are positioned in relation to the French language both in virtue of their roles and cultures and by the particular style and orientation of our approach.

Although several examples of 'slang' can be found in the material selected, there are no examples of dialect, no forms of French spoken outside the '*hexagone*', few if any samples of the codes of minority groups, and no extracts of the electronically mediated register which is currently transforming the language more quickly than any formally recognised institution. To that extent, the book is conservative. It invokes an image of the French language which is essentially fixed in its habits and systems of control, one in which change is seen in relation to a written standard being overtaken by events but which is still regarded by a core of the French population as the language of the most powerful national institutions – symbolic of national pride and an emblem of French cultural identity. The features and techniques of written style are seen as 'informative' for the Anglo-Saxon learner of French, to the extent that they have been judged to be a central ideological and educational objective for several generations of French citizens. An appreciation of this dimension of French lies, as we see it, at the heart of what the language stands for as a vehicle of communication and the transmission of a culture.

We have not, however, sought to propound a view of French style based on '*l'art de bien écrire*'. The book is not prescriptive, but descriptive. While the ideal of a written standard subsists as a construction of French civilisation, a *culture mosaïque* which finds daily expression in a multiplicity of written and visual arte-facts challenges and comments ironically on it. In Part 1, we wanted to point this out and to imply that an appreciation of the quality of written prose does not preclude an awareness of its relative status. Neither have we sought to present style as primarily a matter of individual choice. On the contrary, a constant theme running through our analysis has been the inseparability of choice and context, of linguistic self-determination and the discursive forces which condition the way in which texts are formed. Our second aim has therefore been to go beyond purely linguistic awareness and what has traditionally been regarded as the domain of stylistics. As well as being interesting in their own right as samples of written language, the style and discursive structure of texts provide an insight into a society in constant mutation. Their construction is the product of the dynamic between writers and institutions and between institutions themselves. It is also the consequence of the interaction between institutions and real or implied readers. We have sought to explain and illustrate the inevitability of this interdependence with reference to the linguists and philosophers whose work brought the social groundedness of discourse to the consciousness of the wider academic community.

In situating our approach theoretically in relation to established schools, we wanted to provide readers with some insight into the background of stylistics as a field of study. The picture has inevitably been a partial one and scarcely does justice to the complexity of the field. We did not, for example, attempt to explain why it is that an author such as Bally (1963, 1970), who was primarily interested in the spoken language, should have been identified by successive generations of French linguists as part of the mainstream of French literary stylistics. Neither did we explore the analogies between the work of Spitzer (1948, 1970) and more recent analysts of linguistic change such as Fairclough, though these would have been relevant to a discussion about how new generic forms replace old and, in doing so, cause the cultural perceptions of communities to evolve. Nor finally, did we consider why, notwithstanding the work of French discourse analysts like Maingueneau (1987), the influence of Michel Foucault and the increasing body of work in discourse analysis worldwide should have had only a limited impact on the approaches taken by scholars and teachers working in French stylistics today. In choosing examples of practitioners and theoreticians, we have selected figures whose approaches corresponded most closely to our own. Underpinning our whole approach has been the hope that the schism between stylistics and discourse analysis can be overcome and that a critical understanding of poetic and conative texts can be embraced within a more unified and socially informed investigation.

The continued separation between stylistics and discourse analysis probably results from the extent to which literary culture and the discursive practices which this implies remain embedded in French educational institutions, a thesis explored in detail by Bourdieu (1982) and placed in context by Williams (1999). It is nevertheless true that the dichotomy between humanistic and social approaches to text analysis is being broken down. The environment is changing and new courses are being created which fill the discursive space we have sought to identify. In this book, we have set the context and background for this debate and, more importantly, defined the principles on which it is based. For reasons of space, we have not presented a detailed analysis of the current changes in the teaching of reading and writing in France. These deserve to be the object of more specialised academic research.

Converting the principle of eclecticism into a practical methodology has forced us and the other contributors to the book to confront the contradictions inherent in combining sociolinguistic awareness and linguistic pedagogy. If you approach a text as an act of social communication, then the features you identify and the order in which you describe them have to be informed by a coherent explanation of the relationship between the actual or implied interlocutors and the 'grammar' of the text which is being studied. Text grammar should not be seen as a self-contained, independently describable system whose categories and figures of speech exist in a world which is separate from the context in which they are being applied. It should be pragmatic and flexible. Yet, in order for texts to be comprehensible, the principles underlying their construction must by definition be systemic and coherent; the relationship between textual construction and communication must be rule-governed in the sense that it follows a discernible pattern. Beyond these theoretical concerns, it is also pedagogically important to offer a methodology that students can readily apply and for the set of examples provided to be sufficiently comprehensive to act as a source of reference.

Part 2 of the book has therefore been an attempt to make sense of the relationship between function and structure. We have sought to make readers aware of the value of stylistic features as instruments of social interaction, while locating them within a theoretical framework which lends itself to practical application. Throughout the history of rhetoric, these different priorities have always been at odds with each other. At its most basic, rhetoric has been reduced to a set of tools or samples, a sequence of features or figures of speech which the student could be trained to turn to good effect. In this restricted form, it has, at various moments in history, fulfilled a vital but ultimately limited educational purpose, enfranchising individuals but containing their cultural scope. In its fullest sense, however, rhetoric has had a wider and more enlightened goal. Ever since

Aristotle, creative proponents of rhetoric have seen discursive structure as integral to all forms of communication, whether initiated by individuals or the product of social and ideological forces. The means have been inseparable from the ends and as such have been informed by philosophy and ethics.

Our approach has aimed to place rhetorical method within the context of modern theories of discourse. Within the methodology we have proposed, positioning and deixis have been the pivotal elements. The reference to stylistic features and the order in which they have been treated have been subordinated to the way in which they engage readers and, in so doing, situate a text within a discursive space. The relationship between authors or institutions and readers is therefore not the only interpretation which we have given to the term 'positioning'. How the text locates itself stylistically in relation to other texts has been equally important and has meant that the internal coherence and originality of the text under consideration have had to be examined. While seeking to offer a range of examples which illustrate the stylistic potential of the language, we have had to strike a balance between the text as communication and the text as a structural entity which is more or less differentiated from other texts in the same genre.

In taking an essentially functional approach to the identification and analysis of textual structure, we have followed Foucault's precepts in *L'Archéologie du Savoir* (1969). Individual syntactic elements such as pronouns or tense, for example, are not presented as grammatical categories but as expressions of a communicative relationship which can only be understood in the context of the text as a whole. Features like rhythm and sentence structure have had to be described as independent phenomena, but always with reference to their value as cohesive elements or as markers of register. In this way, features of style are not simply structural entities but indices of culture whose significance extends well beyond the text in which they occur.

The art of commentary lies in reconciling the task of identifying features with that of demonstrating their value in context. The cliché that all features of a text are significant is trivial, but it does identify the problem faced by the analyst and particularly by the student who feels bound by an obligation to conform to academic stereotypes. It is clearly not enough to identify textual features – even selectively. The real goal is to define their social and aesthetic relevance and this task is inevitably partial in the sense that it is itself ideologically informed. Like any form of criticism, commentary is recursive and reflects the values of the commentator as much as those of the writers and institutions responsible for the creation of the original text. Authors of a book on commentary can define a set of objectives and provide a methodological framework but they cannot put words in the mouths of commentators. These must speak for themselves.

That is why, in Part 2 of this book, we wanted to offer a range of examples which would illustrate different styles of style analysis. These reveal the ideological perspectives of their authors and should themselves be read and evaluated critically. One of the greatest problems in undertaking commentary and particularly in using it as an educational instrument is reductionism – the danger of re-narrating texts or of offering explanations which are grounded in oversimplified theories of society. In acknowledging the scope of individuals to explain the positioning of different texts with their own voices, we have approached text analysis from a decentred point of view. The texts selected for analysis are fragments of an exploded culture in which discourses and social structures are interrelated in infinitely variable ways. Moreover, the perceptions and cultural positioning of commentators are themselves necessarily different. It is the method and, above all, the objective of analysis which we have regarded as consistent. The conclusions which analysis draws cannot be anticipated or prescribed.

The image of French society which emerges from the texts we have considered is one which is seeking to reinterpret and make sense of the past in a present marked by instability and uncertainty. This perspective is, of course, in large part a function of the texts which have been chosen for analysis. But the style as well as the topics of the texts reveal a world-view through their representation of different aspects of contemporary life: historical events, gastronomy, theatre and performance, urban exclusion, language, sport, tourism and travel, lifestyle, business and the cult of the *patron*. The view of France is of a country which seeks to understand the past as a means of coming to terms with the complexities of the present and future. The life of the underprivileged and young unemployed in the urban ghettos is expressed in a prose of yearning which enters the mind of the subject, while in fashion ads, language and image become symbols of themselves in a world of signs in which potential consumers participate in a collective *jouissance*. Similarly, the euphoria at France's victory in the World Cup of 1998 is identified with the country's desire to become a multicultural community, prepared to pay lip-service to a new ideal of integration but in reality unable to escape from the pressures of an unforgiving economic environment. The press portrays business barons as paternalistic visionaries, driven by imperialistic ambition to sustain national pride yet never losing the common touch. But it glosses over the social consequences of their ruthlessness for their own employees and hints darkly at the problems posed by succession.

Within an environment of externalisation and exclusion, there is evidence in the texts of the attempt to rediscover traditional values – but in a modern idiom. The view of language is essentially centralising, Walter's prize-winning style making a self-consciously popular appeal to the traditional interest in a national institution and doing so from a position of knowledge and authority. That of gastronomy shows the urge to reinvent the authentic flavour of the French provinces – '*La France Comme Autrefois*' – while travel within France recaptures the paradoxical contrasts in the rhythms of contemporary life but in playful and inconclusive fashion. Similarly, while the language of performance is much in evidence in all the texts, most notably in the treatment of fashion and sport, the rediscovery of the *Comédie-Ballet* and the *Baroque* bears witness to a preoccupation with the authentic recreation of the past. Nostalgia suggests a need to find security and a sense of identity in former institutions, re-narrated in a language which appeals to the contemporary consciousness. Even the portrayal of the French Revolution seeks not so much to confirm a new thesis as to refute the certainties of a previous one. It does so in a style which draws attention to itself and reminds the reader of the fragility of historical theory. The power of rhetoric is used to full effect. But overlaying it is a sense of irony and a consciousness of the role played by language in giving meaning to the present through explanations of the past: a deconstructed representation of heritage which, in the place of certainty, offers a dynamic of open-ended interpretation.

In describing nations as imagined communities, Benedict Anderson (1983) transfers the concept of nationhood from the physical reality of geographical boundaries and the practical implementation of laws, religions and institutions to the psychological domain of discourse. Communities of the imagination are constantly being redefined by the texts of daily communication which transfigure collective memories through the prism of the present. As Billig (1995: 8) puts it, '[National identity] is to be found in the embodied habits of social life. Such habits include those of thinking and using language.' It is through text that populations are led to 'enhabit' identities and ideologies. Modes of thought and behaviour become 'turned into routine . . . with the result that the past is enhabited in the present in a dialectic of forgotten remembrance' (1995: 42). The range of texts through which these processes are realised is infinite, as is the nature of the processes themselves. National identity does not reside simply in texts which refer explicitly to identity issues. The language of communal identification is an inherent characteristic of the discursive environment as a whole.

As Foucault pointed out in *L'Archéologie du Savoir* (1969), the method required to understand the processes of discursive construction should be based on systematic and microscopic analysis. Texts relate to each other, to themselves, to an objectively real or imagined reality, and at the same time mediate communication between personal and institutional interlocutors. In so doing, they constitute a social reality which is reconstructed differently every time they are read and interpreted. A wider view of the ways in which discourse operates on collective consciousness can only be arrived at by looking at the minutiae of texts and, in theory, any text can be revealing. Billig (1995: 106–107) and others such as Fairclough (2000) emphasise the centrality of deixis – the use of the definite article and the pronouns 'we', 'you' or 'they' – in defining the identity of their readerships, thereby reinforcing a sense of collectivity and, by definition, also of exclusion. But this is only one highly visible way in which discourse contributes to the processes of defining and dividing groups in society. The 'ideational/ referential', 'textual/intertextual' and 'poetic' functions of text are often less overtly deictic and more deeply embedded in the structural properties of style

(Van Leeuwen 1995). It is precisely this which makes it important to recognise their realisation in language. They are themselves the products of convention and thus reinforce the insider–outsider relationships which texts form with their readers and with each other.

We have not, in this book, claimed to offer a complete 'analysis' of French society or of the French language. We have hoped rather to provide readers with an insight into the way in which the features of French written discourse construct a social reality and to describe a method which will enable them to approach written French 'critically'; that is, in a state of mind which is as aware of its own cultural groundedness as it is of the contexts in which texts are produced. Our aim is that readers should bring this awareness and an enhanced understanding of the French language to their readings of other texts, that they will be encouraged to distance themselves from the effects which texts have on them and to evaluate these in a spirit of informed scepticism which does not preclude pleasure.

We also hope that in considering the way in which social attitudes are moulded by cultural artefacts, readers will not cease to interrogate the relationship between written language and aesthetic value, to ask what it is which makes some texts more 'effective' than others, to seek constantly to understand the nature of coherence and its relationship with linguistic form. In this aspect of the production of text, it is assumed that individual human vision contributes to the formulation of ideas in language. In becoming aware of the role played by written discourse in social conditioning, individuals will be better equipped to make choices of their own to the greater good of themselves and of the communities to which they belong.

Appendix
The French phonetic alphabet

Consonants

[b]   balle
[d]   dent
[d]   dent
[f]   fin
[g]   gare
[k]   comme
[l]   lait
[m]   mère
[n]   non
[ɲ]   signe
[p]   peu
[ʀ]   rade
[s]   cime
[ʃ]   chou
[t]   ton
[v]   vie
[z]   zèle
[ʒ]   je

Semi-consonants or semi-vowels

[j]   hier
[w]   oui
[ɥ]   lui

Vowels

Oral vowels

[a]   papa
[ɑ]   lâche
[ə]   de
[e]   les
[ɛ]   bête
[i]   fit
[o]   faux
[ ]   mort
[y]   fut
[u]   fou
[ø]   peu
[œ]   feuille

Nasal vowels

[ɑ̃]   banc
[ɔ̃]   bon
[ɛ̃]   vin
[œ̃]   un

Glossary

Accent in stylistics, the syllable which receives the main or secondary stress in a word or sentence. More generally, the way sounds are pronounced in speech.

Acronym the designation of a social category or institution by the first letters of its title (e.g. DTI = The Department of Trade and Industry, *SNCF = Société Nationale des Chemins de Fer*).

Active voice where the action of the clause is attributed to the subject, e.g. *Les guérillas investirent la ville* (cf. **passive voice**, **transitive verb**).

Adjective the class of words used to describe nouns, normally in terms of what they do, what/who they are, what people think of them, what they are made of, what they look like, etc.

Adverb the class of word which provides further information about verbs or which qualifies or defines the meaning of a clause (e.g. *souvent, savamment, infiniment*, etc.).

Adverbial phrase a phrase governed by an adverb (e.g. *en tant que tel . . ., à vrai dire . . .*).

Agency the fact of taking an initiative or causing something to happen. The person or social institution who is responsible for carrying it out is known as the agent. Grammatically speaking, the subject of a sentence is normally the agent. The term 'agency' implies an active force which may change situations or the attitudes of actors within or outside the world of the text.

Allegory a sustained discourse on a topic dealing with moral, psychological or theoretical issues where the subject matter is represented in physical or animate terms. Typically, an allegory is a form of metaphor which is extended consistently over the full length of a narrative (e.g. the novel *La Peste* by Albert Camus).

Alliteration the repetition of consonants at the beginning of words in a sentence or line of poetry.

Anaphora the repetition of words in the initial position of sentences or phrases. The effect of anaphora is to enhance the coherence of the message and normally increases its impact. Anaphora may also be a form of co-reference in which a linguistic feature (typically a pronoun) refers back to a noun which has occurred earlier in the text, so causing the text to 'hang together'.

Antithesis   the deliberate juxtaposition of two phrases or clauses having opposite meanings in order to heighten the contrast between them (e.g. *nous avons longuement discuté du bonheur et du malheur, de la paix et de la guerre*).

Antonomasia   a form of **metonymy** where the name of a person or institution becomes so closely associated with a given trait of character or behaviour that it is used as a substitute for it (e.g. 'He's a right Scrooge', meaning that the person concerned is mean and stingy).

Apodosis   the fall in **cadence** in the breath group which normally marks the end of the sentence in French, following a series of progressive rises in intonation to the acme, or high point, in the sentence.

Apposition   a structure in which words of the same type are placed side by side, often in order to express a relationship whose meaning is not made grammatically explicit (e.g. *Une campagne choc* cf. **ellipsis**).

Aspect   expressions such as the forms of verbs or adverbs which define the duration of an action or event (e.g. the difference between *ils allaient vite* and *ils allèrent vite*, or between the adverbial expressions *tout d'un coup* and *pendant longtemps*).

Assonance   the repetition of similar vowel sounds in a sentence or line of poetry (cf. **alliteration**).

Auxiliary verb   a verb which is used to support or qualify another verb (typically forms of the auxiliary verbs 'to be' or 'to have' followed by a participle) (cf. **main verb**).

Bienséance   a seventeenth century French term which refers to the principle of respecting good taste or appropriateness.

Binary rhythm   the combination of two similarly structured phrases forming a rhythmic group consisting of two main stresses (e.g. *de gestion et de direction des entreprises*; *le pour et le contre*) (cf. **parallelism**, **antithesis**).

Breath group   the division of the sentence into syntactic units which correspond to natural rhythmic pauses marked by a rise or fall in the level of the voice.

Cadence   the melodic articulation of the sentence which results from the way in which the voice rises and falls within breath groups. It is normal in French for the breath groups to increase in length as the sentence progresses (the *loi de longueur*), a phenomenon known as *cadence majeure*. Conversely, a decrease in length is termed *cadence mineure* and normally occurs at the end of the sentence (cf. **protasis**, **apodosis**).

Chiasmus   a figure of speech in which two normally similar structures are placed next to each other in the formation A . . . B/B . . . A (e.g. *'elle avait les* *cheveux soyeux, roses les joues'*, where the adjective *'roses'* in the second phrase is placed before the noun *'joues'*, so bringing the two adjectives *'soyeux'* and *'roses'* together and placing the emphasis on the final word.

Circumlocution   a general stylistic feature which consists in using a more extended form of words than is strictly necessary (cf. **periphrasis**).

Closure   the way in which the end of a text or paragraph is marked stylistically (cf. **marked, cadence, coherence, foregrounding**).

Code   the language or dialect spoken by a definable community or social group (cf. **register**).

Code-switching   the act of changing from one language or dialect to another, normally within the same text.

Coherence   the underlying logic of a text or the combination of features which make it aesthetically meaningful. A text may be apparently incoherent but have an underlying artistic unity which appeals to the imagination. This too is implied by the term 'coherence'.

Cohesion   the linguistic features which promote coherence. At the sentential level, these may be grammatical elements such as coordination or subordination. At the textual level, 'cohesion' commonly includes the use of 'cohesive devices' such as demonstrative adjectives or pronouns, the repetition of words or phrases and adverbial phrases of emphasis or opposition, all of which bind a text together and lend it coherence.

Collocation   in general terms, the words most commonly used in association with other words or, in a stylistic sense, the bringing together in phrases or sentences of words or particular parts of speech.

Complement   the elements in a clause which complete the meaning of another constituent. In the sentence *'Il est riche'*, *'riche'* is the complement of the verb *être*. In the noun phrase *'la destruction de la ville'*, *'de la ville'* may be defined as the complement of the noun *'destruction'*.

Complex sentence   any sentence that consists of two or more clauses.

Conative   the elements within a text which focus on the addressee, i.e. which lend the text the function of convincing or persuading readers to change their point of view. The term was coined by Jakobson (1960) to define one of six major functions of language.

Concept   an abstract object or idea referred to by a word.

Confirmatio   rhetorical term referring to the argument in favour of the main proposition or thesis presented by a speaker or writer.

Conjugation   the process whereby the form of a verb is changed in order to express number, person, tense, voice and mood.

Conjunction   a class of words used to connect words or structures to each other (cf. **coordination**).

Connotation   that part of the meaning of a word which evokes associations beyond its primary meaning (cf. **denotation**).

Constituent   a word or phrase which combines with other words and phrases to form a sentence (e.g. subject, verb, object, complement and adverbial).

Context   in a specifically linguistic sense, context refers to the environment in which a particular feature or structure is used (i.e. its position in relation to other sounds, words or sentences). In a broader sense, context means the non-linguistic environment in which the communication takes place (cf. **context of situation**, **context of culture**).

Context of culture   the wider cultural environment in which a linguistic exchange or written text is located.

Context of situation   the immediate situation of a text or verbal exchange in terms of the physical and social conditions in which it is produced and interpreted.

Coordination   the linking together of two main clauses of equal status, typically by means of 'and' or 'but'.

Critical discourse analysis   an approach to the analysis of spoken and written text which describes the way in which discourse moulds and reflects power relations between different social groups.

Dative   the case used to express a relationship of indirectness between a verb and its object (e.g. *je lui ai parlé* – where *lui* is in the 'dative' case).

Declension   the process whereby the endings of nouns, pronouns, articles and adjectives change in order to express number, gender and case.

Deixis   expressions which locate an object, person or concept in space or time. Examples of deictic expressions typically include demonstrative adjectives and pronouns ('this', 'that', etc.), verb tense and adverbs of time ('today', 'tomorrow' . . .), though in the widest sense the term can be said to cover the function of any grammatical element – such as the definite article – which identifies a referent and situates it in relation to other referents within a real or fictional context.

Demonstrative   a type of adjective or pronoun which is used to distinguish one noun from another or to draw attention to an object, person or concept which has already featured in the text (e.g. *ce, cette, ces / celui-ci, celui-là,* etc.) (cf. **deixis, coherence, cohesion**).

Denotation   that part of the meaning of a word which designates that to which it refers; the primary meaning of the word (cf. **connotation**).

Determiner   term in linguistics normally used as an alternative to the word 'article' – *le, la, les / un, une, des,* etc.

Deviation   the way in which the linguistic features of a particular text differ from what can be described as the linguistic 'norm' or 'standard' of the language. In a more narrow sense, the term refers to the individual features within the text (a striking image, word-order changes, etc.) which stand out from the linguistic patterns established by the text (cf. **foregrounding**).

Diachronic   literally, 'through time'; the term is used to describe the process of linguistic change as it affects sounds, words and their meaning and grammatical features (cf. **synchronic**).

Dialect   any variety of a language where the combination of pronunciation, grammar and vocabulary forms a system which is peculiar to a given region and/or linguistic community.

Discourse   a piece of language consisting of more than one sentence (cf. **text**) which has an interactive function in society. The term may be applied to both spoken and written language. In modern linguistic terminology, 'discourse' has taken on the particular meaning given to the French word '*discours*' by Michel Foucault (1969, 1971), viz. the shared characteristics of a set of 'texts' which define the activities and influence of an identifiable social group (e.g. '*le discours de la publicité*'), hence ' discourse analysis'.

Disposition (Latin *dispositio*)   one of the major fields of rhetoric, *dispositio* concerns the overall organisation – or outline – of discourse: the choice of proposition, the structure of the argument, etc.

Ellipsis   the omission of words or phrases in a sentence to form a clipped, abbreviated style. Ellipsis is common in journalistic French, where main verbs are often left out to produce a sentence dominated by one or more noun phrases.

Elocution (Latin *elocutio*)   one of the five main areas of traditional rhetoric, *elocutio* concerns the selection and arrangement of words and sentences in discourse. It is the domain of rhetoric most closely associated with *style*.

Emotive   the term given to those elements of the text where the emphasis is on the speaker or writer: normally those elements which express personal feelings and opinions.

Euphemism   a form of understatement in which a word or phrase is substituted for one which might be thought too harsh or offensive.

Exordium   rhetorical term referring to a speaker or writer's introduction to the theme or topic of a text.

Expletive   an exclamation or swear word used to express an emotional reaction.

Explication de texte   the educational technique derived from rhetorical approaches to text analysis in which students describe the structure and stylistic features of a text. Adopted as a method by state education in France, it is used as a means of promoting literacy and the capacity for aesthetic appreciation.

Fiction   discourse which is understood to represent characters who did not exist and events which did not take place in reality. 'Real' characters and events may nevertheless be incorporated into fictional narratives. In such cases, it is normally recognised that the primary function of the discourse is to entertain, convey a moral message or achieve an original form of aesthetic expression rather than to portray an objective view of the facts. In practice, the distinction between fiction and non-fiction is complex, frequently contentious and ultimately a matter of emphasis (cf. **literature**).

Figure of speech   features of construction which make communication more effective through a combination of clarity, elegance and impact. In traditional rhetoric, figures of speech were part of *elocutio* and formed the basis of style. They include features involving both the meaning of words (e.g. **metaphor**, **metonymy** and **simile**) and the patterning of syntactic structures (cf. **scheme**, **trope**).

Foregrounding   the combination of stylistic features which causes a word, phrase or sentence to stand out from the rest of the text. Foregrounding may result from the single occurrence of a given feature or may be achieved through repetition (cf. **anaphora**, **parallelism**).

Fricative   the term used to describe the sound of a consonant resulting from the partial interruption of the airstream by different vocal organs.

Function   the term used to define the objectives of a message within a given communicative context.

Gender   In grammatical terms, the division of words into masculine, feminine or neutral categories. Otherwise, a term applied to features of texts which position readers as 'men' or 'women'.

Genre   the 'type' of text to which a given extract of spoken or written discourse can be said to belong. A 'genre' is characterised by its overall structure, by the context in which it occurs and by identifiable stylistic features which are common to a number of texts.

Gradation   the organisation of discourse into a sequence of examples or arguments which increase in intensity as the discourse continues.

Grammar   the systematic organisation of language which is normally divided into four component parts: sounds (phonology); the way in which words change their form as a function of meaning (morphology); the structure of sentences and their interrelationships (syntax); and the structure and expression of meaning (semantics). Often, the term is used to refer exclusively to the combination of morphology and syntax.

Grammatical   a term used to describe a sentence or expression which is judged by a native speaker to be well-formed according to the rules of that language.

Homonym   words which are pronounced the same but which have different meanings (e.g. *croit*, which may mean either 'believes' or 'grows') (cf. **synonym**).

Hyperbole   deliberate exaggeration or overstatement.

Ideational   the elements within a text which have to do with content or ideas. The term was used by Halliday to refer to one of three dominant functions of text (cf. **interpersonal**, **textual**).

Ideology any system of ideas which contributes to the establishment and reproduction of social structures and processes.

Illocutionary force the extent or manner in which an action takes place as a direct consequence of something being said. The term may be used in a general sense to describe the impact which an utterance or text has on the real world.

Imperative an expression or mood of a verb which carries the force of a command (cf. **mood**).

Implied reader the notional reader whose identity is implied by the genre, period, structure and language of a text.

Indirect object an object, normally expressed in the dative case or introduced by the preposition 'to'/*à* which is in an indirect relationship to a verb (e.g. *je le lui ai dit*, where *lui* is the indirect object pronoun).

Inferencing the process of drawing conclusions about writer–reader relationships and contexts of situation and culture on the basis of the limited information provided by a text.

Infinitive a form of the verb which does not provide any information about the verb's subject (e.g. *aller, descendre*). In theory, the number of possible subjects can be said to be infinite.

Inflection the changes in the endings of verbs, adjectives and nouns which express notions of case, gender and number and thereby make explicit the relationships between constituents in a sentence (cf. **suffix**).

Interlocutor any person who takes part in a conversation or a reader – actual or implied – whom a written text may be said to be 'addressing'.

Interpersonal the term given by Halliday to refer to those elements of a text which focus on the relationship between the addresser and addressee (cf. **ideational, textual**).

Intertextuality the notion that any text available to a given community is related to other texts in the sense that it may be written in response to them, contain similarities of style or tell the same story in a different way. Similarly, texts are open to constant reinterpretation as their position within the culture of the receiving community is changed by the production of new texts.

Intransitive verb a verb which, under normal grammatical conventions, does not govern an object (e.g. *aller, sembler*).

Inventio the first of the areas of traditional rhetoric, *inventio* is the term used to refer to the choice of subject matter and the approach which the speaker or writer takes towards it.

Irony a general or particular feature of discourse which consists in saying the opposite of what is meant, normally for humorous effect.

Koïné the dialect recognised as the institutionally 'approved' language within a speech community, as prescribed, for example, by the national educational system.

Lexicon/lexis   the vocabulary of a language. The term 'lexical item' may be used to refer to words which have meaning as they stand (nouns, adjectives, verbs), as opposed to 'functional' or 'syntactic items' (determiners, prepositions, pronouns), which define grammatical relationships. Hence 'lexical field', which refers to the collectivity of words relating to a given area of meaning, either within a language as a whole or within a text.

Literature   a broad term used to describe texts which conform to conventional criteria of aesthetic or expressive quality (cf. **fiction, poetic**).

Litotes   a figure of speech which consists in saying less to mean more (e.g. '*Elle l'aimait un tout petit peu*', meaning in fact '*Elle l'aimait beaucoup*').

Main clause   the principal clause of a complex sentence. In the sentence: '*L'homme qui portait des pantalons rouges est allé en ville*', '*L'homme est allé en ville*' is the main clause – as opposed to the **subordinate clause** which in this case is '*qui portait des pantalons rouges*'.

Main verb   the verb which expresses the main action, event or state in a sentence – as opposed to the **auxiliary verb** (*avoir, être*), which defines or qualifies it.

Marked   a term used to describe any structure or form, but especially word order, which does not conform to the basic or normal pattern either of the language in general or of the language of a given text – as opposed to 'unmarked' (cf. **deviation, foregrounding**).

Memoria   the term from rhetoric used to describe the process of learning a text by heart. The notion of *memoria* emphasises the close relationship between style and memory. Through a balanced combination of originality, rhythm and coherence, a well-constructed text should be memorable.

Metafunction   the term used by Halliday to refer to the three high-level functions (**ideational, interpersonal, textual**) which are present to varying degrees in all messages.

Metalanguage   the language or terminology used to talk about language. The term 'metalingual' is used by Jakobson (1960) to refer to those elements within a text which define or explain the language used in other parts.

Metaphor   the use of a word from one lexical field to replace a word from another field which would normally be expected in a given context. Used to provide added figurative effect to a text by creating an unusual association between the two elements concerned (e.g. *les chandelles de la nuit se sont éteintes*, where '*les chandelles de la nuit*' = *étoiles*). A major property of style and of language in general, since it reveals how, in representing reality, the human imagination interacts with the need for symbolic clarity (cf. **metonymy, trope**).

Metonymy   the replacement of one term by another where there is a physical or cause–effect relationship between the two terms (e.g. '*boire un verre*',

where the container, – '*verre*', – replaces the content – '*bière, vin, eau*', etc.)
(cf. **metaphor, trope**).

Modal verb   one of a closed set of verbs used to express possibility, permission, mood and obligation (e.g. *devoir, pouvoir, vouloir*). Normally used with another verb, in which case it may be described as a 'modal auxiliary'.

Mood   the category of verb conjugation which defines the state of mind of a speaker/writer. There are generally thought to be five moods: 'indicative', which conveys certainty or objective fact; 'interrogative', which implies a request for information; 'imperative', which seeks to impose an obligation on the listener/reader; 'subjunctive', which is used to convey uncertainty and strength of feeling; and 'conditional', which may express a speaker/writer's attitude towards the future.

Morpheme   the smallest unit of grammar in a language. Words may consist of one morpheme only (e.g. '*jeu*') or of two or more (e.g. '*jou + er*'; '*inter + nation + al*').

Morphology   the area of grammar concerned with the structure of words (cf. **grammar, syntax**).

Narratio   rhetorical term referring to that stage in a discourse which follows the introduction and develops the topic or main idea of the text.

Nominalisation   the process whereby a noun is created from one or several other parts of speech, e.g. *anéantissement* (from *anéantir*) (cf. **verbalisation**).

Nominative   the case or form of the declension of a noun or pronoun which designates it as the subject or agent in a phrase or clause. '*Je*' is the nominative form of the first person pronoun, '*me*' being the form which represents the accusative and dative.

Noun   the class of word used to name persons, objects or concepts. Nouns can be described as 'animate' or 'inanimate', and 'countable' or 'non-countable'. Nouns may function as either the subject or object of clauses and may be formed from other parts of speech, by **nominalisation**.

Noun phrase   any phrase containing a noun. The most frequent structures of noun phrases are: determiner + noun = '*la maison*'; determiner + adjective + noun – '*la belle maison*'; determiner + noun + complement – '*l'anéantissement de la nation*'.

Object   the constituent of a sentence which has an action performed on it by the subject of the verb. Objects may be direct, in which case they are represented in the accusative or indirect, when they are represented in the dative.

Onomatopoeia   when the sounds of words imitate the phenomena to which they refer. Onomatopoeia may be described as 'primary' when the word is a more or less exact replication of the sound (e.g. *glou-glou*), or 'secondary' when the word evokes the sound of its referent more indirectly (e.g. *tinter, craquer, miauler*).

Oxymoron   the juxtaposition of two terms which are mutually contradictory (e.g. *une amitiè d'une douceur amère*).

Parallelism   the repetition of identical syntactic structures within texts (cf. **coherence, cohesion, pattern**).

Paraphrase   a rewriting of a text which seeks to represent that text's meaning as exactly as possible in another form of words.

Passive voice   where the form of the verb represents the subject of the verb as being acted upon. The verb is usually conjugated with the auxiliary *être*, 'to be' e.g. *La ville fut investie par les guérillas* (cf. **active voice**).

Pattern   the repetition of structures (notably of word order and rhythms) within a text (cf. **coherence, cohesion, parallelism**).

Periphrasis   a figure whereby, instead of using a simple term to designate an object or concept, a more extended and complicated form of words is deployed (e.g. *alma mater* for 'university') (cf. **circumlocution**).

Personification   portraying abstract referents in human and personal terms and using language which implies a human relationship with the objects or concepts concerned.

Peroratio   the rhetorical term referring to a speaker/writer's summing up or conclusion.

Poetic   the term used by Jakobson (1960) to refer to those properties of a text which lend it coherence and so enhance its aesthetic quality (cf. **literature**).

Positioning   the way in which the style and construction of a text implies that a reader adopt a certain point of view towards its content or towards characters within the text. Advertisements, for example, 'position' implied reader/viewers as potential consumers of the product being advertised. The term may also be applied to the physical or psychological position of characters within a text in relation to each other (cf. **role**).

Possessive   adjective or pronoun which expresses a relationship of belonging between a subject and a referent: e.g. *mon, le mien*.

Pragmatics   the field of linguistic study which considers how language is used in communicative situations. It is concerned especially with the way in which context affects the choices made by language users.

Predicate   that part of a clause which complements the subject. In traditional grammar, sentences were described as consisting of a subject and a predicate.

Prefix   a verbal constituent (affix) placed at the beginning of a word so as to give it a specific meaning (e.g. *international*, *omniprésent*, *préposition*).

Preposition   the class of word used to express a relationship of position with respect to other words (e.g. *dans, sous, à*, etc.).

Prepositional phrase   a phrase containing a preposition (e.g. *à travers champs; sans façons*).

Presupposition   the information implied by a given statement which needs to be taken into account for the statement to be fully understood.

Pronoun   a class of word which stands in place of a noun. The standard forms of pronoun are: personal (*je, tu, il, elle* . . . / *moi, toi, lui, elle* . . .), impersonal (*il/le*), possessive (*le mien, le tien, le sien*), and relative (*qui, que, dont*).

Pronunciatio   rhetorical term referring to the manner of delivery in the oral presentation of text: a combination of tone of voice, accent, stress, intonation and pace of speech.

Protasis   the stepped rise cadence over a succession of breath groups to a high point in the sentence, after which the level of the voice tends to falls towards the end (cf. **cadence, apodosis**).

Quantifier   a determiner which defines the quantity of nouns (e.g. *beaucoup, trop, tous, certains*).

Reference   the relationship between words and the objects or concepts to which they refer.

Referent   any object, person or concept which is referred to by a word.

Refutatio   rhetorical term which refers to the argument against the main point being expressed by a speaker/writer; a stage in the presentation of a topic which shows that the speaker/writer is aware of the counterarguments but is able to demonstrate their lack of validity by considering them alongside the arguments which support his point of view.

Register   a socially defined variety of language (e.g. of a profession or other form of social group) (cf. **code, dialect**).

Relative clause   a type of **subordinate clause** introduced by a relative pronoun.

Rhetoric   the art of representation in speech and writing for specific social purposes. First established as a method of training in public speaking by the ancient Greeks and subsequently developed and extended as an educational discipline under the Roman Empire, rhetorical principles were preserved in Byzantium and by the Church through the Middle Ages. From the sixteenth century onwards, and particularly after the Revolution of 1789, it became – and still remains – one of the cornerstones of the French educational system.

Rhythm   the stress patterns in words or sentences.

Role   the physical or psychological position of characters within a text in relation to each other and to the actual or implied reader (cf. **positioning**).

Scheme   a rhetorical term used to refer to the organisation of sentences and their combination in rhythmic and syntactic patterns (cf. **parallelism, pattern, coherence, cohesion**).

Semantic field   an area of meaning, e.g. *bleu, blanc, rouge* all belong to the field of colour.

Semantics   the branch of linguistics and philosophy which is concerned with the formulation of meaning in language.

Sentence   a unit of syntax consisting of one or more clauses. The foundation of thought and expression in language. Sentences may be simple (consisting of a single clause) or complex (where two or more clauses are linked though coordination, or where one or more clauses are subordinated to a main clause).

Shift   the process whereby a sound changes over time. In stylistics, the transfer of a word from one syntactic category to another (e.g. from verb to noun – *le vouloir*, *l'avant*).

Simile   an expression in which an item from one lexical field is compared to an item from another (cf. **metaphor**).

Speech act   an utterance which is considered within a communicative context in terms of the intention of a speaker and the effect of the utterance on the listener.

Stress   a combination of volume and pitch which causes a syllable to receive greater emphasis within a word or sentence.

Stylistics   the study of the relationship between, on the one hand, the structure of texts and the combination of linguistic features they contain and, on the other, the effects they have on an implied reader.

Subject   the noun or noun-equivalent in a sentence, with which the verb is made to agree. All sentences traditionally constitute a subject and a **predicate**.

Subjunctive   the form of verbs which expresses fear and uncertainty, necessity, will and command, e.g. *Il faut que tu viennes* (cf. **mood**).

Subordinate clause   a clause contained or embedded within another to form a complex sentence (cf. **main clause, relative clause**).

Suffix   a constituent placed at the end of a word designating aspects of its meaning such as gender, number or size, and defining its syntactic relationship with other words within a sentence (cf. **inflection, prefix**).

Superlative   the form of an adjective or adverb which describes the highest degree of quality (e.g. *le train le plus rapide du monde*).

Syllable   an open vowel or combination of vowels and consonants, normally articulated in a single expulsion of breath, which may be used to divide a word or sentence into constituent parts.

Synchronic   literally 'at the same time'; the term used to describe language as a structural system composed of interrelated elements which can be studied by artificially viewing a linguistic system as static.

Synonym   a word which has a similar or identical meaning to another, e.g. 'big', 'large' (cf. **homonym**).

Syntax   the branch of linguistics which is concerned with the grammatical structure of clauses and sentences (cf. **grammar**).

Tautology   the use of terms which are redundant in the sense that they repeat something which has already been said in other terms. The figure is used typically for the purpose of deliberate exaggeration or overstatement.

Tense   the category of conjugation which expresses the time at which an action takes place (cf. **aspect**).

Ternary rhythm   a rhythmic grouping of three even stresses, normally in successive phrases within the same sentence, e.g. *le <u>sens</u> des responsabilités, le <u>souci</u> de la communication, la <u>passion</u> d'entreprendre* (cf. **binary rhythm, coherence, cohesion, parallelism, pattern**).

Text   a technical term normally used to refer to stretches of language consisting of more than one sentence, though any coherent message (even one comprising only one phrase or clause or a disconnected series of phrases or clauses, such as road signs and menus) is also covered by the term (cf. **discourse**).

Textual   the term given by Halliday to refer to that function of a discourse which makes it 'hang together' as a text, i.e. the grammatical features which enable it to 'make sense' (cf. **ideational, interpersonal**).

Transitive verb   a verb which expresses agency between a subject and a direct object.

Trope   the technical term in rhetoric used to refer to figures of speech involving the comparison of two lexical fields or the transfer of meaning from one lexical field to another (cf. **metaphor, metonymy, simile**).

Variety   the way in which the form of discourse varies in different situations, according to the human and physical context, the medium of communication, the degree of formality expected, and so on (cf. **code, register**).

Verb   the class of words used to express an action, event or state (cf. **auxiliary verb, main verb, modal verb, transitive verb, intransitive verb**).

Verbalisation   the process whereby verbs are created out of other parts of speech such as adjectives or nouns (e.g. *purifier* from *pure*, *solutionner* from *solution*) (cf. **nominalisation**).

Word   the smallest unit of grammar which expresses meaning when it stands alone.

Bibliography

Amon, E. and Bomati, Y. (1995) *Vocabulaire du Commentaire de Texte*, Paris: Larousse.

Anderson, B. (1983) *Imagined Communities: Reflections on the Origin and Spread of Nationalism*, London: Verso.

Apollinaire, G. (1913) *Alcools*, Paris: Mercure de France.

Aristotle (1991) *The Art of Rhetoric* (ed. and trans. H. Lawson-Tancred), Harmondsworth: Penguin.

Augé, M. (1992) *Non-Lieux: Introduction à une Anthropologie de la Surmodernité*, Paris: Seuil.

Bally, C. (1963) *Traité de Stylistique française*, Vol. 2, 4th edition, Geneva: Georg.

—— (1970) *Traité de Stylistique française*, Vol. 1, 5th edition, Geneva: Georg.

Barthes, R. (1957) *Mythologies*, Paris: Seuil.

—— (1970) *L'Empire des Signes*, Paris: Flammarion.

Baudrillard, J. (1986) *Amérique*, Paris: Grasset.

Bétourné, O. and Hartig, A. (1989) *Penser l'Histoire de la Révolution: Deux Siècles de Passion Française*, Paris: La Découverte.

Billig, M. (1995) *Banal Nationalism*, London: Sage.

Bourdieu, P. (1982) *Ce que Parler Veut Dire: l'Economie des Echanges Linguistiques*, Paris: Fayard.

Braudel, Fernand (1986) *L'Identité de la France*, Paris: Arthaud.

Brillat-Savarin (1826) *La Physiologie du Goût*, Paris: A. Sautelet.

Brunot, F. (1947) *Histoire de la Langue Française des Origines à 1900: le Dix-Septième Siècle*, Paris: Colin.

Bühler, Karl (1934) *Sprachtheorie: die Darstellungsfunktion der Sprache*, Jena: Fischer.

Camus, A. (1947) *La Peste*, Paris: Gallimard.

Chomsky, N. (1957) *Syntactic Structures*, The Hague: Mouton.

—— (1965) *Aspects of the Theory of Syntax*, Cambridge: MIT Press.

Cicero, M.T. (1970) *Cicero on Oratory and Orators* (ed. and trans. J.S. Watson), Carbondale, Ill.: Southern Illinois University Press.

CNRS (1971–1994) *Trésor de la Langue Française*, Paris: CNRS/Gallimard.

Conley, T.M. (1990) *Rhetoric in the European Tradition*, Chicago: University of Chicago Press.

Cook, M. (1993) *French Culture Since 1945*, Essex: Longman.

Cressot, M. (1969) *Le Style et ses Techniques: Précis d'Analyse Stylistique*, Paris: PUF.

Dauncey, H. and Hare, G. (1998) '"Dans la Cour des Grands": France 98', *Modern and Contemporary France* 6(3): 339–350.

Deloffre, F. (1970) *Stylistique et Poétique Françaises*, Paris: SEDES.

Diderot, D'Alembert (1751–1788) *Encyclopédie ou Dictionnaire Raisonné des Sciences*, Paris: Briasson &c.

Dine, P. (1998) 'Sport and the State in Contemporary France: From *La Charte des Sports* to Decentralisation', *Modern and Contemporary France* 6(3): 301–312.

Dixon, P. (1971) *Rhetoric*, London: Methuen.

Duras, M. (1960) *Hiroshima Mon Amour: Scénario et Dialogues*, Paris: Gallimard.

Eliot, T.S. (1963) 'The Waste Land', in *Collected Poems 1909–1962*, London: Faber and Faber.

Eskenazi, F. (1988) 'Furet, Roi de la Révolution', *Libération*, 20 October 1988.

Fairclough, N. (1989) *Language and Power*, London: Longman.

—— (1992) *Discourse and Social Change*, Cambridge: Polity.

—— (1995) *Critical Discourse Analysis: The Critical Study of Language*, Essex: Longman.

—— (2000) *New Labour, New Language*, London: Routledge.

Floch, J.-M. (1990) *Sémiotique, Marketing et Communication*, Paris: PUF.

Forbes, J. and Kelly, M. (1995) *French Cultural Studies: An Introduction*, Oxford: Oxford University Press.

Foucault, M. (1966) *Les Mots et les Choses*, Paris: Gallimard.

—— (1969) *L'Archéologie du Savoir*, Paris: Gallimard.

—— (1971) *L'Ordre du Discours*, Paris: Gallimard.

Fowler, R., Hodge, B., Kress, G. and Trew, T. (1979) *Language and Control*, London: Routledge & Kegan Paul.

France, P. (1972) *Rhetoric and Truth in France: Descartes to Diderot*, Oxford: Clarendon.

Furet, F. (1978) *Penser la Révolution Française*, Paris: Gallimard.

Gaxotte, P. (1928/1970) *La Révolution Française*, Paris: Fayard.

Greimas, J. (1970) *Du Sens: Essais Sémiotiques*, Paris: Seuil.

Grimod de la Reynière (1803–1812) *Almanach des Gourmands*, Paris.

Grunig, B.-N. (1990) *Les Mots de la Publicité*, Paris: CNRS.

Halliday, M.A.K. (1971) 'Linguistic Function and Literary Style: An Enquiry into the Language of William Golding's *The Inheritors*', in Seymour Chatman (ed.), *Literary Style: A Symposium*, New York: Oxford University Press.

—— (1975) *Learning How to Mean: Explorations in the Development of Language*, London: Edward Arnold.

—— (1978) *Language as Social Semiotic: The Social Interpretation of Language and Meaning*, London: Edward Arnold.

—— (1987) 'Introduction', in D. Birch and M. O'Toole (eds) *Functions of Style*, London: Frances Pinter.

Hutcheon, L. (1988) *A Poetics of Postmodernism: History, Theory, Fiction*, London: Routledge.

Jakobson, R. (1960) 'Closing Statement: Linguistics and Poetics', in T.A. Sebeok (ed.), *Style in Language*, Massachusetts: MIT, pp. 350–377.

Judge, A. and Lamothe, S. (1995) *Stylistic Developments in Literary and Non-literary French Prose*, Lewiston/Queenston/Lampeter: Edwin Mellen Press.

Kantorowicz, E. (1957) *The King's Two Bodies*, Princeton N.J.: Princeton University Press.

Keat, R. and Abercrombie, N. (1991) *Enterprise Culture*, London: Routledge.

Kress, G. (1989) *Linguistic Processes in Sociocultural Practice*, 2nd edition, Oxford: Oxford University Press.

Kristeva, J., Rey-Debove, J. and Umiker, D. (eds) (1971) *Essays in Semiotics*, The Hague: Mouton.

La Bruyère, Jean de (1688) 'Des Ouvrages de l'Esprit', in *Les Caractères ou les Moeurs de ce Siècle* (ed. Garapon) (1962), Paris: Garnier.

La Fontaine (1668/1934) 'Le Loup et l'Agneau', in *Fables*, Paris: Larousse.

Lacan, J. (1966) *Ecrits*, Paris: Seuil.

Lawson-Tancred, H. (1991) 'Introduction', in Aristotle, *The Art of Rhetoric*, Harmondsworth: Penguin.

Le Clézio, J.-M. (1982) *La Ronde et Autres Faits Divers*, Paris: Gallimard.

Leech, G. (1970) ' "This bread I break" — Language and Interpretation', in D.C. Freeman (ed) *Linguistics and Literary Style*, New York: Holt, Rinehart and Winston, pp. 119–128.

—— (1983) *Principles of Pragmatics*, Harlow: Longman.

Lefevere, A. (1992) *Translation, Rewriting and the Manipulation of Literary Fame*, London: Routledge.

Lévi-Strauss, C. (1955) *Tristes Tropiques*, Paris: Pion.

Levin, S. (1973) *Linguistic Structures in Poetry*, The Hague: Mouton.

Littré, E. (n.d.) *Dictionnaire de la Langue Française*, Paris: Hachette.

Maingueneau, D. (1987) *Nouvelles Tendances en Analyse du Discours*, Paris: Hachette.

Massialot (1691) *Le Cuisinier Roïal et Bourgeois*, Paris: Charles de Sercy.

Mazaleyrat, J. (1974) *Eléments de Métrique Française*, Paris: Colin.

Mennell, S. (1993) 'Food and Wine', in Malcolm Cook (ed.), *French Culture Since 1945*, London: Longman, pp. 176–191.

Mermet, G. (1996) *Francoscopie 1995*, Paris: Larousse.

Moirand, S. (1988) *Une Histoire de Discours: Une Analyse des Discours de la Revue 'Le Français dans le Monde 1961–1981'*, Paris: Hachette.

Molinié, G. (1993) *La Stylistique*, Paris: PUF.

Nora, P. (1984) *Les Lieux de Mémoire*, Vol 1, *La République*, Paris: Gallimard.

Nora, P. (1986) *Les Lieux de Mémoire*, Vol 2, *La Nation*, Paris: Gallimard.

Le Nouvel Economiste, July 1998, 1107, Paris: Publications du Nouvel Economiste.

Ogilvy, D. (1983) *Ogilvy on Advertising*, London: Pan.

Ohmann, R. (1970) 'Generative Grammars and the Concept of Literary Style', in Freeman, D. (ed), *Linguistics and Literary Style*, New York: Holt, Rinehart and Winston.

Owen, D. (1998) 'Fairy-tale Victory Changes Political Mood and Outlook', *Financial Times Survey: France*, 14 October 1998.

Pinker, S. (1997) *How the Mind Works*, New York: Norton.

Pudlowski, J. (1994) 'La Brie comme Autrefois', *Le Point*, 1 October 1994, Paris: Le Point.

Quintilian, M.F. (1920–1922) *The Institutio Oratoria* (trans. H.E. Butler), London: Heinemann.

Riffaterre, M. (1959) 'Criteria for Style Analysis', *Word* 15: 154–174.

—— (1971) *Essais de Stylistique structurale*, Paris: Flammarion.

Rhetorica ad Herennium (1954) (trans. H. Caplan), London: Heinemann.

Robert, P. (1964–1970) *Dictionnaire Alphabétique et Analogique de la Langue Française*, Paris: Société du Nouveau Littré.

—— (1970) *Dictionnaire Alphabétique et Analogique de la Langue Française: supplément*, Paris: Société du Nouveau Littré.

Rochefort, C. (1961) *Les Petits Enfants du Siècle*, Paris: Grasset.

Saussure, F. de (1916/1973) *Cours de Linguistique Générale*, Paris: Payot.

Schama, S. (1989) *Citizens: A Chronicle of the French Revolution*, London: Penguin.

Segalen, V. (1978) *Essai sur l'Exotisme, une Esthétique du Divers*, Paris: Fata Morgana.

Short, M. (1996) *Exploring the Language of Poems, Plays and Prose*, Harlow: Longman.

Soboul, A. (1948) *La Révolution Française (1789–1799)*, Paris: Editions Sociales.

—— (1962) *Précis d'Histoire de la Révolution Française*, Paris: Editions Sociales.

—— (1965) *La Révolution Française*, Paris: PUF.

—— (1982) *La Révolution Française*, Paris: Editions Sociales.

Spitzer, L. (1948) *Linguistics and Literary History*, Princeton: Princeton University Press.

—— (1970) *Etudes de Style Précédé de 'Leo Spitzer et la Lecture Stylistique'*, ed. Jean Starobinski, Paris: Gallimard.

Sterne, Laurence (1768) *Sentimental Journey Through France and Italy*, London: Penguin.

Thorne, J. (1970) 'Stylistics and Generative Grammars', in Freeman, D. (ed.) *Linguistics and Literary Style*, New York: Holt, Rinehart and Winston, pp.182–196.

Urbain, J.-D. (1991) *L'Idiot du Voyage: Histoires de Touristes*, Paris: Pion.

Van Dijk, T. (ed.) (1985) *A Handbook of Discourse Analysis*, London: Academic Press.

—— (1995) 'From Text Grammar to Critical Discourse Analysis', University of Amsterdam, unpublished paper.

Van Leeuwen, T. (1995) 'Representing Social Action', *Discourse and Society* 6(1): 81–106.

Walter, H. (1988) *Le Français dans Tous les Sens*, Paris: Laffont.

Williams, G. (1999) *French Discourse Analysis: The Method of Poststructuralism*, London: Routledge.

Williamson, J. (1978) *Decoding Advertisements*, London: Marion Boyars.

Zeldin, T. (1983) *The French*, London: Collins.

Films referred to in the text

Les Amants du Pont-Neuf (1991), dir. Leos Carax.

The Asphalt Jungle (1950), dir. John Huston.

The Blackboard Jungle (1955), dir. Richard Brooks.

La Haine (1994), dir. Mathieu Kassovitz.

Index

Note: references to main extracts of texts analysed are in **bold**; *f, g* and *t* refer to figures, glossary and tables.

Exploring French Text Analysis

This work fills a huge gap . . . It combines well established approaches to text analysis . . . with some of the newer approaches . . . it is refreshing to see a work of this sort that focuses on French.

Linda Waugh, *Cornell University*

Exploring French Text Analysis introduces advanced students to the critical understanding and appreciation of written French. The book outlines the background to stylistics and critical discourse analysis and invites readers to combine both approaches in their close reading of French texts.

The authors provide a clear framework for analysing written French critically. A series of commentaries by different contributors offers a variety of models for readers to review, imitate and discuss.

The texts commented on have been carefully chosen to illustrate key features of written French style and to present different perspectives of French national identity. They include advertisements, newspapers, magazines, travel writing and contemporary fiction, and cover a range of topics such as food, sport, language, history, marginalisation and the cult of the *patron*. The book also includes a comprehensive glossary of technical terms.

Robert Crawshaw is Senior Lecturer in European Languages and Cultures and Head of French and **Karin Tusting** is a Teaching Assistant and Research Officer in European Languages and Cultures. Both teach at Lancaster University.

Exploring French Text Analysis

Analysis

Interpretations of national identity

Robert Crawshaw and Karin Tusting

London and New York

First published 2000
by Routledge
11 New Fetter Lane, London EC4P 4EE

Simultaneously published in the USA and Canada
by Routledge
29 West 35th Street, New York, NY 10001

Routledge is an imprint of the Taylor & Francis Group

Typeset in Perpetua by RefineCatch Limited, Bungay, Suffolk
Printed and bound in Great Britain by Biddles Ltd, Guildford and King's Lynn

British Library Cataloguing in Publication Data
A catalogue record for this book is available from the British Library

Library of Congress Cataloging in Publication Data
Crawshaw, Robert H.
    Exploring French text analysis: interpretations of national identity / Robert
    Crawshaw and Karin Tusting.
        p.   cm.
    Includes bibliographical references and index.
    ISBN 0-415-18407-X (H) – ISBN 0-415-18408-8 (P)
    1. French language – Discourse analysis. 2. French language – Style. 3.
    Ethnicity – France. I. Tusting, Karin, 1973 – II. Title.

    PC2434.C73 2000
    440'.1'41 – dc21   99-053738

ISBN 0–415–18407–X (hbk)
ISBN 0–415–18408–8 (pbk)